WELLSPRINGS

WELLSPRINGS

A NATURAL HISTORY OF BOTTLED SPRING WATERS

Francis H. Chapelle

Illustrations by Katy Flynn Brown

RUTGERS UNIVERSITY PRESS

NEW BRUNSWICK, NEW JERSEY, AND LONDON

Library of Congress Cataloging-in-Publication Data

Chapelle, Frank.
 Wellsprings : a natural history of bottled spring waters / Francis H.
Chapelle ; illustrations by Katy Flynn Brown.
     p.   cm.
 Includes bibliographical references and index.
 ISBN 0-8135-3614-6 (hardcover : alk. paper)
 1. Bottled water—United States—History.   2. Drinking water—
United States.   3. Water-supply—United States.   I. Title.
 TD223.C434 2005
 628.1'12—dc22

                                                        2004025316

A British Cataloging-in-Publication record for this book is available from
the British Library.

Manufactured in the United States of America

For Leanndra Marie,
Child of my heart

CONTENTS

ILLUSTRATIONS

FIGURES

TABLES

PREFACE

The young woman, dressed in a sharp-looking business suit, paused as she strode by the airport concession stand. Her eyes passed swiftly over the rows of fruit juice, soda, and bottled water arranged neatly on the cooler shelf. She frowned a bit, as if impatient with herself, and then picked out a brightly labeled bottle of spring water. Moving to the checkout line, she paid for it quickly and stepped out into the terminal to join her fellow travelers, wasting no time.

Although this particular businesswoman spent very little time procuring her bottled water, the water itself took a considerable amount of time getting to her. It all started fifteen thousand years ago when the glaciers covering most of North America began to melt. Much of the meltwater simply ran off into streams, rivers, and lakes. Some, however, percolated deep into the earth and began a long journey though the glacial sediments and sandstones underlying what was to become Pennsylvania. As the water filtered slowly through the ground over the millennia, it was cleansed of particulate matter and microorganisms. In addition, small amounts of rock were dissolved, giving the water just enough calcium, magnesium, and bicarbonate to produce a clean, crisp taste. Finally, thousands of years after the water first seeped into the ground, it reached a gushing spring. Here, some of the water was diverted to a nearby bottling plant, run through a series of progressively finer filters, dosed with ozone to kill any lurking microorganisms, and placed into individual 16-ounce plastic bottles. Within days, this fifteen-thousand-year-old spring water, with its pleasant, clean taste carefully intact, was shipped to market and to the impatient hands of our time-strapped businesswoman.

This is the reality of bottled water in the United States today. On one hand, it often serves people in a hurry, people who have no time to contemplate the source of the water they are drinking. On the other hand, the fact that they choose bottled water over public water fountains suggests a belief that bottled waters are somehow special. Just how special, however, varies widely. Some bottled waters, and not necessarily the expensive ones, are truly rare products of nature. Others are just ordinary municipal water subjected to various chemical treatments. So how do you tell the difference? One way is to consider their natural history.

This book is a natural history of American bottled water. Like most things American, this history is outwardly simple but inwardly complex. The practice of "bottling" water began with the straightforward need of Native Americans for reliable sources of drinking water and the necessity of storing that water for a time. After European immigrants arrived and started building cities, it was continued by people who first used bottled mineral waters as medicines. But by the end of the nineteenth century, bottled water had evolved into a cleaner alternative to often polluted municipal water supplies. The introduction of chlorination in the early twentieth century nearly led to the demise of this fledgling bottled water industry. It was not until the late 1970s when renewed concerns about water pollution and an interest in healthy lifestyles revived the demand for bottled water. Today, millions of Americans consider bottled water to be part of everyday life.

But bottled water is more than just a commodity to be consumed and forgotten before it is even digested. Water is basic to life and survival, and access to usable water is fundamental to human civilization. The efficient allocation, distribution, and control of water supplies in an orderly and fair way is the hallmark of any successful culture. Bottled water is a microcosm of the constant and unending battle over the allocation of water supplies. Does water bubbling from a spring belong solely to the owner of the land where the spring is located? Or, since ground water flows freely beneath property lines, should it be a publicly held resource? If it is a publicly held resource, is it wrong for individuals or corporations to sell spring waters for private profit? On the other hand, does the enhanced availability and choice provided by their bottling of water serve a public need that justifies private profit? This conflict between the public and private utilization of water—which is a central issue facing the entire drinking water industry today—has a long and bitter history. Resolving this conflict, or at least learning to live with it, depends on understanding that history.

We can begin by wondering where bottled waters come from, what distinguishes one from another, and what makes some more desirable than others. In an age when perfectly healthy drinking water can be had virtually free from the tap, it is also natural to wonder just why so many people deem bottled waters to be worth the price.

The short answer to these questions is that different bottled waters have a wide variety of natural histories. Some are spring waters that have circulated deep within the earth for years, decades, or centuries. Depending on the kinds of rocks encountered, and depending on how long the water has circulated, these spring waters can have vastly different chemical characteristics. Other bottled waters are just chemically treated municipal water. Regardless of the source, however, Americans have unprecedented choice in the kinds of drinking water available to them. This choice, this dizzying variety, is one thing that makes bottled waters interesting.

The long answer is less obvious. It begins in the mists of prehistory, continues through the ancient civilizations of Egypt and Rome, moves to Europe during the Middle Ages, and culminates in the rise of rationality and modern science. It can be argued that the practice of bottling water, which has gone on for many thousands of years, mirrors the technological and social development of civilization itself. Many Americans, who tend to think of bottled water as a recent invention, may be startled by that assertion. That being the case, its natural history will take some time to consider.

Hence this book.

ACKNOWLEDGMENTS

This book would not have been written if I hadn't, on a whim, visited Camp Holly Springs, Virginia, in August of 1997. Like most hydrologists, I knew a fair amount about ground water and springs, but virtually nothing about bottled water. When I showed up (unannounced), Dave Dowdy, the owner, dropped everything he was doing to show me around. Beginning at the spring orifice, which his father had engineered thirty years earlier to collect water in a sanitary fashion, he walked me through the bottling process. Dave had designed and built the entire plant himself from scratch, and the joy he took in showing it off—it now employed about a dozen people—was both palpable and impressive. As we went, Dave kept referring to "how we used to do things," a clear implication that the bottled water business hadn't always been so efficient and high-tech. That was the first hint I had that there was a story behind the development of the modern bottled water industry that I had never heard about, and it was Dave Dowdy who got me interested in it.

Over the last few years, I have visited several dozen springs throughout the country that are or have been used as sources of bottled water. Most of the people I met were just as friendly and helpful as Dave Dowdy, and all of them had stories that were worth listening to. In particular, I'd like to thank Jim Tarpley and Linda Adams of Blue Springs Pure H-2-O of Idaho; Bob Hirst, Director of Education and International Member Relations for the International Bottled Water Association; Doug Oberhamer of the Deep Rock Artesian Water Company, Denver, Colorado; Kristen Tardiff of Poland Spring; and Robert Betts of the Hawaiian Natural Water Company. All the members of the Drinking Water Research Foundation, including Jack C. West of U.S. Filter, E. Austin "Dutch" Hess of Hess Machine International, Vincent Ducasse of Group Danone, and Albert D. Lear of Wissahickon Spring Water have been especially helpful. In addition, I'd like to thank Professor Donald I. Siegel of Syracuse University, Dr. Brian G. Katz of the U.S. Geological Survey, and Dr. Stephen C. Edberg of the Yale University School of Medicine for providing technical reviews of the manuscript. Finally, I'd like to thank Dr. William Back, retired Research Hydrologist with the U.S. Geological Survey and my teacher, who first pointed out to me that chemical hydrogeology as a scientific discipline can be traced to the early nineteenth century and human curiosity about the medicinal effects of spring waters.

I A HISTORY OF BOTTLED WATER

1 WATER FROM THE HEART
Why Americans Drink Bottled Water

Bottled water went out of style in America on September 27, 1913. As a consequence, the American bottled water industry, which had thrived for much of the nineteenth century, instantly became obsolete. Just like the buggy whip, which was also on its way toward oblivion in 1913, bottled water became a commodity rendered unnecessary by the brave advance of civilization.

The demise of bottled water in the early twentieth century was due to a breathtaking technical innovation: the use of chlorine to disinfect municipal water supplies. Like many American cities, Philadelphia had suffered greatly from epidemics of typhoid fever and cholera throughout the nineteenth century. By 1900, the new science of microbiology had identified the cause of these diseases to be waterborne bacteria named *Salmonella typhi* and *Vibrio cholorae*, respectively. Furthermore, microbiologists had learned that both of these bacteria were easily killed, or at least inactivated, by exposure to chlorine. Engineers responsible for the municipal water supply of Philadelphia began experimenting with adding chlorine to drinking water in 1909. By 1913, they had worked out a method for using liquid chlorine that was much more efficient than previous methods involving solid hypochlorite compounds. In late September of that year, the first permanent chlorine water treatment plant in America was installed at Philadelphia's Belmont Filters. By the end of the year, all of Philadelphia's municipal water was chlorinated, and other American cities rushed to follow suit.[1]

The Brave New World of chlorinated tap water had begun.

Prior to 1913, one way to procure relatively clean drinking water in American cities was to buy bottled water. City life had numerous advantages, including the efficient conduct of commerce and social contact. But it also had one very large disadvantage. Having so many people and animals living closely together made it virtually impossible to obtain clean water. Rivers, streams, and wells rapidly became contaminated from the feces of humans, horses, dogs, cats, rats, and whatever other creatures happened to be around. Municipal water supplies, which relied on water drawn from rivers or wells, were routinely contaminated by fecal material. Most of the time, healthy people could deal with routine contaminants, such as *E. coli,* which are transmitted by fecal matter. But when the water became contaminated by *Salmonella typhi* or *Vibrio cholorae,* which were spread by the fecal matter of infected people, it was dangerous to everybody.

The practice of bottling water in the United States began about 1820 when an enterprising preacher named Rev. D. O. Griswold began to bottle the naturally effervescent spring waters of Saratoga Springs, New York. At first, this sparkling water seems to have been used primarily as a cure for upset stomachs. In fact, the good reverend sold the water under the name of "Doctor Clark." But gradually, as glass bottles became cheaper and more widely available in the middle 1800s, bottled spring waters came to be viewed less as medicines and more as sources of relatively clean drinking water.

As the nineteenth century progressed, heavy five-gallon glass water bottles became increasingly common in American cities. Distributing water in large containers, which had begun long before in Europe, was one way to avoid waterborne diseases such as typhoid fever. Various enterprising individuals made a business of finding and bottling clean water collected from springs or wells in the countryside and transporting it to the cities. In the days before the availability of motor vehicles, this was a tough, demanding job. Motorized trucks made the job easier, but the sheer physical effort involved in loading and unloading heavy five-gallon glass bottles filled with water meant that it was a business reserved for strong men who were willing to work hard.

But it was profitable. Because most city water was always more or less contaminated with various microorganisms, bottled "drinking water" began to appear on the dinner tables of rich and not-so-rich city dwellers. By the end of the nineteenth century, bottled water was thought of as a desirable amenity rather than a luxury. Providing bottled water to the cities, therefore, was a very good business.

All this changed with chlorination. Suddenly, safe drinking water could be had straight from the tap. As you might expect, the consumption of bottled water dropped precipitously, and within a couple of years the bottled water industry in America had virtually ceased to exist. Part of this was due to the convenience of having relatively clean water available straight from the tap. But there was more to it than just convenience. Chlorinated tap water was a novelty. It was a symbol of the bold progress of American society. It was a sign that technology could conquer all the problems of humankind. As a consequence, chlorinated municipal water became stylish and was considered more desirable than old-fashioned bottled water.

The bottled water industry in America, which had grown slowly over much of the nineteenth century, was shunted aside by this rising tide of progress. But it did not disappear entirely. Rather, its focus shifted toward providing drinking water to factories, shops, and other businesses that could not or would not invest in decent plumbing. The few stubborn people who stayed in the bottled water business concentrated on this lower-class and much less profitable drinking water market. Thus was born, incidently, the American tradition of workers gathering "around the watercooler." In this humble fashion, the bottled water industry in America limped along through most of the twentieth century.

The near-death experience of the American bottled water industry in the early twentieth century has largely been forgotten these days. Paradoxically, at the beginning of the twenty-first century, many Americans consider bottled water to be a necessity of life. To them, the idea of taking a drink of chlorine-laced tap water, or even of using tap water to make the morning coffee, is . . . well, unthinkable. They prefer the taste, the predictable chemical quality, and, let's face it, the image of bottled water.

This willingness to pay for bottled water, which can be anywhere from 250 to 10,000 times more expensive than municipal water, has entirely resurrected the bottled water industry. In 1960, annual sales of bottled water in America were less than $50 million. By the year 2000, bottled water sales exceeded $5 billion. Like the phoenix rising from the ashes, the bottled water industry has risen from obscurity to unprecedented heights of profitability.

The question is *why?* Why is it that so many Americans with access to unlimited quantities of inexpensive, good-quality tap water choose to drink bottled water? What circumstances have led the bottled water industry, which was practically killed by the technical innovation of chlorination, to make such a spectacular comeback?

Sometimes this is not much of a mystery. In Orlando, Florida, for example—the home of Disney World—much of the municipal water is drawn from deep wells pumping the underlying Floridan aquifer. This is perfectly good water, but it often contains noxious hydrogen sulfide gas. Hydrogen sulfide, although harmless in the small amounts found in Floridan aquifer water, smells and tastes like rotten eggs. Water treatment plant operators work hard to remove the sulfide from treated water. The problem is, the human nose is exquisitely sensitive to hydrogen sulfide and can detect it at concentrations as low as 2 parts per billion. Thus, even if water treatment is 99 percent effective, detectable traces of hydrogen sulfide can still get into tap water. The "sulfur" taste of Orlando's water does not bother everybody, and it certainly is not unhealthy. But some people just don't like it. The obvious alternative is bottled water, which many people use as a matter of course. In this case, when there is an obvious issue of taste, the widespread use of bottled water is perfectly understandable.

New York City is a different story. Much of New York's water supply is brought to the city via aqueducts from the nearby Catskill Mountains. This is some of the best drinking water in the world. Because the Catskills remain relatively pristine, chemical and biological contaminants in the water are virtually nonexistent. Furthermore, the underlying sandstones and shales provide just enough calcium, magnesium, and potassium to give the water a strikingly fresh, clean flavor. Because of all these factors, and because the city aggressively screens its water for potential chemical and biological contaminants, New York City is widely considered to have the best municipal water supply in the entire world. Yet bottled water consumption in New York is as high as or higher than it is in much of the rest of the United States. The Perrier fashion that began in the 1970s, when Upper East Side sophisticates competed with each other for just that right air of elegance, sophistication, and conspicuous consumption, started in New York City. Apparently, the best municipal water in the world was not quite good enough for everybody.

By the simple criteria of water quality, therefore, the use of bottled water in New York City just doesn't make sense. Municipal water in the Big Apple is as good as or better than some brands of bottled water. So, if the only reason people drink bottled water is to procure high-quality drinking water, bottled water consumption in New York should be virtually nil. But it's not. There has to be something else going on. There must be another attraction, some other motivation, some other incentive at work here. Otherwise, the widespread popularity of bottled water in New York and in countless other places in the United States, just doesn't make sense.

What is going on?

We do have one clue to work with, and it has to do with style. When the New York yuppies (young urban professionals) began sipping Perrier, Poland Spring, and Evian back in the 1970s, drinking water from small, individual-serving bottles was a novelty in the United States. The old days of the nineteenth century, when bottled water was fairly common, had been entirely forgotten. Americans were used to having water served in restaurants, of course, but normally this was just a glass of tap water. Upscale bars and restaurants found that serving bottled water, which has long been the custom in Europe, gave an aura of elegance and epicurean sophistication that suited yuppie tastes.

So bottled water became trendy in the 1970s. It became stylish. This association of bottled water with wealth and sophistication, which helped propel the U.S. bottled water industry out of its small-time niche status to a big-time moneymaker, is intriguing. It is tempting to simply write this off as human fickleness or even shallowness. But that notion does not quite stand up. Water styles, whether they include bottles or not, are part of every human society. These styles may appear whimsical—New York's Perrier-swigging yuppies are sufficient evidence of this—but if you dig a little deeper, you will find that they also have a solid core of practical necessity.

Take, for example, the water "style" of Thailand.

Thailand is located in Southeast Asia and is a very hot, very humid place for most of the year. Because of this, and because Thais are a notably hardworking people, having readily available drinking water to stay properly hydrated is a necessity of life. Over the centuries, as far back as human memory can reach, the Thais have practiced a unique and fascinating solution to their water-delivery problem. The custom revolves around earthenware water jars, or *maaw nahm*, which Thais traditionally place outside their homes in shaded but accessible places.[2] The purpose of these ceramic vessels, which typically hold five or ten gallons of water, is to provide cool, clear drinking water for passersby and travelers in need of refreshment. From a strictly practical point of view, the maaw nahm simply provide a necessary commodity. In such a hot, humid climate, working people need to drink water continuously in order to avoid dangerous dehydration.

But from a cultural point of view, the maaw nahm are something else altogether. They are an expression of community. They show concern for the welfare of others. And, because we are dealing with people here, they also express the prosperity, good taste, and sophistication of the owners. This, of course, is the way human culture works. If a particular behavior or attitude happens to be important and needed in society, it is actively encouraged by consensus. In other words it becomes stylish, with the fashion being enforced by peer pressure. This is the case with the maaw nahm. Given Thailand's hot, humid climate, an efficient water-delivery system was necessary. Thai society responded by inventing the maaw nahm and by making them fashionable.

Over the centuries, the custom of providing water freely to neighbors, friends, and strangers alike has become deeply embedded in Thai society. Part of the Thai ideal for a good person involves what they call the *nahm jai,* literally the "water heart." People with good nahm jai are those who unfailingly provides good, healthy drinking water to all who pass by their homes. Giving water is an expression of hospitality, warmheartedness, and benevolence.[3] The quality of the water provided, as well as the quality of each individual maaw nahm, reflects on the quality of the household. Thus, the family that provides particularly excellent, abundant drinking water in its maaw nahm is considered to "give water from the heart." To maintain a maaw nahm, and to keep it stocked daily with freshly drawn well water or newly collected rainwater, is thus an expression of responsibility, of community, of care for humanity. There is nothing whimsical or shallow about this at all.

Water from the heart is at the very foundation of human civilization.

But while the maaw nahm have a practical, serious function in society, they also tend to be fun. After all, as long as people have to do something, they can generally find a way to enjoy it. Thus it is with the maaw nahm. Many of these clay ceramic jars are intricately decorated with elaborately incised patterns or are supported by equally elaborate figurines. The playfulness and fun involved in these decorations are evident. It is clear that having a beautiful, visually striking maaw nahm is a source of pride to an owner. It is equally clear that taking a drink of water from a beautifully designed, attractive maaw nahm is also enjoyable. Many maaw nahm are real works of art. One can imagine the pride a family would have in commissioning a potter to design, build, and decorate a particularly attractive maaw nahm. One can also imagine the more or less friendly competition between households to have the best maaw nahm and the best drinking water in the neighborhood. It is the Thai equivalent of keeping up with the Joneses.

Thais also delight in building niches for their maaw nahm. The hot, direct sunlight in Thailand makes it desirable to keep the water jars elevated above the ground and to cover them with roofs. These niches can be as simple as a bit of corrugated tin or as elaborate as a specially designed water house. These water houses, or *bahn nahm*, are kept simple and peaceful, and they seem to encourage a certain amount of Buddhist reflection.[4] Verses painted on small signs often surround the bahn nahm, with sayings such as:

If you let cloudy water settle, it will become clear.
If you let your upset mind settle, your way will become clear.

As urbanization has overtaken Thailand, the use of the maaw nahm has declined. These days, you need to travel to less-developed northern Thailand to see them in any abundance. But the cultural conviction—that is, the style—that water is an important part of hospitality has not changed. Upon arrival at a house or apartment, friends and strangers alike are still offered water by the thoughtful host. Failure to do so would be considered impolite, and the host would risk being described as *mai mee nahm jai*, or "one who has no water heart." These days, however, it is bottled water that is usually offered. In other words, as the use of the maaw nahm has declined, the use of bottled water has risen proportionally.

This cultural switch to bottled water in Thailand is striking. In the year 2000, Thailand ranked sixth in the world for both total and per capita bottled water consumption. Considering that the population of Thailand is only about 60 million people, the fact that Thailand's use of bottled water rivals that of Japan (126 million people) and even China (1.1 billion people) is remarkable. But if you consider the place that high-quality drinking water has in Thai culture, which places a premium on offering and receiving water in social situations, it makes perfect sense.

Clearly, the popularity and consumption of bottled water in Thailand can be traced to the cultural importance of water and traditional Thai values. It is worth asking, therefore, if similar cultural forces might be at work in the United States and whether these forces might explain the otherwise puzzling popularity of bottled water. Can it be that the Perrier-swigging yuppies of the 1980s were expressing a cultural memory deeper and more fundamental than conspicuous consumption?

Well, perhaps.

We can start with the fact that water in nature is not usually clean. Water, after all, is a very good solvent and will dissolve just about anything it comes in contact with. In addition, running water tends to pick up sand and mud, neither of which contributes to cleanliness. Stagnant water is usually less muddy, but it also facilitates the decay of plant material into a tea-colored brew of humic acids. But most of all, water is the natural dwelling place for swarms of microorganisms. These bacteria, algae, fungi, and viruses—often as many as 100 million *per milliliter*—can live in water that is hot or cold, clear or muddy, rapidly flowing or stagnant. They can live in desert pools where water temperature exceeds 140°F, or on frozen tundras where temperatures dip below −50°F. We like to think that water drawn from unpolluted rivers, streams, and lakes is naturally pure and fit for human consumption. Sometimes it is, but this is not common. Water, by its very nature, is often very dirty.

And people just make things worse. Before the rise of civilization, when humans lived in small nomadic bands that moved from place to place, disposing of human wastes was not much of a problem. After a week or two in any given location, when the accumulation of urine and feces became objectionable, the tribe just pulled up stakes and left. But when people began to farm for a living, and villages and towns grew up, the wastes just accumulated in shallow pits, open sewers, and cesspools. It was not just human excrement, either. Goats, donkeys, horses, cattle, chickens, geese—as well as the mice and rats that thrived in the accumulated filth—all contributed their fair share. Inevitably, these fermenting masses of waste washed into nearby rivers and streams or seeped down to the underlying water table. So, if you combine the natural tendency of water to pick up sediment, solutes, and microorganisms with the mounds of filth generated by human and animal habitation, you can begin to appreciate how rare clean, drinkable water has been for much of human history.

Like the Thais with their maaw nahm, every civilization had to come up with a solution to the problem of providing reasonably clean drinking water. The Romans are justly famous for the huge aqueducts that they built to bring fresh water from the mountains into Rome. These aqueducts, which during their heyday carried several million gallons of water per day, were a major factor in making the marshy areas around Rome habitable for large numbers of people.

Unlike the aqueducts of Rome, most of the prechlorination methods for providing drinking water have been forgotten over the years. Some of those that are remembered, however, were, like the Thai maaw nahm, really ingenious. Take, for example, the filter cisterns of Venice.[5]

The city of Venice was founded in the fifth century A.D., just as the Roman Empire was crumbling. According to tradition, Venice was originally built on a hundred islands near the shores of the Adriatic Sea. This made the city easier to defend from barbarian marauders, but it also made it difficult to obtain drinking water. The Venetians, who were as ingenious and resourceful as any people who ever lived, quickly came up with a unique solution to their problem. It started with simple rain cisterns, designed to collect falling rainwater. But water that lies stagnant in cisterns soon spoils, growing large populations of algae and bacteria that eventually render the water undrinkable. A partial solution was to bury the cisterns in the ground, where cooler temperatures and isolation from sunlight discouraged the growth of algae. At some point, however, some unknown genius came up with the idea of coupling cisterns with a built-in filter system. A conical hole was dug to a depth of about ten feet and a narrow cistern placed in the center. The bottom of the cistern was perforated to allow water to flow in and the conical hole filled with clean, fine sand. When completed, most of the water resided in the porous sand rather than in the open cistern. This not only increased the storage capacity of the cistern; it kept the water cool and discouraged the growth of microorganisms. The real technological innovation, however, was to continuously filter particulate matter such as microorganisms out of the water. As water was withdrawn from the cistern, it was replaced by water that had been filtered through the sand. These filter cisterns were recharged by rainfall (during wet weather) or from barrels of water ferried from the mainland (during droughts). Either way, the incoming water was filtered and, at least by the standards of medieval Europe, was marvelously clean and fresh.

Like the Thais and their maaw nahm, the Venetians took pride in the appearance of their filter cisterns, which by the sixteenth century had became objects of art. One visitor to Venice early in the seventeenth century, a gentlemen named Thomas Coryat, described the cisterns in the Ducal Palace of Venice as follows: "In the middest of the court there are two very goodly wels which are some fifteen paces distant, the upper part whereof is adorned by a very faire work of bronse that incloseth the whole Well, whereon many pretty images, clusters of grapes, and of Ivy berries are very artificially carved." [6]

The filter cisterns in Venice were also places where people gathered to talk, gossip, and flirt with members of the opposite sex. Like the Thai owners of the maaw nahm, Venetians who owned filter cisterns gained public stature from their physical beauty and the excellence of the water contained therein. Public cisterns were carefully maintained in the same way, since they were a reflection of the opulence and prosperity that was the Republic of Venice. It was not uncommon for musicians, equipped with their newfangled violins, to give impromptu concerts near the cisterns. These Italian violins, which were the seventeenth century's equivalent of today's electric guitar, were much louder and boisterous than the viols they replaced. As such, they were suited for outdoor concerts, something the Venetians delighted in. Playing music in the vicinity of the cisterns was a sure way to procure an audience, and it was one way for young violinists to gain a reputation. Many of Antonio Vivaldi's more than two hundred violin concertos, which were the hot pop music of the 1700s, were rendered in this fashion.

But as delightful as stories like this are, filthy drinking water was the norm in most of Europe from the Middle Ages right up to the twentieth century. The effects on the populace of this poor water quality varied from being lethal, as happened during the cholera and typhoid fever epidemics that boiled up regularly, to simply causing chronic intestinal upset and dysentery. Wealthy Europeans of the nobility, however, had a solution to this problem.

They visited the springs.

Although it is true that many natural waters tend to be dirty or only marginally clean, there are exceptions. About 98% of water that falls as precipitation on land quickly runs off into streams and rivers and just as quickly picks up the sediments, the organic matter, and the microorganisms that make it dirty. However, a very small percentage of the water seeps downward through the soil and becomes ground water. Again, most of this shallow ground water soon discharges into various surface-water bodies. Only minute percentage of this shallow ground water continues to seep downward until it finally recharges the aquifers that underlie much of the earth. Water in these deep aquifers usually moves very slowly, often as little as one foot per year. As this water slowly seeps along, any organic matter, sediment, or microorganisms that it might be carrying are filtered out, effectively cleansing the water. The process is a lot like what goes on in the filter cisterns of Venice, only it goes on for much longer periods of time and is much more effective. Water that discharges from such deep aquifers into natural springs or artesian wells is usually free of objectionable particulate and organic matter. In addition, if the water came into contact with rocks having a favorable chemical composition, it will contain just the right proportion of dissolved minerals to produce a pleasant flavor.

Take, for example, the story of Perrier.[7]

If you believe the legends (and it is often wise not to), Hannibal drank from a curious pool of water on the Languedoc plain in what is now southern France when he crossed the Alps to invade Rome in 218 B.C. The pool, which was fed by spring waters seeping through a small crack in the earth's surface, had the curious property that, not only was it excellent drinking water, it was naturally effervescent. Much later, in 1884, a Dr. Louis Perrier leased the spring and began to market its water for drinking.

The desirable chemical properties of Perrier water can be traced to a highly unusual confluence of geologic circumstances. The Languedoc plain is underlain by gravels of glacial origin that function as a productive aquifer. These gravels, in turn, are overlain by deposits of clay, which were probably deposited by a lake that formed after the most recent ice age ended. This clay acts like a cork, allowing the underlying waters to become pressurized. The water in the gravel aquifer has three distinct sources. One source is just rainwater seeping from the surface. Another is water flowing from a fractured limestone aquifer underlying the Garrigues Hills north of the Languedoc plain. Finally, hot, mineralized water seeps upward from a deep volcanic aquifer. This hot volcanic water is saturated with carbon dioxide gas, which gives the water its natural effervescence.

If any of these three water sources were taken by themselves, they would be either unremarkable (the rainwater) or undrinkable (the volcanic water). The water seeping from the land surface would certainly be a worthwhile resource, but it would be indistinguishable from any well water in the region. Similarly, the water from the fractured limestone would be usable, but, like most water from limestone aquifers, it would probably be unpleasantly hard. Finally, the volcanic water would be highly mineralized. But if these three waters are mixed in the proper proportions, as happens naturally in the gravel aquifer underlying the Languedoc plain, they become a healthy and delightful drinking water.

Clearly, the natural hydrologic and geologic circumstances that produce Perrier water are unusual. But it is also true that virtually all springs that produce high-quality drinking water are, in their own ways, unusual. Most springs tap shallow ground water that is not only unremarkable in its composition but can also easily be contaminated from surface sources. But springs that tap deeply circulating ground water that is free of organic matter and fecal microorganisms, and which has a pleasing and healthy amount of dissolved minerals, can produce very good drinking water.

Throughout the last two thousand years, Europeans of means traveled to such springs to take advantage of their healthy properties. One hears a lot about "healing springs," the idea that waters from certain springs can cure a variety of human ailments. In some cases, it is possible that trace minerals present in spring water can help cure or at least help alleviate the symptoms of some human diseases. But the more common mechanism at work was simply that these spring waters were relatively clean. They did not contain the fecal matter and festering microorganisms that laced the everyday drinking water consumed even by affluent Europeans. Upon arriving at a spring and ingesting for a day or two water that was free of fecal bacteria, the effects on the digestive tract would be striking. The more-or-less chronic digestive upset, the loose bowels, the unpleasant gas would disappear. It is no wonder that spring waters were considered to be healing.

In due course, visiting springs to take advantage of the healthy, clean water became part of established medical practice.[8] It also became fashionable. Traveling to springs was an expensive, exhausting, and time-consuming endeavor. People who had the means could visit springs regularly. But for everyday people, working people, such expense was out of the question. Since common people were so naturally excluded, these springs became the meeting places for the rich and affluent members of society. Being "seen" at the springs was a statement of economic and social status.

So it is no mystery that the fashion of "taking the waters" came to be associated with wealth and sophistication. But even rich people could not spend all their time in the remote, often mountainous terrain where high-quality springs tend to be found. So, if the people could not come to the springs in order to enjoy clean, contaminant-free water, was it possible for the springs to come to the people?

This, actually, is what led to the development of Perrier as a high-end bottled water. Impressed by the waters being bottled by Dr. Perrier, an Englishman named St. John Harmsworth realized the economic potential of the operation and bought the springs. Harmsworth continued using the name "Perrier", however, since it had acquired a reputation. In the early twentieth century, the far-flung British Empire had a particularly bad problem with drinking water. Local waters in India, Afghanistan, and eastern Africa were often so contaminated that they could not be rendered drinkable even by mixing in a liberal dose of whiskey or gin. Harmsworth, taking advantage of the English affinity for things Continental, marketed bottled Perrier throughout the empire as a healthy—and high-class—source of drinking water. By 1930, the Perrier Company was selling 18 million bottles of water per year, much of which was being exported to expatriate Englishmen throughout the world.[9]

So, by the early twentieth century, all the ingredients for a successful bottled water industry were in place. There was a long European tradition of using spring waters as a health supplement; doing so was strongly associated with fashion and the upper crust of society; and there was a real need. Clean drinking water was in short supply, and bottled waters were a convenient and fashionable way to satisfy this need. In the United States, meanwhile, numerous bottling operations were already supplying clean drinking water to various cities. There was Saratoga Springs, New York, which began to bottle naturally carbonated water as early as 1820. There was Poland Spring, Maine, which began bottling water as a cure for kidney ailments in 1844. There was Mountain Valley Spring water, from Hot Springs, Arkansas, which began bottling operations in 1871. There were countless other local bottling operations in business by 1900, all catering to customers who either considered the waters to be medicinal or could not get acceptably clean drinking water any other way. By all accounts, bottled water was very much an up and coming industry.

But then disaster struck. This disaster, this cataclysm, this haymaker, was the introduction of chlorinated municipal water in American cities. As we have seen, Philadelphia instituted chlorination in 1913. Other cities soon followed suit, and by 1941, 4,590 of the 5,372 water treatment systems in the United States were using chlorination.[10] Within a few short years, an important reason for using bottled water in the first place—procuring a source of relatively uncontaminated drinking water—evaporated. Now, for the first time in human history, clean potable water could be had by just about anybody in the United States. But even more then that, chlorination was seen as being "modern." It was a triumph of American ingenuity and technology over the most pervasive problem in human history.

Chlorinated municipal water was in style.

This just about killed the bottled water industry in America. Most local bottlers went out of business. Even the larger and well-established bottling operations, notably Saratoga Springs, Mountain Valley, and Poland Spring, had to cut back production precipitously. By the 1940s, the bottled water industry was serving only a small niche of users, often farmers or small business owners who could not get clean water any other way. The bottled water business consisted mainly of small bottlers who spent most of their time tooling around the countryside in beat-up trucks delivering five-gallon jugs of water to machine shops, factories, or isolated farms. None of this did much to enhance the stylishness of bottled water in the eyes of big-city sophisticates.

But what goes around comes around, and by the 1960s there were rumblings of dissatisfaction on the water front. Years of dumping untreated sewage effluents and industrial wastes in American rivers had seriously degraded the quality of the water. Since these obviously polluted rivers were also sources for municipal drinking water, people began to get a queasy sense that maybe their water, even when chlorinated, was not so clean after all.

In addition, the "modern" aura of chlorinated water had faded with time. Whereas the sometimes pungent odor of chlorine had at first seemed excitingly new, it never caught on as being truly desirable. Municipal water had other problems as well. Pipes that distributed the water tended to become clogged with sludge and precipitates, so they needed periodic cleaning. This cleaning generally served to stir up the accumulated solids in the pipes, causing hours or days in which the tap water was badly discolored. Local officials piously saying that "it isn't harmful" did not help matters much. The water looked and tasted disgusting. Furthermore, the fact that tap water was delivered through those same pipes even when the water was not discolored made it unpalatable to many people.

By the 1970s, the environmental concerns over water pollution, combined with a growing realization that chlorinated tap water was not the panacea that it had once been thought to be, began to revive the dormant bottled water industry in America. Also, some people had tired of soda pop over the years. Many of these people were health conscious and tended to gravitate toward bottled water as a naturally low-calorie beverage that did not contain artificial ingredients. One catalyst was Perrier's decision in 1977 to launch a nationwide, $5-million advertising campaign.[11] Perrier's strategy in the United States was to introduce—or, more accurately, reintroduce—the concept of the single serving of water in an attractive, handheld bottle. Perrier's timing, which was probably more fortuitous then visionary, could not have been better. It caught a market already primed by concerns about pollution and poor-quality tap water, and it caught the yuppies just as they were beginning to flex their consumer muscles. The distinctive green-glass Perrier bottle was cool, it was sophisticated, it was European, it was expensive. It was all the things the yuppies wanted in a lifestyle-defining product.

In the end, it was a rout. Sales of Perrier skyrocketed, and the rest of the American bottled water industry slipstreamed easily behind. Since 1980, sales of bottled water have increased steadily in the United States. As recently as 1990, finding bottled water in convenience stores among the racks of soda and beer was unusual. Nowadays, bottled water can be bought just about everywhere.

The rows and rows of neatly packaged bottled waters that you will find today in any grocery story can be viewed simply as one more slickly marketed, overhyped, flashy product. On the surface, bottled water might seem like one more example of Madison Avenue creating a need in the heads of mindless consumers. After all, selling something like drinking water, which can be had virtually for free, is surely the epitome of marketing genius.

But when it comes to water, we are not dealing only with what you see on the surface. Hidden deep below is a wellspring of human history and culture. While the outward fashion may seem whimsical and shallow, the underlying water consciousness has very, very deep roots. It is entirely true that the modern success of bottled water in the United States depends heavily on clever marketing. It is less well understood that such marketing could not work without this invisible, deeply ingrained, cultural reverence for pure water. This water consciousness, which in the case of the United States can be traced directly to long European tradition, was the well waiting to be tapped by Perrier's marketeers. It may have been marketing genius, but it did not come out of nowhere.

In the end, it is the history of human society, and the natural history of particular waters, that explains the allure of bottled water. This, in turn, is what makes bottled waters interesting. There are millions of springs in the United States alone, but only a tiny fraction produce water of sufficient quality that can be sold in competition with inexpensive tap water. What is it about these waters that makes them so unique and so desirable? Why is it that people buy them? Is it the waters themselves, or is it the mystique surrounding them? Or, is it simply how these waters are packaged, marketed, and sold? As it turns out, all of these apply, but the proportion varies from spring to spring, from source to source, and from market to market. If you don't look carefully at the natural history, these questions cannot be answered.

What follows, therefore, is a natural history of bottled water. This is partly a history of human customs and technology, and how circumstance has drawn people and certain springs together. But it is also a history of the waters themselves. Some waters come from deep, hot recesses of the earth; others originate high in cold mountains. Some waters are ancient, having seeped through the earth for thousands of years; others are virtually newly fallen rain or recently melted snow. In the end, it is how these waters interact with the earth that determines their chemical purity. Just as important, though, it is how people have interacted with these waters—often over thousands of years—that affects how interesting they are. It is entirely analogous to the Thai and their maaw nahm or the Venetians and their filter cisterns. People like their water to be clean and stylish, preferably both.

Modern American and Thai traditions are literally worlds apart. And yet the parallel between bottled water use in both societies is striking. Water is important to people, and thus it is an important part of human society. In both societies, how people use water reflects their lifestyles, their personal beliefs, their economic prosperity. The popularity of bottled water in Thailand and the United States is simply a reflection what water really means to people.

It is water from the heart.

2 MYTHS AND MYSTERIES
The Geology of Springs

Just after daybreak, an old-model car with a beat-up finish pulled into the dirt parking lot and stopped next to a small headstone. At first glance, the headstone appeared to mark a grave. The driver, a woman who looked to be about fifty years old, stepped out of the car, walked around to the back, and opened her trunk. In the trunk were ten or twelve empty milk jugs. One by one, she carried the jugs down to the spring, which was hidden by the early morning mists. She filled them with bubbling spring water and returned them to the car. In five minutes the water jugs were filled and neatly arranged in her trunk. Her routine complete, she got back into her car, started it, and pulled away from the headstone, which, as it happens, did not mark a grave. The headstone read:

God's Acre
Healing Springs
Deeded to Almighty God,
to be used by the sick and afflicted
by
L. P. "Lute" Boylston
July 21, 1944

By local reckoning, anywhere from a dozen to more than two hundred people a day (depending on the weather and season) visit Healing Springs, located near the little town of Blackville, South Carolina. Most of these people bring an assortment of jugs and bottles to be filled with water for use at home. Some wade or even bathe in the shallow pool that surrounds the springs. These springs, like so many others throughout the United States, are the stuff of local legend and history.

The story of Healing Springs begins in about 1750 when a man named Nathaniel Walker received a king's grant of land along the South Edisto River in South Carolina. One day, while exploring the land, Walker happened to see an Indian bathing in a pool of water. Intrigued, Walker approached the Indian and, using signs, asked him where the waters came from. The Indian replied that the waters came from the Great Spirit and that they could heal sickness and injuries. Walker, apparently convinced by the story, traded a sack of maize to a band of local Indians in return for the spring. The Indians, who almost certainly did not understand the concept of owning or selling land, much less owning or selling a holy spring, happily took the maize and went on their way.

That part of the story may or may not be true. As with most stories of healing springs, it is almost impossible to separate history from legend. But one part of the Healing Springs story can be verified from documentary evidence. In 1782, during the Revolutionary War, British soldiers garrisoned in Charleston made a raid on some suspected patriots near Blackville. The resulting battle, locally called the Battle of Slaughter Field, left six British soldiers so badly wounded that their companions feared to move them back to Charleston. Instead, they were left at Healing Springs, where they drank the water, bathed, and rested. In a few weeks, as is actually documented in the garrison records of Charleston, all six soldiers returned to duty, their wounds healed. Thus began the legend of the Healing Springs of South Carolina.

The legend grew over the years, with literally hundreds of stories of miraculous healings being attributed to drinking or bathing in the spring waters. In 1907, a gentleman named Lute Boylston, the owner of the springs, tried to capitalize on the water's fame by bottling and selling it. There was ample precedent for this. After all, Saratoga Springs, Poland Spring, and countless other spring waters had been bottled and sold for much of the nineteenth century as "healing" waters. But by 1907, demand for curative bottled waters in the United States was waning. One reason was that medical science had actually advanced to the point where it could do more good then harm, and thus there was less need for medical miracles. Another reason was a series of articles written by Samuel Hopkins Adams for *Collier's* magazine.[1] Adams, who was one of history's notable muckraking journalists, was unhappy with the traffic in what were called "patent medicines." These were proprietary formulations that were touted to cure everything from headaches to cancer. These medicines were extremely popular, and in 1906 Americans spent more than $80 million on them. Adams's series, called "The Great American Fraud," exposed these medicines for what they were—drinks composed mostly of herbs, alcohol, and opiates that could effectively intoxicate people but were generally worthless as medical therapy. Most Americans were shocked and scandalized by these revelations. Adams himself did not directly attack "healing" bottled waters, but they were guilty by association. When Boylston launched his enterprise of bottling water from Healing Springs in 1907, he was selling to an already shrinking market. After three hard years of work collecting the water in green glass bottles (which are collector's items today) and hauling them to Charleston and other cities, the Healing Springs Bottling Company went out of business.

But the renown of the Healing Springs water in the countryside around Blackville continued to grow during the twentieth century, so much so that Boylston began to worry what would happen to the spring when he died. Convinced that the water was a gift from God, Boylston had the novel idea of giving it back to the Almighty. In his will, which was executed in 1944, one acre of land surrounding Healing Springs was left to God. The deed in the county courthouse actually lists the owner of the property as "God Almighty."

There are hundreds of springs across the United States that, like the Healing Springs of South Carolina, have varying reputations for their holy, healing, or magical waters. This has had a profound impact on the bottled water industry. The purveyors of many famous bottled waters—Saratoga Springs, Mountain Valley Springs, and Poland Spring are obvious examples—originally got started in the business to fill the demand for such "healing" waters. Many more bottling operations—Lute Boylston's operation at Healing Springs being one example—tried and failed to capitalize on their "healing" reputations. Although bottled waters are not marketed as medicines anymore, it would be foolish to ignore the lingering association between spring waters and health. It would also be foolish to ignore the fact that this is not a significant factor in the bottled water industry today. Twenty-first-century America is a rational, technological society, and the advances made by modern medicine in saving and improving lives can only be described as miraculous. Why, then, are there still so many "healing springs" throughout the United States? What is it about springs and spring waters that touch such a superstitious nerve in so many people?

We can begin by considering the stone circles of Great Britain. There are over nine hundred stone circles known in the British Isles, and as far as archaeologists can tell, they were built in the late Bronze Age between 2500 and 1000 B.C.[2] Just what they were used for has been the subject of massive speculation over the years. It does seem that at least some of them, like Stonehenge, were astronomical devices, designed to keep track of the summer and winter solstices. But they also appear to have been the foci of outdoor worship, although the rites and deities being honored have faded from human memory. One aspect of the stone circles that is not widely known is that they often have wells associated with them.[3] One such well, found at Wilsford near Stonehenge, had been dug to a depth of hundred feet. The effort and technology involved in sinking a shaft hundred feet below the land surface is mind-boggling. These shafts, which have been found throughout Britain, are as impressive a technical accomplishment as are the standing stones themselves. Upon excavation, the Wilsford shaft was found to contain the remains of buckets and a rope. But it also contained amber beads, pottery, and wooden objects. Because this particular well was found in a burial mound, it seems to have had a religious purpose in addition to possibly being a source of water. Some archaeologists interpret these wells or shafts, of which more than hundred have been found, as indicating a desire to communicate with spirits living beneath the earth. If that interpretation is correct, then the association between wells and the spirit world can be traced back at least 3,500 years.

The custom of trying to propitiate subterranean spirits by making offerings at wells can be traced back even further in human history. Prior to Christianity, the Roman religion was based on the belief that natural objects were inhabited by spirits. Since springs were natural objects, it stood to reason that they too would have various spirits associated with them. It was common practice for Romans to give offerings (sacrae stipes) to the spirts of springs and wells in order to gain their favor.

There is some remarkable archeological evidence for this.[4] In 1852, the Jesuit owners of a celebrated sulfur spring named Sorgenti di Vicarello, located on the western shore of the Lake of Bracciano near Rome, resolved to repair the ancient masonry surrounding the well. They hired a team of masons, who began the project by diverting the upwelling spring waters and draining the ancient well. At the bottom of the well, which was only a few feet below the former water level, the masons came across a layer of brass and silver coins dating from the fourth century A.D. Below this was a layer of gold and silver coins, minted by various emperors, dating from the first and second centuries B.C. By now, as you can imagine, the masons were digging with real enthusiasm. Unfortunately, however, the archeological value of what they had found was the last thing on their minds. Next, they came to a layer of silver coins dating to the Roman Republic, probably 200 or 300 B.C. Underneath this was a layer of bronze coins, sextants, and tripods dating to the late Bronze Age, which would be about 2000 B.C.

Seeing that they had come to the end of the gold and silver, the masons divided their booty and hid most of it. Only then did they inform the local priest, Padre Marchi, of what they had found. By the time the good padre arrived, most of the gold and silver was gone. Nevertheless, the impatient masons had left behind several hundred coins, which they apparently judged to be less valuable or, more probably, just could not carry away in time. Some of these coins, known as *aes grave signatum,* were among the first coinage used in Rome. At the bottom of the well, there was a layer of "gravel" that the masons had ignored completely as being worthless. When Padre Marchi looked at it, however, he realized it was a collection of arrowheads and knives made out of beautifully polished stone. Clearly, the spring of Sorgenti di Vicarello had been the site of votive offerings to gods and spirits at least as far back as the neolithic Stone Age, which could make these artifacts older than ten thousand years.

By the time the Romans conquered Britain in 50 A.D., both the Roman and Briton cultures had a long history of revering water, wells, and springs. Springs and wells were considered to be inhabited by spirits, which could be either good or bad. Since these wells and springs were important sources of drinking water, there was good reason to try to keep these deities happy. It became the custom to give these water spirits small gifts of cloth, coins, food, or pins. Furthermore, the individual tastes of the water spirits were taken into careful consideration. Some wells, for example, might have a spirit that liked bits of cloth, and thus there is the "rag well" in Northumbria. Another might be particularly fond of cheese, and thus there is the "cheese well" of Peeblesshire in Scotland. Another might like pins, and thus there is a "pin well."

When Christianity was brought to Britain in the second or third century A.D., the association between springs, wells, and deities was already deeply ingrained in the culture of the native Britons. As the population converted to Christianity, there was no particular reason to alter these customs. Baptism, the most fundamental of Christian sacraments, involves the use of water, and the New Testament frequently uses the imagery of water as a symbol of life. In the Gospel of John, for example, the writer records how Jesus met a woman at Jacob's Well in the town of Sychar, Samaria, and told her: "Everyone who drinks this water will be thirsty again; but whoever drinks the water I shall give will never thirst; the water I shall give will become in him a spring of water welling up to eternal life" (John 4:13–14). Clearly, the early Christians were entirely comfortable associating water and God, so it's not surprising that the Romans continued to offer sacrae stipes at the spring of Sorgenti di Vicarello long after they had became Christians. Nor is it surprising that the Britons held on to their customs of revering wells and springs. The image of water providing life, and even eternal life, was one that resonated with the everyday experience of people in the ancient world.

What Christianity did do, however, was to shift the worship away from pagan water deities and focus it instead on God. Saint Columba, who was the first Christian to evangelize Scotland in the sixth century, once came upon a spring reputedly inhabited by a particularly evil spirit.[5] The local Scots were greatly afraid of this spirit and carefully provided it with offerings and worship in order to keep it from becoming troublesome. According to legend, this spirit would attack anyone who drank the water or washed in it so that they were "struck by demonical art, and went home either leprous or purblind." Saint Columba, an Irishman who was no doubt well acquainted with water worship, turned this to his advantage. He blessed the spring in the name of Christ and proclaimed that the demon had been expelled. Then he drank the water and washed his hands and feet in it. To the astonishment of the people, Saint Columba was unaffected by the water. They took this as clear evidence of the strength of the Christian God, and of Saint Columba's power to drive out demons. This, in turn, helped Saint Columba to convert the local pagans into good Christians.

Virtually all the early Christian evangelists in Ireland and Britain are associated with stories of miraculous dealings with springs and wells. Saint Cuthbert, the patron saint of Northumbria, managed several miracles associated with springs.[6] One of these occurred after he retired from the priorship of the Lindesfarne monastery, resolving to spend his last years praying in solitude. He withdrew to Farne Island, two miles from Lindesfarne, which was said to be haunted by evil spirits. But Cuthbert drove the spirits away and set about building a cell to live in. Unfortunately, Farne Island lacked fresh water. However, in response to Cuthbert's prayers, a spring arose in the floor of his cell. The Venerable Bede, who wrote the story of Cuthbert's life in 716, remarks: "This water, by a most remarkable quality, never overflowed its first limits, so as to flood the floor, nor yet ever failed, however much of it might be taken out: so that it never exceeded or fell short of the daily wants of him who used it for his sustenance." But the miracle did not end there. In the twelfth century, a particularly vicious Viking by the name of Eistan of Norway was ravaging the coast of Northumbria. Eistan landed on Farne Island and destroyed the homes of the hermits living there, no doubt looking for booty. When the Vikings tried to resupply their ship with water from Saint Cuthbert's well, however, the well went dry. The spring was apparently unwilling to give any help to heathen pagans.

Over the years, as numerous saints roamed the landscape, blessing wells and springs as they went, traditions of holy and healing wells accumulated in Great Britain. It is easy, in these days of broad-spectrum antibiotics, to smile at these beliefs. But for most of human history, with medical science likely to do more harm than good, healing wells were an important resource in the event of sickness or injury. Hundreds of these springs and wells dot the countryside of Ireland, England, Wales, and Scotland to this day. The folklore of these springs, many of which were specific for specific human ailments, is a subject of intense interest to many Britons to this day.[7] And who can blame them? These stories of holy and healing springs go so far back into human history, and are such a pervasive part of our culture, that it's no wonder they continue to fascinate.

In light of this, it is no particular surprise that when Nathaniel Walker first was introduced to the Healing Springs, South Carolina, in 1750, he was perfectly willing to believe that the waters could be healing. Coming from good English stock, Walker would be fully aware of how springs and spring waters could effect miraculous cures. The Scotch-Irish, who were already moving into South Carolina by 1750, were equally acquainted with these traditions. When the Boylston family acquired the Healing Springs in the 1800s, having a healing spring that belonged to Almighty God seemed perfectly natural.

The traditional mythologies that surround wells and springs can be traced to two historical realities. First, springs were an important source of water, sometimes unusually clean water, for people who very much needed it. Second, the source of the waters issuing from springs or tapped by wells could not be directly observed and was therefore deeply mysterious. We need search no further than this combination of necessity and mystery to understand why these mythologies arose and why they persist to this day.

Mountains, in this context, were thought to play a role analogous to that of the alembic flasks used by alchemists to distill and condense water.

But the beginning of the Italian Renaissance produced other, less biblical explanations for the origin of springs. One such explanation was espoused by Bernard Palissy (1514–1589), who believed that waters were cycled out of the oceans by evaporation followed by condensation into rain and snow. Palissy published his ideas in a book about springs in which he writes:

> The sun's heat, dryness and the heavy winds blowing toward the land cause the evaporation of great quantities of water from the ocean, which water gathers in the heavens in the form of clouds which speed from one coast to another like heralds sent by God, and when it pleases God that the clouds (which are nothing more than bodies of water) should become dissipated, these let their water fall all over the earth in the form of rain. Having made the question of the origin of springs the subject of close and long continued study, I have learned definitely that these take their origin in and are fed by rain and rain alone.[13]

The tone of Palissy's book, which is written in the form of a dialogue between a person called "Theory" and another called "Practice," is striking. In this dialogue, it is always Practice who is instructing Theory, not the other way around as favored by the ancient Greek and Roman philosophers. This, in turn, was very much in keeping with the new spirt of the Renaissance. Palissy was a potter by trade, a business in which close observation and a practical mind-set was a necessity. In this spirit of practicality, Palissy took the trouble to go into the mountains and observe directly how water behaves. What he saw was that "these rain waters rushing down the mountain sides pass over earthy slopes and fissured rocks and sinking into the earth's crust, follow a downward course till they reach some solid and impervious rock surface over which they flow untill they meet some opening to the surface of the earth, and through this they issue as springs."[14]

So, by the seventeenth century, there were two competing theories for the origin of springs. One was the holes-in-the-seafloor theory that had developed in the Middle Ages; the other was the rainfall-percolating-into-the-earth theory outlined by Palissy. The controversy intensified when, in 1664, a Jesuit priest named Athanasius Kircher published a book titled *Mundus Subterraneus*, which codified the hole-in-the-seafloor theory and actually showed pictures of huge whirlpools thought to exist on the floor of the sea.

The controversy was finally settled by studies conducted near the town of Modena in Italy. Modena was built on a plain about ten miles from the San Pellegrino Alps and had a water supply system that was the envy of the rest of Europe. Anywhere in the vicinity of Modena it was possible to dig a well to a depth of about fifty feet before encountering a hard layer of rock. At this point, it was actually possible to hear water flowing underneath the rock. When the rock was breached with an auger, water would gush upward, filling the wellbore and flowing continuously thereafter. In 1691, a professor at the University of Modena named Bernardino Ramazzini wrote an account of the "Wonderful Springs of Modena." In it, he describes how wells were bored and interprets the origin of the spring waters using Kircher's framework: "Though I derive the Original of our Fountains from the Seas first, then from some Cistern of water plac'd in our Mountains, into which the Vapors, sent up the enclos'd Heat, are returned in the Form of Waters." [15]

Ramazzini's report drew the attention of another academic named Antonio Vallisnieri, who was the president of the University of Padua at the time. Vallisnieri, a true rationalist at heart, resolved to settle the origin of the Modena spring waters once and for all. He reasoned that if Kircher's theory was correct, one should see evidence of spring waters being forced *out* of the ground in the mountains. One the other hand, if Palissy was right, one should see evidence of rainwater draining *into* the ground in the mountains. Upon hiking into the San Pellegrino Alps, Vallisnieri was surprised to see that, though there were extensive snowfields that were melting in the hot spring sun, there were very few streams running down the mountain. When he expressed his surprise to some passing shepherds, they led him to several places where the meltwaters could be seen draining into fissures in the rocks. The water ran downhill, alright, but it was moving under the ground, not over it. Kircher, apparently, was wrong.

In fairness to Athanasius Kircher, one must admit that oceanographers in the twentieth century have found that seawater really does percolate through porous volcanic rocks present on the seafloor, becomes heated at depth, and then is discharged as submarine springs. The water being discharged from these submarine hot springs, however, is just heated seawater, not fresh water that has condensed from heated steam as Kircher envisioned.

By 1750, a few people in Europe, a very few people, had a reasonably clear idea of how springs formed. One of these people was an English farmer named Joseph Elkington (1739–1806), who became interested in ground water while attempting to drain wetlands so that crops could be grown.[16] Elkington noticed that springs invariably were located at the foot of hills, and he clearly understood that it was rainwater falling on the hills that fed the springs. Elkington's description of spring waters is remarkably clear and straightforward, even by modern standards: "Springs therefore originate from rain water falling upon such porous and absorbent surfaces, and subsiding downwards through such, till, in its passage, it meets a body of clay or other impenetrable substance, which obstructs its farther decent, and here, forming a reservoir."[17]

But most people who used spring and well water on a daily basis in the eighteenth century still held on to the mystical traditions that had been handed down for hundreds of years. Part of this was because traditional beliefs do not change very rapidly. But a large part was because the new understanding of springs was still very incomplete. What was missing was a way to understand the hidden, underlying structure of the earth and thus visualize how ground water moved and circulated.

This was not a small problem. The hidden depths of the earth were largely unexplored and, given the technological limitations of the time, virtually unexplorable. True, people could see rocks and sediments at the land surface, but it was not at all clear how they were related to the underlying structure of the earth. Miners had been boring shafts into the ground for centuries, but this was difficult and expensive, and miners were unlikely to share any observations that might help competitors find valuable metal ores or coal. Without an understanding of the underlying structure of the earth, it was impossible to study the movement of ground water to springs and wells.

The solution to this problem came from an entirely unlikely source. In 1769, a boy named William Smith was born in Churchill, Oxfordshire, to parents of modest means.[18] He lost his father at an early age and was raised by an uncle who had a farm nearby. From a very early age, Smith had an interest in the fossils found in that part of England. His uncle, the farmer, thought this interest to be foolish and

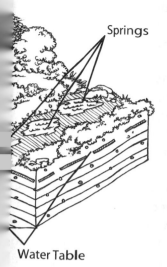

Springs

Water Table

e the land surface intersects the
·ey

gy at Stanford University, con-
h to understanding springs and
simplest circumstance that can
ion that allows the water table
:learly, water discharging from
:o the land surface and is there-
er common spring-generating
eable sands or sandstones at the
ible shales or clays (fig. 2.2). In
l surface percolates downward
ipermeable zone. At this point
.ard a spring.
es 2.1 and 2.2 are closely con-
:ermittently, depending on the
ilogic circumstances, however,
water being raised to the land
irs when rainwater seeps into
:he dip of a permeable geologic
:ture in the earth's crust where
ist each other) (fig. 2.3). In this
vhich may have spent decades,
irough the ground, can travel

tried to steer him in a more practical direction. So, at the age of eighteen, Smith became an assistant to a local surveyor.

The end of the eighteenth century in England was a time of massive
technical and social change. While coal was abundant in the English
countryside, moving this coal to textile factories using horse-drawn
carts was virtually impossible. With the construction of canals, however, it became possible to move large quantities of coal quickly and
cheaply to the new factory towns. Smith, with a background in sur-
veying and a keen interest in geology, was well placed to make a living
evaluating local coal reserves and building new canals to bring this coal
to market.

In 1791, at the age of twenty-two, Smith went to Somerset to survey and evaluate the coal reserves of a local landowner. In doing so, he
learned something that the local miners had known for generations:
the succession of strata in the coal beds was virtually identical in each
mine. As a surveyor of canals, Smith was accustomed to noting and
mapping the kinds of rocks encountered at the land surface. But as he
went from mine to mine in the Somerset district, and as he saw how
the stratigraphic succession of the coal seams was so predictable, he had
a sudden insight. By mapping the distribution of rocks on the surface,
and by measuring the angles at which the rocks dipped into the ground,
he could visualize the underlying structure of the earth.

This was an astonishing idea, and one of great practical use. In de-
signing canals, for example, it enabled him to make sure there would
be stone of sufficient quantity and quality for building locks and dams.
It allowed him to plan for efficient excavations, and it helped him to
find the best foundations for bridges. But, just as important, it allowed
him to evaluate issues of water drainage. Managing water was critical
to building and maintaining canals, and Smith devoted careful attention to learning how water circulated and moved in the subsurface, a
subsurface that he could now "see" by mapping the surface expression
of rock formations and extrapolating below. One of the first practical
applications of his insight was to drain the great Prisley Bog in 1806,
converting it into highly productive agricultural land. This notable
success made him highly sought after, and he traveled all over England
taking on similar engineering projects. These travels, in which he kept
careful records of the rocks he found, eventually led to his *Geologic
Map of England*, published in 1815. This was the crowning achievement
of his life, and one that earned him the title "father of English geology."

But it was his knowledge of ground water, and hence his exp[e] managing it, that most often kept Smith gainfully employed. [W]he the famous hot springs at Bath failed, leading to general lame[nt] and the real possibility of financial ruin for the local economy[, and] the mystical traditions surrounding the hot springs of Bath, [some of] which predated the Romans, you can imagine how the failur[e of the] spring waters to flow affected the countryside. If the hot waters [of Bath] were a gift from God, was not their failure a sure sign of G[od's dis]pleasure? Would not interfering with the spring's flow be inte[rfering] with the Almighty's will? There was, in short, a general wail[ing and] gnashing of teeth.

Smith, with his clear understanding of the underlying stru[cture of] the earth and with a basic knowledge of how the flow of groun[d water] reflects this structure, was not impressed by these superstitiou[s ideas.] After considerable resistance from the local population, he was a[ble] to excavate to the bottom of the spring. Using his knowledge [of min]ing practices to advantage, he soon discovered what the real p[roblem] was. Rather than an angry and vengeful God, Smith and his wo[rkers] found that the culprit was an ox bone. Somehow, the bone had [fallen] into the main water channel that fed the spring and blocked [it. The] spring waters had obligingly formed a new channel that drai[ned] the waters before they could reach the surface. Smith soon sea[led] the new channel, and in a matter of days he restored the spring[.] In fact, the flow actually increased. Many people, including B[ernard] Palissy and Antonio Vallisnieri, had contributed to a rational [under]standing of how springs work. William Smith was one of the [first to] use this understanding to solve practical problems concerning g[round] water and springs.

Smith's insights made it possible to use geologic maps to vi[sualize] the hidden subsurface. Direct methods for penetrating and obs[erving] subsurface rocks—that is, drilling technologies—were still som[e way] away. Most water wells were excavated by hand with picks and sh[ovels,] and digging a well more than ten or twenty feet deep was a difficu[lt and] dangerous undertaking. People in Europe had been experim[enting] with drilling methods at least since the eleventh century, but i[n 1859] they remained relatively crude. This all changed in 1859, when [Edwin] Drake successfully managed to drill an oil well in Pennsylvania.

It was no particular secret that there was oil hidden belowg[round] near the little Pennsylvania town of Titusville. Oil of remarkabl[e qual]ity oozed out of the ground in several places, but the flow was n[ot]

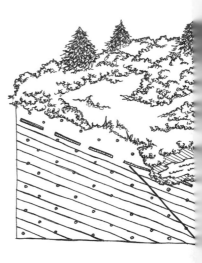

FIGURE 2.1 How springs develop whe[n the] water table. Source: U.S. Geological Sur[vey.]

Stanley N. Davis, a professor of geol[ogy, con]tinued developing this rational approa[ch to] spring waters.[20] According to Davis, th[e] cause a spring is a topographic depres[sion] to intersect the land surface (fig. 2.1). [The water in] such springs is very closely connected [and there]fore very easily contaminated. Anot[her such] circumstance occurs when highly perm[eable rocks at the] land surface are underlain by imperme[able rocks. In] this case, rainwater falling on the lan[d moves downward] until its movement is resisted by an i[mpermeable layer, and] the water turns laterally and moves to[ward the surface.]

Both kinds of springs shown in figu[re 2.1 are con]nected to the surface and often flow i[n response to the] amount of recent rainfall. Different g[eologic conditions] can lead to deeply circulating ground[water at the] surface. One common mechanism oc[curs when water in] the ground, is carried downward along [a permeable] unit, and then encounters a fault (a fr[acture where] subsurface rocks have broken and slid [past each other). In this] case, deeply circulating ground water[may spend years,] centuries, or even millennia moving [through the]

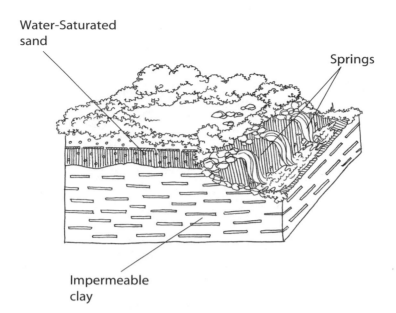

Water-Saturated
sand

Springs

Impermeable
clay

FIGURE 2.2 How springs develop where permeable sandstones overlie impermeable shales. Source: U.S. Geological Survey

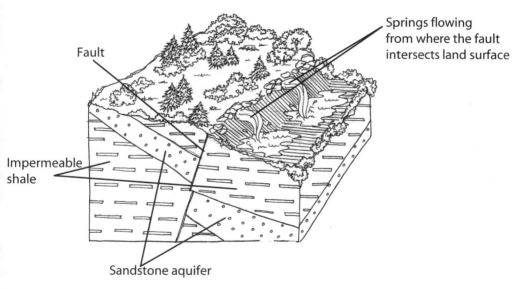

Fault

Springs flowing
from where the fault
intersects land surface

Impermeable
shale

Sandstone aquifer

FIGURE 2.3 How geologic faults can bring deep ground water to land surface, where it discharges from springs.

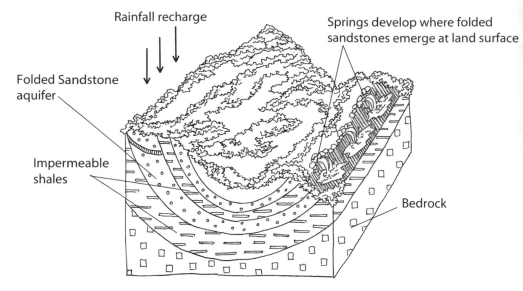

Rainfall recharge

Springs develop where folded
sandstones emerge at land surface

Folded Sandstone
aquifer

Impermeable
shales

Bedrock

FIGURE 2.4 How folded rocks can bring deep ground water to land surface, where it discharges from springs. Source: U.S. Geological Survey

along the fault and be brought to the land surface, where the water discharges as springs.

Faults are not the only underlying structure that can bring deeply
circulating water to the surface. In many parts of the country, layers of
sediments or sedimentary rocks have been crumpled and folded by the
movement of the earth (fig. 2.4). In these cases, the downward dip of a
permeable sandstone can carry water deep into the earth. In the same
way, however, as the sandstone bends back toward the land surface
(fig. 2.4), water can return to the surface, where it can discharge from
springs. Again, it can take hundreds or thousands of years for water to
move from where rainfall recharges the aquifer to where it ultimately
discharges from a spring.

In both shallow-circulating (figs. 2.1 and 2.2) and deeply circulating
(figs. 2.3 and 2.4) springs, it is the force of gravity that causes water to
percolate into the ground. When by various geologic circumstances the
water level in the aquifer is higher than the land surface, and when
there is a conduit allowing water to flow naturally, the result is a
spring. But with deeply circulating ground water, what happens if the
water level in an aquifer is higher than the land surface but there is no
fault or other structure acting as a conduit to allow flow to the surface?
In this case, if a well is drilled into the formation, the water will flow

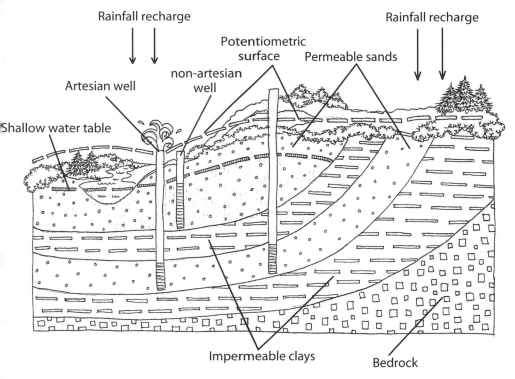

FIGURE 2.5 The relationship between artesian and nonartesian wells. Source: U.S. Geological Survey

naturally from the well (fig. 2.5). This is the definition of *artesian water*, and wells that tap this water are called *artesian wells*. Clearly, though, in most places where a well is drilled to the water table, the water will not come to the surface under natural pressure. In these wells, water can still be obtained; it is just that the water has to be pumped to the surface artificially (fig. 2.5). This is the definition of *well water*.

From the standpoint of what would be desirable for drinking water, it is clear that deeper-circulating spring, artesian, or well waters are less likely to be contaminated from animal or human wastes at the land surface than shallow-circulating springs. Conversely, deeper-circulating ground waters have had much more time to react chemically with rocks in the subsurface and are often more mineralized than shallow-circulating waters. In fact, many shallow-circulating waters are virtually pure rainwater or snowmelt. When this water is uncontaminated by microorganisms or chemicals originating at the land surface, it can make excellent drinking water whether it is produced from springs or wells. The ways in which different geologic settings can produce spring waters with various chemical properties are virtually endless.[21]

As the sun slowly rose over the Healing Springs of South Carolina, a steady stream of people in cars pulled into the parking lot and trudged down to the spring. Back in the days when Lute Boylston dreamed of bottling and selling the water, the spring had bubbled to the surface at the bottom of a shallow and muddy depression. To make collecting the water easier and more sanitary, Boylston drove several wellpoints (per-forated tubes) into the ground. These wellpoints were then connected to a series of spigots, from which bottles and jugs are easily filled. The spring water, however, still forms one or more small, shallow pools. Most of the people coming to the spring are intent on filling their jugs as quickly as possible and driving off to work or home. A few, however, take the time to wade in the shallow pools. Later in the day, the few children who come, often accompanying a parent or grandparent, hap-pily splash and play in the water. Occasionally, solemn-faced adults will sit or lie in the pool for a few minutes, allowing the spring waters to wash over them. These unfortunates, who suffer from a variety of ailments, will tell you that the water makes them "feel better." So the legend of Healing Springs continues, and probably will forever.

A careful inspection of geologic and topographic maps suggests how the Healing Springs were formed, and why the waters continue to flow.[22] Blackville is located in the Atlantic coastal plain and is underlain by sediments that have washed out of the mountains to the west over the last 70 million years. Over the millennia, the level of the sea has risen and fallen dozens of times. The sediments underlying Blackville represent at least two cycles of sea-level rise and fall. About 36 million years ago, the area near Blackville was submerged beneath the sea, and the sediments being deposited were mostly fine-grained clays. These sediments, which are about sixty or seventy feet thick, are known today as the Dry Branch Formation. As sea level fell, the sediments became progressively sandier, reflecting the deposition of beach sands. These sandy sediments, which are about fifty feet thick, are known today as the Tobacco Road Sand. Finally, overlying the Tobacco Road Sand are even younger (5 million years old) deposits of river sands and gravels known as the Upland Unit.[23] The distribution of these geologic units acts as a natural water-catching, spring-making machine (see fig. 2.2).

As rain falls on the sandy and very permeable Upland Unit sediments, water percolates vertically into the ground. Because the Tobacco Road Sand is also very permeable, water easily flows through these sediments as well. However, water does not flow easily through the relatively impermeable clays of the Dry Branch Formation. This causes the water to stop flowing downward, forcing it in a lateral direction parallel to the impermeable clay. Where the sand-clay boundary intersects the land surface on the side of a hill, the water bubbles out of the ground as the Healing Springs. This confluence of geologic and hydrologic circumstances, which are clearly "visible" from looking at a geologic map,[24] is the origin of the Healing Springs of South Carolina.

But, as is often the case, there is more to the Healing Springs than meets the eye. The limestones that make up part of the Dry Branch Formation have, over time, been progressively dissolved by percolating rainwater. As they have dissolved, conduits to deeper underlying geologic units seem to have formed. This appears to provide a source of deeper, more ancient water (see fig. 2.3) that bears the chemical signature of dissolving limestone. The waters discharging from the Healing Springs, therefore, appear to be a complex mixture of young, shallow water with older, deeper water.[25]

The hydrologic framework of Healing Springs also suggests a reason why people have come to consider the spring water to be so healthy. Blackville is located in the low country of South Carolina, which is characterized by an abundance of swamps and wetlands. These wetlands contain masses of decaying plants and trees, which in turn produce tea-colored humic acids. It is these humic acids that cause the so-called blackwater streams characteristic of the low country. The water is not actually black, but it is visibly discolored. The water also contains large numbers of microorganisms and is not very healthy or pleasant to drink.

In contrast, the water that issues from the Healing Springs is cool and clear. As rainwater percolates into the Upland Unit and then into the Tobacco Road sand, the water is naturally filtered. Whatever organic matter and microorganisms the water picked up at the land surface are removed, and all of this produces spring water that is delightfully clean. During colonial times, people who were used to drinking water from blackwater streams or from shallow, easily contaminated wells would have considered Healing Springs water a luxury. They also would have observed that people who drank Healing Springs water regularly were noticeably healthier then other, less fortunate folks. There is absolutely no mystery as to why this clean, clear, healthy spring water would, over time, earn a reputation for being "healing."

Hydrogeologists and engineers, who have spent years studying in college and graduate school, often have little patience with the aura of mysticism that surrounds places like Healing Springs. Physicians also worry that belief in the healing powers of spring water might keep people from seeking medical help when they need it. These attitudes are understandable, but they miss an important reality. Myths and legends about gods, spirits, and springs are thousands and thousands of years old. Furthermore, traditions about how spirits and God can work through spring waters to heal the ailments of the faithful are just as old. Rational hydrogeology, on the other hand, cannot be traced back much further than William Smith in 1800, a mere two hundred years ago.

If history teaches us anything about human behavior, it is that people are loath to part with their cherished traditions, particularly traditions that bring comfort and hope. The people who fill their jugs and bottles at Healing Springs, and the people who bathe in the waters, come away comforted. They feel good about it, just as they feel good repeating stories describing miraculous healings said to have happened at the spring. Rationality, hydrogeology, and modern medicine are marvelous and useful inventions. But as long as people are comforted by drinking and washing in spring waters, they will continue to do it.

And the legends will continue as well.

3 MEDICINES AND MIRACLES
The Chemistry of Spring Waters

The patient was a shy teenaged girl. She sat with her eyes lowered as her mother, a formidable, no-nonsense German Frau, explained the problem to Dr. Kreysig. She has no strength, her mother was saying, she mopes about all day, she is not interested in anything, and she never exercises anymore. This was quite unlike her, the mother continued, remembering the happy, active child her daughter had once been. So the question was, were these the symptoms of a physical ailment—as the mother suspected—or were they just the natural result of adolescent petulance? In this year of 1820, teenagers were just as prone to exasperating their parents as they are today.

Dr. Kreysig listened to the mother's description of symptoms without comment. Then, with the mother's permission, he stood up from his desk and sat next to the young girl. To his practiced eye, there was nothing obviously amiss. Her skin was pale but clear, her breathing was easy, and her heart beat normally.

But there was, perhaps, one thing.

Turning the young girl's face to the light flooding in from the window, Dr. Kreysig could just barely see the greenish tint of her skin. After a few more minutes of asking questions and watching carefully, the diagnosis became clear. The young girl was suffering from chlorosis, a form of anemia that was common among young European women in the nineteenth century. Happily, however, thanks to the medical technology of the day, there was a cure. Dr. Kreysig turned to the mother.

"She must go to the springs of Eger, in Bohemia, to take the waters," the doctor intoned. "I will give you precise instructions on which spring waters she is to take, how much of each she is to drink, and how the dose will change as the treatment continues. These instructions you will follow exactly. The treatment will last for at least two weeks and perhaps as much as a fortnight."

The mother nodded in satisfaction, as if she had suspected as much all along.[1]

In nineteenth-century Europe, chlorosis was a fairly common condition among young women beginning the rigors of puberty. One symptom of chlorosis, and the one from which the name of the ailment comes, is a slight greenish tint of the skin. We now know that chlorosis is a kind of anemia caused by iron deficiency. But, as was common in the medical practice of the early nineteenth century, it was not particularly clear what was cause and what was effect. In 1824, Dr. Kreysig wrote:

> Chlorosis is generally considered as a nervous disorder, to which young females are liable . . . at the age of puberty; because the formative fluids, in consequence of neglect of education . . . are rendered imperfect, and the glands and intestines have become obstructed.[2]

In other words, Dr. Kreysig did not have a clue as to what caused chlorosis. But while he was not sure what caused it, he did know how to treat it. For many years, physicians had observed the effects of spring waters on particular diseases. Certain conditions, it was noted, responded favorably to certain mineral waters. The waters of Eger, for example, had several unusual properties that were of medicinal interest. This is how Dr. Kreysig described them, using the medical jargon of the time:

> The Eger is a chalybeate abounding with carbonic acid, of a most efficacious kind. It differs from Pyrmont and Spa, in containing a great proportion of soda and Glauber's salt; and is therefore ranked amongst the resolvent strengthening wells.[3]

The term "chalybeate" refers to water containing relatively high concentrations of dissolved iron. The reference to "carbonic acid" indicates that the water was naturally effervescent, a characteristic often associated with medicinal properties. These waters also contained "soda," or dissolved sodium, and "Glauber's salt," an iron precipitate. The medical significance of chalybeate waters was that they were observed to help people suffering from anemia. Dr. Krisig went on to describe the use of iron-bearing waters to treat chlorosis:

> The cold chalybeates are in general justly considered as strengthening. . . . The iron, which, in chlorotic subjects, sometimes produces, in the course of a few weeks, so healthy an appearance, combined

with feelings of vigor and strength, does not effect this in all cases when the vital powers are truly depressed.[4]

So it is easy to see why Dr. Kreysig would prescribe the water of Eger to a young teenaged girl exhibiting symptoms of chlorosis. It is also interesting to note, as his last comment indicates, that the good doctor was under no illusions that chalybeate waters were a cure-all. While such water might help someone suffering from simple chlorosis, it would not necessarily help with more complicated afflictions (such as clinical depression) that produced similar symptoms.

In 1820, the various medicinal effects of different spring waters were well known, having been cataloged for centuries. What was new, however, was the science of analytical chemistry. Beginning about the middle of the eighteenth century, several scientists including Joseph Priestly, Antoine Lavoisier, Henry Cavendish, and John Dalton had revived the atomic theory of the elements and shown that most chemical substances were compounds containing two or more different elements. By 1820, analytical chemists such as the Swede Jons Jakob Berzelius (1779–1848), who contributed to analyses listed in Dr. Kreysig's treatise, had compiled fairly accurate tables of atomic weights. They also had fairly good wet-chemical methods for selectively precipitating dissolved solids such as sodium, calcium, magnesium, iron, bicarbonate, and sulfate from water so that these substances could be dried and weighed. This made it possible, for the first time in human history, for people to actually analyze mineral waters for the kinds and amounts of dissolved solids they contained. So, in addition to cataloging the medicinal effects of different spring waters, Dr. Kreysig was able to provide chemical analyses of them as well. Even though the chemical technology was crude by modern standards, and even though the units of analysis (grains of solute per pound of water) sound odd to the modern ear, the water analyses provided by Dr. Kreysig immediately show why the waters of Eger were so useful in the treatment of chlorosis. Specifically, they contained relatively high concentrations of dissolved iron. This iron, in turn, was just what people suffering from simple anemia needed in their diet. The fact that the iron was dissolved helped as well, since this made it easier to assimilate. For young ladies suffering from chlorosis, the waters of Eger were the best and highest-tech medicine available at the time.

Other spring waters described by Dr. Kreysig had entirely different medicinal effects. For example, the waters of Carlsbad were famous for treating stomach ailments. Dr. Kreysig commented: "Although not so refreshing to the taste as the chalybeates, these waters [of Carlsbad] are still drunk with pleasure by the patients; and notwithstanding they commonly operate as purgatives . . . and I have even frequently witnessed, that relief has been obtained in pains of the stomach."[5] In other words, the waters of Carlsbad acted as a gentle laxative "capable of relieving the bad humors, and returning the intestinal organs to their proper balance." A glance at the chemical analysis of these waters given by Dr. Kreysig in his book shows why. The waters of Carlsbad contained large amounts of "carbonate of magnesia" and "sulfate of soda." Translated into the jargon of modern chemistry, the Carlsbad waters contained more magnesium sulfate than the other waters in Dr. Kreysig's treatise. These days, magnesium sulfate can still be purchased in drugstores under their traditional name of "Epsom salts," and they are still used as laxatives. When an invalid took a dose of Carlsbad spring water, he or she was taking a naturally occurring solution of Epsom salts, and the results were entirely predictable.

In these days of medical sophistication, it is easy to smile at how nineteenth-century physicians used spring waters as medicines. But considering the bleak state of medical science at the time, and considering that these waters *did* have medicinal effects that were entirely reproducible, they were arguably as useful as anything else that was available. If the tendency was for people to use the waters as cure-alls, trying them for ailments that the waters could not help (such as heart disease, kidney failure, or cancer), then perhaps they can be excused on the grounds that there was simply no alternative. The bottled water industry in Europe began by bottling, shipping, and selling the waters of Carlsbad, Eger, and countless other springs as medicines. In fact, the custom of drinking mineral waters is still enthusiastically practiced in Europe today. While mineral waters are no longer marketed as specific medicines, drinking them is still widely thought to be a wholesome and healthy habit.

The connection between the development of analytical chemistry and the medicinal uses of spring waters is intriguing.[6] For example, in 1767, a gruff and unpleasant man named Joseph Priestly took up residence near a brewery in Leeds, England. This led to his interest in the "fixed air" that was generated in the brewing vats. At one point, Priestly dissolved the gas in water and noted that this produced "an exceedingly pleasant sparkling water, resembling seltzer water." In other words, Priestly had discovered why "sparkling" spring waters sparkled in the first place. They contained "fixed air." A few years later, the French chemist Antoine Lavoisier identified Priestly's "fixed air" as carbon dioxide, or, as Dr. Krisig called it, "carbonic acid."

It did not take long for people to see the economic potential of artificially carbonating water. Natural carbonated waters could be had by bottling the spring waters of Carlsbad or Eger, of course. But bottling and shipping these waters was extremely expensive, and thus they were available only to the privileged classes. However, in 1781, an English apothecary named Thomas Henry published a paper titled "An Account of a Method of Preserving Water at Sea, to which is added a Mode of Impregnating Water in large Quantities with Fixed Air. For the Use of the Sick on Board of Ships and in Hospitals." If naturally effervescent spring waters were good for sick people, the thinking went, then artificially produced effervescent waters might be good as well. Also, since carbonic acid is a mild antiseptic, artificial carbonation would certainly help preserve water stored in casks at sea.

Another motivation for producing carbonated waters for use on ships was that they were thought to prevent scurvy.[7] Scurvy, which led to infections, loss of teeth, uncontrolled bleeding, and other debilitating symptoms, was a large problem for the British navy. When deprived of fresh food for months at sea, entire crews became ill. This, in turn, made it very difficult to service Britain's far-flung empire. In the early 1700s, a Dutch writer named Johannes Bachstrom concluded that scurvy "is solely owing to a total abstinence from fresh vegetable food, and greens; which is alone the primary cause of the disease." Later, a British navy surgeon named James Lind noticed that oranges and lemons could cure scurvy. But there were other competing theories as well. One of these was that carbonated waters could prevent the disease.

The question, however, was how to produce carbonated water at sea most efficiently and cheaply. Thomas Henry's method worked, but it required the use of cumbersome equipment. In the 1780s, a professor of chemistry named Torbern Bergman (1735–1784) proposed a simpler method for producing carbonated water. Professor Bergman suggested combining lime juice and sodium bicarbonate (baking soda) to produce effervescence. Professor Bergman then suggested that this mixture "be swallowed during the effervescence" in order to take full advantage of the medicinal benefits of carbonation. This, in turn, would prevent scurvy.

The professor was spectacularly right. In experiments carried out by the British navy at sea, the treatment was soon shown to prevent scurvy. As it turned out, however, this had nothing to do with effervescence, baking soda, or carbon dioxide. Rather, the acidic lime juice used to produce the effervescence contained vitamin C. The British navy began using lime juice to prevent scurvy in the 1790s, by which time the experiments had shown that the baking soda did not add anything to the effectiveness of the treatment. It was not until the 1930s that scurvy was shown to be a vitamin C deficiency, which finally explained why lime juice could prevent it. It is an interesting quirk of history, however, that the discovery of a treatment for scurvy is intertwined with the perceived medicinal properties of carbonated spring waters.[8]

Although the supposed medicinal benefits of artificially carbonated water did not quite pan out, it did taste pretty good. In 1783, Jacob Schweppes, a friend of Joseph Priestly, began producing "aerated" water for sale in Geneva, Switzerland. In 1792, the Schweppes Company opened a factory in London to produce artificially carbonated water, a commercial operation that continues to this day. Clearly, the carbonated beverage industry can be traced back to the insights of the first scientific chemists who worked out the chemical properties of carbon dioxide. Just as clearly, the carbonated beverage industry slipstreamed behind the business of bottling and selling spring waters as medicines.

The bottled water industry in the United States began, just as it did in Europe, as a means to deliver waters with medicinal properties to people who could not afford, or whose poor health prevented, travel to mineral springs. If the state of medical practice was crude in Europe in 1820, it was even worse in America. There were only two medical schools in the United States at the time, and most "doctors" learned their trade as apprentices to country physicians. There is considerable debate among medical historians as to whether the doctors of the time did more harm than good. Some studies suggest that people who either could not or would not see doctors actually had a better chance of survival then those who submitted to a doctor's care. It is almost certainly true, for example, that George Washington's last, fatal illness—probably a simple case of strep throat—was greatly exacerbated by his being bled by a local doctor. Fear of doctors was common and often justified. For this reason, many people opted to medicate themselves. This, in turn, led to a market for the "wonderful" healing waters bottled at various mineral springs.

In the United States, the first mineral waters to be exploited for medicinal use came from Saratoga Springs, New York.[9] The word Saratoga is a Mohawk word that has been translated in a number of ways including "the place of the beavers" or "the place of swift waters" or, as is the sentimental favorite, "the place of the medicine waters of the Great Spirit."[10] Clearly, the Native American population of New York knew all about the healing waters of Saratoga Springs long before Europeans came along. In fact, the first recorded European visitor to the springs was a gentlemen named Sir William Johnson, who was taken there in 1767 by Native Americans to try to cure an old leg wound. Apparently the treatment was successful, and the fame of Saratoga Springs waters as a cure for just about any ailment spread rapidly. By the 1790s, an inn was built to accommodate the influx of visitors seeking to use the waters. This inn is said to have housed such notables as George Washington (who was a prodigious traveler) and Alexander Hamilton.[11]

But, just as with many springs in Europe, it was quickly observed that the chemical composition of the waters of Saratoga Springs varied from place to place. Furthermore, and again just as in Europe, this variability indicated different medical uses for the different spring waters. One of the first descriptions of the Saratoga Springs waters, written by one Dr. Stoddard in 1806, is essentially a prescription:

> Each spring has the salts and solutions in different proportions which gives it a peculiar virtue and adapts it more particularly to certain forms of disease. Columbian Spring is a fine chalybeate tonic, gives tone and strength to the stomach, and improves the condition of the blood by increasing the number of red blood corpuscles. It is useful in all diseases characterized by impoverished condition of the blood. Dose: From half a glass to one glass before meals; its use is better preceded by cathartic water. Hawthorne Spring as a cathartic is unrivaled in potency by any spring in Saratoga, and in this its danger lies. It is highly beneficial in dyspepsia, chronic constipation, gout, rheumatism, and in liver and kidney difficulties.[12]

The similarities of this prescription to Dr. Kreysig's regimen—especially using waters from one spring as a source of iron to "improve the condition of the blood" and using other waters as a laxative—are striking. This is no coincidence. It simply reflects the fact that, in those days, spring waters were viewed as an accepted part of medical practice. Furthermore, just like their European colleagues, American physicians were keen to learn why different waters had different medicinal effects, and they turned to chemical analysis of the waters to address these questions.

These analyses, performed by a physician named John Steel, clearly showed that the composition of waters produced from different springs varied considerably.[13] While these differences were initially of purely medical interest, they did make people wonder just why this should be so. Why was it that springs or wells just a few hundred feet from each other were so different in chemical composition? Why did some springs, such as High Rock Spring and Washington Spring, contain relatively high concentrations of sodium, calcium, and magnesium, whereas other springs, such as Sulfur Spring, contained much less? Why did Sulfur Spring have so much more hydrogen sulfide than other springs? Why did some of the waters have more natural effervescence than others? Why did waters from High Rock Spring contain iodine, a mineral of considerable medical interest, whereas others did not? Until quantitative chemical analyses of these waters became available in the early nineteenth century,[14] nobody even thought to ask these questions, and many more years would pass before they could be answered in any satisfactory way. And, as is often the case in science, the beginnings of this understanding started in an unexpected and humble way.

In 1920, about a hundred years after people like Dr. Kreysig, Jons Berzelius, and John Steel began analyzing spring waters for concentrations of dissolved solids, a young geologist named B. Coleman Renick, working in Montana, noticed something strange. He was compiling a survey of wells in an area near Miles City, Montana, for the U.S. Geological Survey. This survey included logging the depths of wells and noting the rock units that each well penetrated. But also, since it was now good professional practice, Renick collected water samples and had them analyzed for the kinds of dissolved solids they contained.

As he had come to expect, calcium, magnesium, sodium, and bicarbonate comprised most of the dissolved solids in the water. What was curious, however, was that water from the shallower wells—those less then about a hundred feet deep—contained roughly equal amounts of calcium, magnesium, and sodium. Conversely, the deeper wells—those more than a hundred feet deep—yielded water that contained sodium but virtually no calcium and magnesium.[15] It was almost as if there were two separate water-bearing zones, one yielding calcium-magnesium water and the other yielding sodium water. But, as a good geologist, Renick knew that the wells all penetrated the same geologic units. What could be going on?

Although the people living in the area did not have the wherewithal to analyze their water, they did know that the properties of the water changed with well depth. Water that contains high concentrations of calcium and magnesium interferes with the action of soap, making it "hard" to wash clothes or dishes or anything else. Dissolved calcium and magnesium ions each carry two positive charges and in modern chemistry are abbreviated Ca^{2+} and Mg^{2+} respectively. These relatively strong charges attract and surround soap particles and partially inactivate them. Sodium, on the other hand, has just a single positive charge when it is dissolved in water and is abbreviated Na^+. This single positive charge does not interact as strongly with soap particles, and thus the soap lathers more easily. Waters containing mostly Na^+, since they lack the hardness of Ca^{2+} and Mg^{2+} waters, are referred to as being "soft." The people of Montana, who were using these well waters on an everyday basis, had discovered the difference between the shallow "hard" waters and the deeper "soft" waters long before Renick came along. Furthermore, they greatly favored the deeper soft waters, which were easier to use.

But why were these shallow and deep ground waters so different in chemical character? In the early twentieth century, having relatively accurate analyses of water was still a bit of a novelty. But, now that chemical analyses were available, it was inevitable that people would cease being satisfied knowing just *how* water chemistry varied and begin wondering *why* they varied. B. Coleman Renick was one of the first geologists to try to work out why well water produced from different depths had such different chemical compositions. In his publications as a professional scientist, Renick is mute as to why he began studying this problem. It is a pretty good bet, however, that he was simply curious.

One clue to the differences in chemical composition was that the amount of total dissolved solids did not change appreciably with depth. The shallow waters contained, on average, about 1,400 milligrams per liter (mg/L) of dissolved solids, whereas the deeper waters contained about 1,360 mg/L. In other words, while the shallow waters contained principally Ca^{2+} and Mg^{2+} and the deeper waters contained principally Na^+, both contained about the same amount of dissolved material. Furthermore, if you took into account the different atomic weights of each element, it was clear that there was exactly twice as much Na^+

in the deeper water as there was Ca^{2+} and Mg^{2+} in the shallower water. Renick, who was aware of recent developments in water treatment technology, thought he knew what was going on.

Hard waters were a problem not only for people in Montana trying to wash their clothes; they were also a problem for engineers producing steam from steam engines. Hard water left a "scale" on the inside of boilers and was considered a major nuisance. In 1907, a chemist named A. Feldoff reported a method of removing Ca^{2+} and Mg^{2+} from boiler-feed waters using "base exchange." If hard waters were reacted with certain sodium-bearing clay minerals, the Ca^{2+} and Mg^{2+} could be removed from solution and "exchanged" for Na^+ according to the simple reactions

$$Ca^{2+}_{dissolved} + Na_2\ clay_{solid} \rightarrow 2Na^+_{dissolved} + Ca\ clay_{solid}$$

and

$$Mg^{2+}_{dissolved} + Na_2\ clay_{solid} \rightarrow 2Na^+_{dissolved} + Mg\ clay_{solid}.$$

When Renick noticed that Na^+ concentrations in the deeper waters were exactly twice the Ca^{2+} and Mg^{2+} concentrations in the shallower waters, as indicated by the proportions given by these two reactions, the answer to the puzzle was clear. Base exchange was occurring naturally in the Montana ground water. Specifically, rainwater percolating into the earth was dissolving Ca^{2+} and Mg^{2+} minerals present in the rocks and produced the hard shallow water. As the water continued percolating downward, however, Ca^{2+} and Mg^{2+} was exchanged for Na^+, producing the softer, deeper water.

The mystery was solved.[16]

The idea that the chemical character of spring waters reflects interactions between water and the rocks through which the water seeps was straightforward enough. In fact, one of the first people to characterize the chemistry of Saratoga spring waters, a medical doctor named Valentine Seaman, wrote in 1809: "all of these substances [iron, lime, salt, and alkali] exist in the bowels of the earth and water, after being loaded with carbonic acid, cannot pass over them without taking up a part."[17] But in the early twentieth century, it was far from clear how specific interactions between rocks and water could explain differences in spring water chemistry. Coleman Renick was one of the first geologists to try to address this issue.

Throughout the twentieth century, as more and more analyses of ground waters became available, it became increasingly clear that the

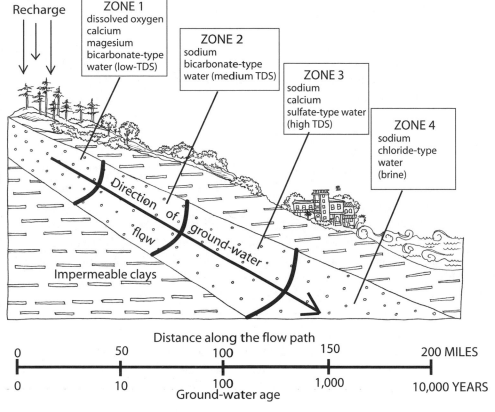

FIGURE 3.1 How ground-water chemistry changes as the water flows progressively deeper into the earth. Source: U.S. Geological Survey.

chemical composition of ground waters followed certain patterns and that these patterns were related to the movement of the water in the subsurface.[18] The most common pattern is illustrated in figure 3.1. Rainwater percolating into aquifers contains atmospheric gases such as oxygen and carbon dioxide and is slightly acidic. This acidic water then dissolves minerals present in the rocks or sediments of the aquifer. This produces relatively dilute ground water containing mostly dissolved calcium, magnesium, and bicarbonate and still containing some dissolved oxygen (zone 1). As water percolates farther into the ground, dissolved oxygen is consumed, and calcium and magnesium tend to be removed by base exchange or by other mineral precipitation reactions. These processes leave a sodium bicarbonate water that no longer has any dissolved oxygen and that may contain dissolved iron and/or sulfide (zone 2). As ground water moves still deeper into the earth, mineral dissolution and precipitation processes lead to increasingly mineralized water characterized by higher sulfate and chloride concentrations (zone 3). Finally, if the ground water travels far enough in the subsurface, the water becomes dominated by the two most soluble ions, sodium and chloride, which can accumulate in concentrations that are as high as or higher than those in seawater (zone 4). This overall pattern has been observed over and over again in many different aquifers,[19] and these zones are referred to by hydrologists as *hydrochemical facies*.[20] The details of this progression vary from place to place, depending on the kind of rocks that are present. But, in general, they are fairly consistent.

But while this overall progression is fairly simple and predictable, the geochemical processes that lead to it are not. During the twentieth century, geologists and chemists labored to understand mineral dissolution processes that control the chemistry of ground water. This effort began with Coleman Renick and other researchers who noticed certain patterns in how water chemistry changed as it flowed in the subsurface and who attributed these changes to simple chemical processes such as base exchange. Gradually, however, this problem was taken over by physical chemists, who used their knowledge of quantitative phase equilibria (chemical equilibria between different phases such as solid minerals and liquid water) to understand how and why ground water chemistry varied the way it did. What they found turned out to be an intriguing mixture of simplicity and complexity, and the findings began in the Sierra Nevada of California and Nevada.

The Sierra Nevada, like many mountain ranges, acts like a giant moisture trap. The winds blowing off the Pacific Ocean often are saturated with water vapor, and when this moisture-laden air hits the mountains, it is forced upward to higher altitudes. At these higher altitudes, the air cools, and its moisture falls out as rain and snow. Much of this precipitation occurs at relatively high altitudes, and much of it falls as snow. A portion of the rainwater, or of melting snow, seeps into the ground and begins to flow downward. Where the water table intersects the land surface, springs develop (figs. 2.1 and 2.2), and there are hundreds of springs in the Sierra Nevada. Some of these springs, incidently, are highly prized as sources of bottled water.

The Sierra Nevada itself is a huge block of granite that geologists call a *batholith*. Two hundred million years ago, tectonic forces fermenting in the earth near the intersection of the North American Plate and the Pacific Plate began to melt sediments and rocks buried miles within the earth. Once the rock melted, this liquid (magma) was less dense than the surrounding unmelted rocks and began "floating" upward. Most of the magma, however, never quite made it to land surface. As this vast plug of molten rock slowly ascended, it cooled and eventually froze in place. As it froze, it crystallized into a block of granite that, since it is very hard and durable, now stands up as a mountain range. Near land surface, this granite is fractured and faulted, and these fractures act as conduits for rainwater and snowmelt to seep into the earth. Where these water-filled fractures intersect land surface (fig. 2.3), springs develop.

For much of the twentieth century, the waters of many Sierra Nevada springs were collected and analyzed by geologists who, like Coleman Renick, were curious about why different springs produced waters with different chemistry. In 1964, a compilation of analyses of these spring waters was published for the first time.[21] In this compilation, the authors (J. H. Feth, C. E. Robertson, and W. L. Polzer) not only attempted to document the chemical composition of the waters but also, like Coleman Renick, tried to explain why the waters had the composition they did.

This approach was simply an extension of work that had gone on now for fifty years. But, on the scale of human history, it represented a sea change in how people thought about spring waters. For hundreds of years, the kinds and amounts of dissolved solids in spring waters were simply a given. The underlying causes of why some spring waters were salty, why others were fresh, why some contained iron or sulfur, were simply not known. For Feth and his coworkers to attempt to understand just why some Sierra Nevada springs were more or less mineralized than others, therefore, was revolutionary.

One thing that made this endeavor possible was the fact that the Sierra Nevada Batholith is composed of rocks of relatively uniform composition. If you look closely at a piece of granite, you will probably be able to discern only three of four different minerals. There is quartz, of course, which has a glassy look. There is a white mineral called plagioclase feldspar and a pink mineral called orthoclase feldspar. Finally, the black flaky-looking mineral is called biotite. There are other minerals present in the rock, of course (such as gold, a mineral of some interest in California history), but they represent such a low percentage of the granite that they do not affect spring water chemistry. Given the relatively predictable composition of the Sierra Nevada granite itself, Feth reasoned that the composition of the spring waters should be predictable as well.

At first glance, this approach seemed to be doomed to failure, since it was immediately clear that no two springs produced water of the same composition. In particular, different springs produced water with higher or lower concentrations of total dissolved solids (TDS). But when Feth and his coworkers looked closer, a pattern emerged. Some of the springs were ephemeral, which is to say they flowed only in the spring-time, when the ground was saturated with melting snow and rain. Other springs were perennial, which is to say that they flowed all year long. Feth noticed that water from perennial springs contained about twice the TDS ($\sim$75 mg/L) as water from the ephemeral springs ($\sim$36 mg/L). In both kinds of springs, however, the proportions of dissolved calcium, magnesium, sodium, bicarbonate, sulfate, and chloride were similar.

In considering the analyses, Feth thought he knew what was going on. Ephemeral springs are ephemeral because their waters do not cir-culate deeply into the subsurface (figs. 2.1 and 2.2). Thus, when it gets dry in the summertime and the water table drops to where it no longer intersects the land surface, these springs dry up. Perennial springs, on the other hand, produce waters that circulate much deeper into the earth, have a longer residence time, and thus react more completely with the underlying granitic rocks (figs. 2.3 and 2.4). This, in turn, ex-plains why perennial spring waters have more TDS then do ephemeral spring waters.

This was a promising start, since it suggested that spring water com-position was not quite as unpredictable as it had first seemed. But the TDS data raised an even more interesting possibility. Since the spring waters were reacting primarily with granite, would it be possible to ex-plain the dissolved solids present in the waters simply by considering how much granite had dissolved? Since granite is composed almost en-tirely of quartz, plagioclase feldspar, orthoclase feldspar, and biotite, maybe *spring water composition could be calculated exactly by con-sidering how much of each mineral dissolves.* This was an extraordi-nary idea. In other words, maybe the varying compositions of the spring waters were not such a deep mystery after all. Maybe they were as pre-dictable and understandable as ordinary arithmetic.

At this point, the problem was taken up by two chemists named Robert M. Garrels and Fred T. Mackenzie. Garrels was a physical chemist by training, and he was used to making complex calculations that related the composition of one phase (water) as it reacted with other phases (the minerals present in the granite). As Feth, Garrels, and Mackenzie had suspected, the composition of the spring waters did turn out to be predictable. But the explanations were not simple.

For one thing, all the minerals in granite are virtually insoluble in pure water. However, water that has been charged with carbon dioxide (CO_2) is slightly acidic and will dissolve some, but not all, of the minerals. Carbon dioxide is present in the air, and it is also present in the soil, so water that has fallen through the atmosphere and percolated through the soil becomes charged with CO_2. Also, the different minerals present in granite dissolve at different rates. Quartz, for example, is pure crystalline silicon dioxide (SiO_2) and is virtually insoluble in water. Thus, while quartz is one of the most abundant minerals in the granite, it does not dissolve sufficiently to affect the chemistry of the spring waters very much.

The most soluble mineral present in granite is plagioclase feldspar, a silicate compound of sodium, calcium, aluminum, and silica that has a rather complicated chemical formula: $Na_{0.62}Ca_{0.38}Al_{1.38}Si_{2.62}O_8$. The next most soluble mineral present in granite is biotite, a compound containing potassium, magnesium, aluminum, and silica that has the chemical formula $KMg_3AlSi_3O_{10}(OH)_2$. Orthoclase feldspar, which contains potassium, aluminum, and silica, is also slightly soluble and has the chemical formula $KAlSi_3O_8$.

You might think that if each of these minerals dissolves in water containing CO_2, predicting the composition of the spring waters would be entirely straightforward. But there's a hitch. None of these minerals, as it turns out, can dissolve completely in CO_2-charged water. Rather, as each of these minerals weather, they leave a residual clay mineral called kaolinite behind. Kaolinite contains aluminum and silica and has the formula $Al_2Si_2O_5(OH)_4$. So, as plagioclase, biotite, and orthoclase are dissolved by CO_2-containing rainwater and snowmelt, some material goes into solution and some remains behind as the weathering product kaolinite. This makes the arithmetic more complicated, but it does not make it impossible. If you know what you are starting with (plagioclase, biotite, and orthoclase) and you know what you end up with (kaolinite and dissolved solids in spring water), you can calculate the amount of each mineral present in the granite that has dissolved. And the question is, do the amounts of minerals dissolving account for the composition of the spring waters?

These calculations, performed by Garrels and Mackenzie in the mid-1960s,[22] begin with the average composition of ephemeral spring waters. First of all, they subtracted out the small amounts of sodium (Na^+), calcium (Ca^{2+}), magnesium (Mg^{2+}), potassium (K^+), bicarbonate (HCO^-), sulfate (SO_4^{2-}), chloride (Cl^-), and silica (SiO_2) that were present in rainfall and snowmelt. Next, they subtracted out the dissolved solids that would be produced by weathering plagioclase to kaolinite. This accounted for all the Na^+ and Ca^{2+} and much of the SiO_2 and HCO^-. The Mg^{2+} and much of the K^+ could be accounted for by weathering biotite to kaolinite, and the rest of the K^+ could be accounted for by weathering orthoclase feldspar to kaolinite. In the end, Garrels and Mackenzie had a small amount of SiO_2 left over, representing about 4% of the original dissolved solids. In other words, it was possible to account for 96% of the dissolved solids found in the spring waters simply by considering reactions between water and granite. Similar calculations could account for the composition of perennial spring waters as well. For perhaps the first time in human history, the mystery surrounding the chemistry of spring waters disappeared entirely.

By the 1980s, the chemical processes that lead to the observed ground-water chemistry in different aquifers throughout the world were being worked out in some detail. As this work progressed, the reasons for the predictable hydrochemical facies that had been observed years earlier (fig. 3.1) gradually became clear. In zone 1, where rainfall and snowmelt percolate into aquifers, dissolution of relatively soluble feldspars or carbonate minerals produces water containing mostly calcium, magnesium, and bicarbonate. As water moves into zone 2, base exchange and precipitation of minerals (often calcite) removes calcium and magnesium and replaces them with sodium. As dissolution of soluble minerals and precipitation of less soluble minerals proceeds, concentrations of sulfate tend to increase (zone 3), finally leaving a sodium chloride water (zone 4) that is similar in composition to seawater.

Inorganic mineral dissolution and precipitation reactions are not the only processes at work deep in the earth. All ground-water systems contain a variety of microorganisms, and the metabolism of these microorganisms has important effects on ground water chemistry. Multicelled organisms (like us) are limited to breathing oxygen in our metabolism. Microorganisms are not so limited. In addition to being able to breathe oxygen, some microorganisms also "breathe" oxidized iron and sulfur compounds. One particular group of microorganisms, of the genus *Geobacter*, "breathe" insoluble iron oxides as they consume

organic carbon, converting the iron into highly soluble ferrous iron according to the reaction

$$
\underset{\substack{\text{ferric} \\ \text{oxides} \\ 4Fe(OH)_{3(\text{solid})}}}{} + \underset{\substack{\text{organic} \\ \text{matter} \\ CH_2O}}{} + 7H^+ \xrightarrow{\text{\textit{Geobacter}}} \underset{\substack{\text{dissolved} \\ \text{iron} \\ 4Fe^{2+}_{(\text{dissolved})}}}{}
$$
$$
+ HCO_3^- + 10H_2O.
$$

It is this process, which most often occurs in zones 2, 3, and 4 (fig. 3.1),
leads to the high-iron chalybeate waters used by Dr. Kreysig to treat
chlorosis.

In modern America, iron-bearing dietary supplements are easily
available, and the use of high-iron waters to treat anemia has ceased
entirely. These days, dissolved iron is primarily considered to be a
nuisance since it stains clothes, sinks, plumbing fixtures, and everything else it comes in contact with. Because of this, most people whose
well water contains dissolved iron use home treatment systems to
remove it.

Another kind of microorganism, from the genus *Desulfovibrio*, also
has an important effect on the chemistry of ground water. In the absence of oxygen, *Desulfovibrio* breathes sulfate and consumes organic
carbon, converting the sulfate to hydrogen sulfide:

$$
\underset{\substack{\text{sulfate} \\ (SO_4^{2-})_{(\text{dissolved})}}}{} + \underset{\substack{\text{organic} \\ \text{carbon} \\ 2CH_2O}}{} \xrightarrow{\text{\textit{Desulfovibrio}}} \underset{\substack{\text{hydrogen} \\ \text{sulfide} \\ H_2S_{(\text{dissolved})}}}{} + 2HCO_3^-
$$

Hydrogen sulfide is an especially bad-smelling compound: it gives water a characteristic "rotten egg" smell and taste. Millions of Americans
who use well water are familiar with the noxious smell of hydrogen
sulfide, and removing hydrogen sulfide from well water is a billion-
dollar-a-year industry in the United States alone.

Finally, another class of microorganisms know as *methanogens* convert organic carbon into methane (natural gas):

$$
\underset{\substack{\text{organic carbon} \\ 2CH_2O}}{} \xrightarrow{\text{\textit{methanogens}}} \underset{\substack{\text{methane} \\ CH_{4\,(\text{dissolved})}}}{} + \underset{\substack{\text{carbon dioxide} \\ CO_{2\,(\text{dissolved})}}}{}
$$

This process can occur in any of the zones but is most characteristic of
the deep zone 4, and this is the ultimate source of much of the natural
gas found in nature.

Now, at the beginning of the twenty-first century, the mystery sur-rounding the chemical composition of well and spring waters is largely a thing of the past. This, in turn, has had an impact on the modern bottled water business. Americans prefer bottled water that contains relatively low concentrations of TDS and contains mostly calcium, magnesium, and bicarbonate. This, in turn, suggests that spring waters emanating from zone 1 of the hydrochemical facies continuum are most often used as sources of bottled water. Water bottlers are fully aware of this, and the market for springs producing bottled water is heavily skewed toward relatively young, unmineralized, oxygen-containing waters. This is one reason, incidently, why springs in the Sierra Nevada are such popular sources for bottled waters.

But this was not the case in the nineteenth century, when waters from Saratoga Springs were the most popular in America. Having examined some of the geochemical processes that progressively change the water composition in ground water systems, and using the generalization that water chemistry tends to evolve similarly in different aquifers, the observed variability in Saratoga Springs waters begins to make sense.

Modern analyses of waters from the Saratoga Springs area show that these waters can be classified based on their chemical composition as "carbonate alkaline saline" waters, "neutral alkaline saline," "saline," and "shallow" ground water.[23] The carbonate alkaline saline waters, for example, contain high concentrations of sodium and chloride, high con-centrations of iron and bicarbonate, and have a high partial pressure of carbon dioxide (pCO_2).[24] The shallow ground waters, on the other hand, have low concentrations of sodium and chloride, low concentrations of bicarbonate, and low pCO_2. Taking a clue from the progression of hy-drochemical facies (fig. 3.1), we would immediately suspect that the shallow ground waters are relatively young, shallow-circulating waters, whereas the saline waters are relatively old, deep-circulating waters. In fact, this is why there is so much variability in the local water chemistry. When the nearby Adirondack Mountains were lifted up by tectonic forces, a series of faults developed in the Saratoga Springs area (fig. 2.3). Deep, ancient waters containing sodium chloride and carbon dioxide (zone 4) move to the surface along these faults where they mix, in vary-ing proportions, with relatively young, shallow waters (zone 2). Because the shallower waters are from zone 2, concentrations of dissolved iron and sulfide are locally high, reflecting the activity of *Geobacter* and *Desulfovibrio* bacteria respectively. Depending on the paths taken by the different waters, and depending on the amount and proportion of mixing, different springs and wells have very different chemical compositions. As in many other naturally effervescing waters, the carbon dioxide appears to come from very deep in the earth indeed,[25] and is associated with the zone 4 waters moving up along the faults.

So the differences in spring water composition found in and near Saratoga Springs, New York, which were so fascinating and so puzzling to people in the nineteenth century, turn out not to be so mysterious after all. The springs are fed by a mixture of waters brought to the land surface from deep within the earth with waters that recently fell as rainwater.[26] This mixing of deep CO_2-bearing waters and shallower waters is what most commonly produces natural effervescence, and this is as true for many European mineral waters as it is for those of Saratoga Springs. The waters of Carlsbad and Eger, used to such effect by Dr. Kreysig, are examples of this general phenomenon, as are the sparkling waters bottled by Perrier in France.

Waters from Saratoga Springs have several medicinal properties that were used by physicians in the nineteenth century. The high iron concentrations present in some of the waters were useful for treating anemia. Those waters with high concentrations of sulfate and magnesium were efficient laxatives. Those waters that were more neutral in pH with high concentrations of bicarbonate were useful for dyspepsia (sour stomach). But most spectacularly of all, some Saratoga Springs waters contain iodine,[27] an element that can prevent and sometimes cure goiters. Before the days of iodized salt, goiters were so common that, in some places, they were considered normal. The fact that some of the waters from Saratoga Springs, the ones that naturally contain iodine, a compound often found in deep zone 4 waters, could cure or prevent goiter was considered a medical miracle in the nineteenth century.

These miraculous medicinal properties—properties that come directly from the underlying hydrology of the Saratoga Springs area—created a ready market for bottled Saratoga Springs waters. By 1856, more then 7 million bottles of Saratoga Springs waters were being produced and sold each year, and they fetched as much as $1.75 per pint (in modern dollars) in New York City.[28] This chemistry, in turn, has greatly affected the history of Saratoga Springs, a cultural phenomenon that continues to this day.[29]

Like most people of the ancient world, the Greek Athenians had a rich variety of myths and legends that they used to explain the puzzling behavior of the natural world around them. One of these stories had to do with a competition between Athena and Poseidon during the founding of Athens.[30] Both gods could see that this new city had the potential to be prosperous. It had a citadel (the Acropolis) so high and strong that it was unassailable. It had access to the sea and thus was well positioned for trade and commerce. Finally, it was populated by inquisitive and intelligent people who were particularly adept at the high-tech art of pottery making. Clearly, this was a city that was going places. If you were a god, this was the kind of city that you wanted to have worshipping you.

But the citizens of Athens, who doubtlessly were just as fickle as people are today, could not decide which of the two gods would be best for the city. So it was decided to have a competition. Each god would use his or her divine powers to provide something for the city. The god who provided the most useful gift would become the patron of Athens.

Poseidon, who was known for his ability to move and shake the earth, thought he knew exactly what the city needed most. Using his powers and expertise in dealing with the subterranean world, Poseidon dug a deep well into solid rock to provide water for the city. Since water was always in short supply, he thought this would guarantee him victory in the competition. But he made a mistake. Since he was also the god of the sea, he preferred salty water to fresh water. Without thinking, he made the well produce salty water according to his own tastes. So, although it was a perfectly good and productive well, it was worthless to the people of Athens, who needed fresh water. Athena, who was known for her wisdom, provided Athens with an olive tree. Olives grew well in the hot maritime climate and provided food and oil that was both nourishing and delicious. Given the choice between olives and salty water, the Athenians chose olives.

Athena became the patron goddess of Athens.

For most of human history, tales like this were all that people had to explain the puzzling chemical composition of water produced from different springs and wells. It has only been in the last hundred years or so that people have begun to work out the hydrologic and geochemical processes that control the chemistry of ground water. While simple human curiosity was certainly a factor in developing this understanding, there was also a fair amount of capitalistic self-interest involved. The idea that chemical analyses of waters could identify what made the waters medicinal raised the interesting possibility that these medicines could be artificially duplicated for sale. As we have seen, whether the ailment was anemia, goiters, or scurvy, this approach eventually led to real medical progress.

The medical use of spring waters has declined over the years as medical technology has improved. Nevertheless, the cultural memory of water as medicine remains. Without quite knowing why, people still consider spring waters healthier than tap water, and they continue to patronize springs such as the Healing Springs of South Carolina year after year. This is also why people still sip mineral waters to ease their tender stomachs. Although Dr. Kreysig and his methods have faded into the mists of time, the memory and practice of "water cures" remains.

And it will for some time to come.

4 THE URNS OF CANA
Evolution of the Bottle

The Egyptian water seller bends under the weight of the urn (fig. 4.1). The water urn, which looks like it holds about five gallons, is balanced expertly on the water seller's back. Even so, the crushing weight is clearly evident. Five gallons of water weigh about forty pounds, and the urn, which is earthenware, probably weighs another twenty. So, conservatively, the water seller is carrying sixty pounds on his back as he begins his rounds to his customers. To our eyes, the angle of his back under the load is sickening. It is interesting to note, however, that the expression on the water seller's face is serene and uncomplaining. One reason for this may be that the Egyptian artist, who captured this moment in history four thousand years ago as a small figurine,[1] simply did not see anything remarkable in what the water seller was doing. Hard labor was part of everyday life for the lower and middle classes, who made up most of ancient Egypt's population. Carrying such heavy burdens was probably considered so normal and so ordinary that the artist just didn't see it as being particularly unusual.

It was just another day at the office.

When the average American sips a bottle of water, it is likely that his or her attention is focused more on the water than on the bottle. After all, the water is the point. It is the consumable, and that is what generally interests people. But without the bottle, the water would never get to the consumer in the first place. These days we are used to having water bottled in space-age plastics that are light, strong, durable, transparent, and can be formed into interesting shapes and sizes. These high-tech materials and high-tech methods for bottle manufacturing have made the storage, transportation, and consumption of bottled water easy and convenient. It should not come as much of a surprise, therefore, that people have always been concerned with ease and convenience. People have always used the best available materials and the

FIGURE 4.1 Figurine of an Egyptian water seller carrying an urn of water on his back. Source: The National Museums Liverpool England

best available manufacturing technologies to store and carry water. This began in prehistory with sewn water skins and has progressed through the development of ceramic pottery, blown glass, and finally plastics. The development of materials and methods for carrying and storing water closely parallels the development of human technology and reflects how important water is to people. It is worth considering, therefore, the history of bottling technology, and also the various materials and methods people have used over the centuries to make bottles. Like so much else in the human experience, this story begins in ancient Egypt.

The figurine of the Egyptian water seller—it probably was used to store perfume or scented water in a wealthy woman's boudoir about 2000 B.C.—records a tantalizing snapshot of the early days of the water delivery business. One of the things that makes it so interesting, apart from showing the obvious difficulty involved with carrying around large quantities of water, is that it shows how important the materials available for storing water are. In 2000 B.C., earthenware was the material of choice for storing water, and this put obvious constraints on how much water could be carried by any one person. Today, the kinds of materials available for bottling water are much more varied than they ever have been. Nevertheless, the materials available for making bottles place constraints on how water can be packaged, stored, and delivered. And this is as true today as it was for the Egyptian water seller in 2000 B.C.

In the modern world, filled with endless kinds of hi-tech plastics, it is tempting to view earthenware jars as being primitive. In fact, earthenware pottery made by people in the ancient world was exceedingly high-tech and was particularly well suited for storing water. In prehistoric times, it is likely that humans stored water in a variety of vessels that included hollowed-out horns, gourds, and various internal organs of animals. Most of the large animals that humans preyed on in prehistory had proportionally large bladders, which were easily removed during the skinning process. These bladders could carry as much as a gallon of water and had the useful characteristic that they were watertight. Various plants that produce large seeds also came into play. Hollowed gourds and coconuts are easily converted into water-bearing vessels.

The technical problem with all of these is that they are made of organic matter, which, unfortunately, also supports the growth of microorganisms. So, even though a gourd or bladder might be filled with perfectly pristine water, the growth of these microorganisms would soon render the water either unpalatable or undrinkable. Just how long "soon" was probably depended on how thirsty the person carrying the water happened to be. It is unlikely, however, that water stored in this manner would remain risk-free to human health for more than a day or two, depending on the ambient temperature.

By 5000 B.C., people had begun to make water-storing vessels out of pottery. Just how or why pottery was first invented and used for storing water has been the subject of much speculation. One idea is that pottery developed from various attempts to make wicker baskets, which were used to carry and store grain, suitable for storing water.[2] Clearly, wicker baskets do not hold water very efficiently. However, if the inside of the basket is coated with clay and the clay allowed to dry in the sun, it can render the basket impermeable to water. The problem, of course, is that once water is put into the dried vessel, the clay will eventually dissolve and turn into a muddy mess. At some point, it was learned that if these clay-lined baskets were burned in an open fire for a day or so, the clay left behind would harden to the point where it could hold water without turning back into mud. Although we will probably never know for sure, it is entirely possible that the need to store water reliably led directly to the art of ceramic pottery.

Ceramic materials, which are made by firing fine-grained clays, have several properties that make them well suited for storing water. While lots of different kinds of clay are used for making pottery, and while these clays have an enormous variety of colors and trace mineral compositions, the bulk chemistry of clays is surprisingly uniform. Clays used for pottery largely contain alumina (Al_2O_3), silica (SiO_2), and water (H_2O). The fact that many clays contain water as an integral part of their crystal structure is one reason they can be molded by skilled potters. The water provides a natural lubrication that allows clay particles to slide and move easily relative to each other, which in turn enables the potter to form the clay into whatever shape is desired. Even when the pot is placed in the sun and thoroughly dried, water remains about 14% of the clay's weight. When the clay is fired, however, most of the water is driven out of the clay's crystal structure. This dehydration can be accomplished at relatively low temperatures ($\sim$1000°C) that can be reached in a wood furnace. As water is driven out of the crystal structure, the remaining aluminum, oxygen, and silica atoms collapse together, filling the voids left by the escaped water. This causes the atoms to intermesh like a basket weave, giving the newly fired pottery its hardness and strength.

This kind of low-fired earthenware, which was the first to emerge in the ancient world of the Middle East about 5000 B.C., has some interesting properties that make it well suited for storing water. First of all, once the silica and aluminum atoms have collapsed into their dehydrated structure, they will no longer chemically absorb water. Water can stand in low-fired pottery vessels indefinitely without chemically altering either the pottery or the water. Second, the firing process not only drives the water out of the clay; it also burns away organic matter. Whatever organic matter is not burned is usually converted to graphite, a relatively nonreactive form of carbon. A newly fired clay vessel, therefore, is virtually free of the chemically reactive organic matter that microorganisms need in order to grow. Thus, unlike gourds or bladder vessels, water can be stored in earthenware for long periods of time without spoiling.

But even better, earthenware pots can actually cool water relative to the outside air, making it much more pleasant to drink. The basket-weave structure of the silica and aluminum atoms of earthenware restricts the movement of water but does not stop it completely. When an earthenware vessel is filled with water, small amounts of water diffuse to the outer surface of the urn. When this water evaporates, it naturally cools the urn's surface and thus cools the water in the urn. Depending on the relative humidity of the outside air, water stored in earthenware urns can maintain a temperature a few degrees cooler than the surrounding air. This was the first "refrigeration" to be invented by humans, and in the hot climate of Egypt and the Middle East, it was highly prized. In fact, low-fired earthenware pots are still used in many parts of the world to keep water cool. The maaw nahm of Thailand (chapter 1) are an example of this.

The importance of water-storing technology in the ancient world, and thus the use of ceramic urns and bottles, often pops up in unexpected and intriguing ways. Beginning in 1875, for example, a series of archaeological excavations was undertaken at Olympia in Greece.[3] The purpose of these excavations was to document the development of the Olympic Games, which began about the year 700 B.C. as a religious festival dedicated to Zeus. One of the most unusual and certainly unexpected findings was the discovery of hundreds of shallow, hand-dug wells. These wells, which contained broken pottery and various other sorts of debris, allow a glimpse into the water-storing technology used in ancient Greece.

Like most places in the ancient world, Olympia did not have a convenient water supply. The Alpheios River is about half a mile away, and a small stream runs to the west of the sanctuary of Zeus. But for the first two or three centuries of the Olympic Games, for the sanctuary of Zeus, and for the nearby stadium where the races were held, these shallow wells were an important source of water. The custom seems to have been to arrive at Olympia a week or so before the games began, dig a few unlined wells down to a depth of ten feet or so, and use this water for the duration of the games. Once the games were over, the accumulated garbage of the last couple of weeks was heaved into the wells, and the wells were abandoned. The pottery shards recovered from these wells have been an archaeological treasure trove, and they clearly link the early Olympic Games with a festival of the god Zeus. But these shards also give a glimpse into the water-storing technology of ancient Greece.

Some of the shards recovered from the wells are the remains of relatively small bottles, much smaller than the one carried by the Egyptian water seller. It is likely that upon arrival in Olympia, these bottles contained wine. But as the games went on and the wine was consumed, the bottles were used to collect and store water from the shallow wells. Greeks seldom drank wine whole in the ancient world, preferring to mix it with water. It seems that the antimicrobial properties of the ethyl alcohol in wine was one of the first water-treatment processes used by humans. Mixed half and half, wine could render not-so-clean water drinkable. One can imagine Greeks who attended the early Olympic Games using these pottery bottles to draw muddy water out of the shallow wells. After the mud settled out, the water could be decanted into a clean bottle, mixed with wine, and consumed with reasonable assurance that it was safe.

The technology of the Greek bottles, however, was different from that of the Egyptian earthenware. For one thing, the Greek pottery was fired to higher temperatures. At these temperatures, which approached 1,200°C, the iron oxide impurities present in most clays begin to melt. This melted glassy substance flows around the silica and aluminum molecules and glues them together. This, in turn, produces pottery that is harder and more impermeable.[4] Although low-fired earthenware jars that "breathe" are useful for cooling water, they are not well suited for long-term storage of wine and oil. The high-fired stoneware bottles and pitchers found at Olympia, while certainly useful for mixing water with wine, were probably designed primarily for storing oil and wine.

The bottles and jars recovered at Olympia show another technological innovation that had an important effect on water storage. Even high-fired stoneware is relatively porous. When filled with a biodegradable substance such as oil or wine, these microscopic cavities can harbor bacteria that can cause spoilage. The Greeks of the eighth century B.C. solved this problem by coating the insides of their bottles with what potters call "slip."[5] Slips are particularly fine-grained clays that remain suspended in standing water after other particles have settled out. These fine clays can then be recovered by first decanting and then evaporating the cloudy water. The Greeks coated the insides of their vessels with slip, which, after firing, assumed a smooth, black, glaze-like surface. This smooth surface, in turn, resisted penetration by oil or wine and helped prevent spoilage. While certainly developed for storing oil and wine, these slip glazes also assisted in the storage of water. After the invention of earthenware, slip glazes were the next important innovation in water-storage technology and, as illustrated in the bottles recovered from Olympia, were widely used by the ancient Greeks.

Although slip glazes can help to seal the surface of stoneware pottery, they are not entirely waterproof. The first documented use of a glassy glaze for ceramics that was completely impermeable to water comes from a tile fragment found in the tomb of the Egyptian king Menes (~3000 B.C.). A glass glaze is formed by melting silica and bonding it to fired clay. Silica by itself will not melt unless a very high temperature (1,700°C) is reached. However, if silica is mixed with alkaline compounds such as borax or baking soda, which are termed *fluxes,* the melting temperature can be lowered to the temperatures used to high-fire stoneware (~1,200°C). Lead oxides are also good fluxes, but lead glazes will leach lead into whatever liquid is stored in the vessel and are not particularly healthy. The ancient Romans in particular were fond of lead glazes, which is one reason lead poisoning was so pervasive in Roman society.

Glazed high-fired pottery is an excellent material for the long-term storage of water and has been used for this purpose in virtually all human cultures for much of recorded history. The first task of any day, usually for the womenfolk, was to take their water urns to the local well, stream, or fountain and to return with enough water to last the day. One can easily imagine that relatively thin-wall bottles were used to carry the water back to the house and that heavier stoneware urns were filled from these bottles. It probably took several trips to secure a day's water supply for a large family. One can also imagine that a relatively light water-carrying bottle was something to be treasured and handed down from mother to daughter.

There is no lack of archaeological evidence for the use of stoneware urns as water-storage devices in the ancient world. But there is documentary evidence as well, sometimes coming from unexpected sources. In the Gospel of John, for example, the first miracle that Jesus performs is turning water into wine at the wedding of Cana. The gospel writer records:

> Now there were six stone water jars there for Jewish ceremonial washings, each holding twenty to thirty gallons. Jesus told them, "Fill the jars with water." So they filled them to the brim. Then he told them, "draw some out now and take it to the headwaiter." So they took it. And when the headwaiter tasted the water that had become wine. (John 2:6–9).

The Gospel of John is famous, in scholarly circles, for recording interesting details of everyday life in biblical times. This passage gives just the briefest hint of the role that water-storing urns played in Jewish households, and it simply confirms what archaeologists find when they excavate sites in the Middle East. The urns of Cana are an example of one of the most important water-storing technologies in human history.

The introduction of glassy glazes essentially perfected the oil-, wine-, and water-storing capabilities of stoneware. It was not long before the use of these glazes, however, led to the development of a brand-new material for storing liquids. This new material was glass.

In the first century A.D., the Roman historian Pliny the Elder recorded the following:

> There is a story that once a ship belonging to some traders in nitrum [borax] put in here [the coast of modern Lebanon] and they scattered along the shore to prepare a meal. Since, however, no stones for supporting their cauldrons were forthcoming, they rested them on lumps of nitrum from their cargo. When these became heated and were completely mingled with the sand on the beach, a strange liquid flowed in streams; and this, it is said, was the origin of glass.

These traders may have been competent sailors, but it is clear that they did not know much about pottery. The reason they were carrying a cargo of nitrum (borax) was that this material was used as a flux to glaze stoneware pottery and thus was fairly valuable. But, if nitrum mixed with sand will produce a fine glaze for pottery, it is just one more step to produce glass.

It took longer to figure out how to mold glass into something useful. Glass begins to show up in the archaeological record of the Middle East about 2000 B.C., but it was not until about 1600 B.C. that people learned how to form glass into beakers and bottles.[6] The technological breakthrough that led to making the first glass bottles was a method called the *core form*. This method involved using an iron rod coated with a mixture of clay and horse dung as a core around which a glass vessel was formed.[7] The core was dipped into a crucible of molten glass in a furnace and turned slowly to coat the core evenly. Once the desired thickness of glass was attained, the core was removed from the furnace and allowed to cool. When the core was exposed to the molten glass, the horse dung would burn away, allowing the iron rod to be extracted from the glass once it had cooled. After the remains of the clay and dung were scraped out, the core-formed bottle was ready for decoration and use.

The core-form method of making glass bottles, which dominated glassmaking for the next 1,500 years, was difficult and expensive. Most of the earliest glass bottles found in Egypt and Iraq appear to have been used to hold precious oils or scents. The idea of storing water in anything as expensive as a glass bottle probably never occurred to anyone.

Glassblowing was invented in the first century A.D., probably in Roman Palestine and Syria, and it revolutionized the glassmaking industry.[8] Whereas core-formed glass was only for the very wealthy, the relative ease of making blown-glass bottles, flagons, and vases made them available to middle-class Romans as well. Still, however, such bottles were primarily used for storing oils and medicines rather than water or wine. It is a general rule of retail sales that the cost of packaging has to be small compared with the cost of the product itself. Certain precious oils, scents, and medicines, carried for hundreds of miles by caravans, were worth so much that it made sense to package them in glass bottles. Although clean water and fine wines were valuable commodities in the first century A.D., they were not valuable enough to be stored in glass bottles.

The collapse of the Roman Empire in western Europe in the fifth century A.D. led to a halt to improvements in glass bottle technology that would last for a thousand years. The story of glass bottles picks up again in the fifteenth and sixteenth centuries, when people rediscovered the recreational value of certain drugs such as tobacco, opiates, distilled spirits, and wine that required long-term storage. The Renaissance is widely considered to be the "rebirth" of learning, art, and culture in western Europe. But people being people, it also involved a rebirth in the use of consciousness-altering substances. Much of the hard evidence for this is recorded by the development of glass bottles to store these various substances.[9]

Throughout most of the Middle Ages, the cultivation of grapes and making of wine had been pursued by monasteries in western Europe. Wine was needed in order to celebrate mass, and several monastic orders quietly developed different varieties of grapes suitable for Europe. By the 1600s, however, the art of winemaking filtered into the secular world, which was more concerned with large-scale wine production, consumption, and intoxication. This revived the need for relatively inexpensive and widely available storage containers, and the glass bottle–making industry shifted in order to fill this need. Wine bottles produced in the early 1600s were free-blown, which is to say they did not use molds or forms, and no two are alike. Some were huge carboys or demijohns holding thirty or forty gallons. Some were squat, bulbous affairs known as "kings's bottles" or "onion bottles" or just "squats." It was not until the mid-1800s that the standard Bordeaux, Burgundy, and German shapes were standardized.

Snuff was another buzz-producing substance that had an effect on bottle-making technology. Tobacco was brought to Europe in 1493 by a Franciscan friar who had observed the Native Americans smoking and snuffing. By 1575, tobacco and snuff were not only known throughout Europe; they were immensely popular. The bottle makers of the day, who were not shy about looking for economic opportunity, began to make free-blown and form-blown snuff bottles.

Distilled spirits also played a role in the development of bottle technology. Prior to 1625, wine and beer were the principal alcoholic beverages available for popular consumption. However, in the mid-1600s, a professor of medicine at the University of Leiden in Holland began experimenting with a concoction designed to improve kidney function and to act as a diuretic. Grain alcohol (ethanol) made by distillation was already known to be an efficient diuretic. The good professor, a gentlemen named Fransico de la Boe (1614–1672), added the essence of juniper berries to enhance the medicinal effect, and gin was born. The first gin was dispensed as a medicine in apothecary shops, but it quickly became so popular that many apothecaries switched over to distilling gin for a living. Gin was much cheaper to make than wine, it packed a much bigger alcoholic punch, and it soon became the favorite drink of the lower classes. William of Orange (William III of England) introduced gin to the upper classes of England, and by the mid-1700s it was the most popular spirit in Britain. The popularity of gin and other distilled spirits fueled demand for glass bottles. Because gin was originally dispensed as a medicine, it was usually sold in square-bodied case bottles. Because their contents were so cheap, these case bottles were also very cheaply made. To a bottle collector, the crudeness of early case bottles is as diagnostic as their distinctive shape.[10]

At first, case bottles were free-blown and then squared by pressing the pliable glass with a wooden paddle. However, as the demand for more uniform, mass-produced bottles increased, case bottles began to be produced from dip molds. Dip molds were another innovation that greatly affected bottle-making technology. With dip molds, less accomplished artisans could rapidly produce serviceable bottles of a relatively uniform size and shape. To produce a dip-molded bottle, the gaffer (as master glassblowers are called) begins with a narrow, free-blown cylinder dipped from the furnace. This cylinder is then lowered into a precast iron mold and inflated. This forces the glass into the deepest recesses of the mold, giving it whatever distinctive shape and outer embossments are carved into the mold. In the eighteenth and nineteenth centuries, bottles were usually dip-blown from two or three molds, and the separate pieces then fused together.[11]

By the middle of the eighteenth century, the booming wine and spirit industry, and the application of dip-molding technology, had the effect of making glass bottles much cheaper. Because of this, it was just a matter of time before this technology was used to bottle water as well. As was the case with gin, however, it was the medicine industry that led to the first widespread commercial bottling of water.

Medical science in the eighteenth and nineteenth centuries was not a particularly high-tech endeavor, and doctors themselves were not held in high esteem. As a consequence, people tended to dose themselves with a variety of concoctions to relive the aches, pains, and intestinal discomfort that all humans are subject to. The names of these *patent medicines*, as nonprescription drugs were called in those days, were as colorful as the glass bottles they came in. Samuel Lee's "Bilious Pills," "Genuine Swaim's Panacea," "Dr. Davis' Pain Killer" (which was 102 proof and, therefore, probably really worked), and "Lydia E. Pinkham's Vegetable compound for Women's Complaints" are representative examples. In this atmosphere of free-wheeling quackery, bottling "mineral waters" as medicines made perfect sense.[12]

For one thing, water from certain springs had real, if modest, therapeutic effects. Some spring waters, for example, contain unusually high concentrations of magnesium and sulfate. Magnesium sulfate, or Epsom salts as it is also known, acts as a laxative. Spring waters that contained this mineral were observed to be "purgative" and were often prescribed by physicians for that reason. Other spring waters contained dissolved iron and were observed to improve the strength of young women who complained of tiredness. In cases of simple anemia, these "iron chalybeate" waters could produce useful results. The best example, however, is iodine. People in the eighteenth century did not know that goiters were caused by the lack of iodine in the diet, but they did observe that water from some springs could prevent and in some cases cure goiters. Because of this, bottling and taking certain spring waters as medicines made at least as much sense as consuming alcoholic concoctions such as Dr. Davis' Pain Killer.

Bottling waters from certain mineral springs and bringing them back from the mountains, where most of these springs tended to be, for sale or home use had gone on in Europe since Roman times. The people doing the bottling, however, were generally wealthy; they could afford not only the transport to and from the springs but the not inconsiderable cost of the bottles themselves. By the beginning of the nineteenth century, however, the application of glass dip-mold technology had dramatically lowered the cost of bottle making. For the first time, the cost of the glass bottle was becoming smaller than the perceived value of certain select mineral waters. This confluence of circumstances, which had taken more than 2,500 years since the invention of glass, was the real beginning of the bottled water industry in America.

In the United States, as in Europe, it was considered fashionable to visit springs "to take the waters." At some of these "watering places," as they became known, this fashion led to the establishment of plush hotels and resorts. Staying at these resorts was too expensive for most ordinary people, but the fashion of doing so created a demand for the "wonderful waters." It was this demand that led to the first bottled water enterprises in America.[13] In 1767, water from a spring in Boston known locally as Jackson's Spa was reportedly bottled for sale. Other water-bottling operations began in a relatively small way in Albany, Philadelphia, and other cities. Some historians credit a Philadelphia druggist name Elie Maglorie Druand as being the first person to bottle mineral water in 1825, although the evidence is murky. It was at Saratoga Springs in New York, however, that these enterprises came of age.[14]

We have already considered the water chemistry of Saratoga Springs water in some detail (chapter 3). Some Saratoga Spring waters are iron bearing, others have more or less carbon dioxide, and some contain iodine as well. In any case, by the standards of the early nineteenth century, there was ample reason to consider these waters medicinal. Sometime around 1820, an enterprising reverend named D. O. Griswold began to sell water bottled from Saratoga Springs. Somewhat later, in 1844, the Mt. Vernon Glass Works Company, which produced dip-mold glass bottles, moved to Saratoga Springs to supply bottles. By 1856, more than 7 million bottles were being produced annually at Saratoga Springs alone.[15]

The bottled water industry in America was launched.

Bottle collectors consider the early Saratoga Springs bottles to be relatively crude in construction and unusually heavy. In any event, there are bottle collectors who specialize in bottles made during the last half of the nineteenth century at or near Saratoga Springs. Names such as "Saratoga Spouting Spring" or "Congress Water" or simply "Natural Mineral Water" are commonly found on these bottles.[16] Because so many of them were made in such quantity, because the workmanship is fairly crude, and because so many of them have been preserved, they are not hugely expensive. An attractive mineral water bottle from this era generally fetches anywhere from $50 to $300 on the open market. However, some of these bottles that exhibit better workmanship are worth more. Bottles made for "Glacier Spouting Spring," a motif with a spouting spring, will fetch up to $2,000.[17]

In this vein, the "Moses" bottles of Poland Spring deserve a special mention. The water of Poland Spring, which is located about twenty-five miles from Portland, Maine, was originally bottled as a kidney medicine. The Ricker family, who started the bottling operation, knew that a particularly attractive bottle could help sell their water. In the Bible story of the Exodus, Moses once procured a water supply for his thirsty and fainthearted Hebrews by rapping his staff against a rock, which immediately produced a spring of water. Inspired by this story, Hiram Ricker, when he opened his resort hotel in 1876, began putting Poland Spring water into bottles made in the shape of Moses. These bottles, which were produced until the 1930s, are real collector's items and can fetch as much as $2,000. What is really interesting about the Moses bottles, however, is that they show how the importance of attractive packaging was recognized very early on in the bottled water industry.

Glass bottling technology came of age in the early 1900s with the development of glassblowing machines. In 1891, Michael J. Owens patented a machine that automatically opened and closed the glass molds used to form bottles. In 1903, the year that the Wright Brothers first flew a powered airplane, Owens developed a fully automatic bottle-making machine. This machine, which was the first revolution in bottle-making technology since the invention of glassblowing, is a monument to modern technology.[18] It served to dramatically lower the costs of bottle making, and variants of this method are still used today. In the 1920s and 1930s, the few water-bottling operations that remained in business following the chlorination revolution turned to this new and cheaper automatic bottle-making technology. But like ceramic urns, glass is heavy. As the water-bottling industry turned away from producing pint- and quart-size containers to larger five-gallon jugs in the mid–twentieth century, the weight of glass bottles became a serious limiting factor in the industry. This, in turn, led people to consider the use of plastics for bottling water.

The first successful commercial use of plastics, curiously enough, did not involve the packaging materials that we are so familiar with today. Rather, it was as a replacement for ivory in the manufacture of billiard balls. In 1868, an inventor named John Wesley Hyatt entered a contest to find a replacement for hugely expensive ivory in the manufacture of billiard balls. A few years earlier, an Englishman named Alexander Parks had shown that nitrocellulose could produce a clear substance he called "plastic," from the Greek word *plastikos*, meaning "pliant." Hyatt combined nitrocellulose with gum shellac as a binder, pressed this substance into molds, and produced perfectly round billiard balls. Hyatt did not win the competition, but it did start him on a lifetime of tinkering with plastics. In 1870, Hyatt replaced the gum shellac with camphor and invented a product he called celluloid.

Other plastics were developed in quick succession. Polyvinyl chloride (PVC), initially discovered in 1838, was investigated as a rubber substitute by a Russian named Ivan Ostromislensky in the 1920s. Polystyrene followed in 1929 and polyethylene in 1939. Because the bottled water industry in those days was virtually nonexistent in the United States, plastics entered the picture very slowly. Prior to 1960, American bottled water was typically delivered in five-gallon glass bottles stoppered with a cork. Plastic caps for the glass bottles did not come along until the 1960s.[19] The conversion from glass to polycarbonate five-gallon bottles in the 1970s was a real revolution in the bottled water industry.

Polycarbonate, which also is known by the trade name Lexan, was invented in 1952 by Dan Fox, a scientist working for General Electric. The legend, which was apparently invented for advertising purposes, is that a cat knocked over a lab beaker onto the floor, and the next morning Dr. Fox noticed that its contents had hardened into a clear, hard plastic. The more mundane truth seems to be that, in fact, a fellow researcher in the lab was the actual culprit who knocked over the beaker. No matter. Polycarbonate, which is hard like glass but will not shatter and is much lighter, was a natural for the bottled water industry, and it led the revolution away from glass toward plastic containers for bottled water.

Numerous kinds of plastics have been tried by the bottled water industry over the years. For a long time, PVC seemed to be the material of the future. Unfortunately, PVC tends to give a "plastic" taste to water, and it never really caught on. High-density polyethylene (HDPE), a material widely used to package carbonated, beverages was used to bottle water as well. By the end of the 1980s, polycarbonate, PVC, and HDPE were the materials of choice for bottling water. Even so, each of these materials had pluses and minuses. Polycarbonate was expensive, relatively heavy, and, while it worked well for five-gallon containers, was not well suited for smaller, single-serving containers. PVC had taste issues, and HDPE tended to be opaque. Opaque containers are not bad for fruit drinks and milk, but people like to see the water they are buying. That way they can verify that the water is crystal clear.

These days, the material of choice for packaging individual servings of bottled water is a plastic called polyethylene terephthalate, or PET. This material is clear, very light, and flexible as well. It was invented by a DuPont engineer named Nathaniel Wyeth in 1968. Wyeth was trying to develop a plastic bottle that was strong enough to contain the pressure of carbonated beverages without puffing up like a balloon or even exploding. He started working with nylon, which he knew got stronger as it was stretched tighter and tighter. To do this, he developed a preformed mold, much like the molds used by glassmakers of the nineteenth century, into which nylon was forcibly extruded in order to make it stretch. It worked, alright, but Wyeth reasoned that it would work better if the material was more elastic than nylon. After trying polypropylene, another popular plastic of the day, Wyeth developed PET. The resulting product was an extremely thin and light bottle. It was very strong and resilient, and crystal clear. And, just as important for the bottled water market, PET does not impart an unpleasant "plastic" taste to water.

And yes, in case you are wondering, Nathaniel Wyeth is the older brother of Andrew Wyeth, the famous American painter.

Plastics have lots of advantages over glass when it comes to packaging water. Chief among these is weight. An empty five-gallon glass water bottle weighs about twenty pounds, and carrying a full one around is pretty close to the burden endured by our Egyptian water seller with his ceramic water jar. There is also the ever present danger of breakage. When a five-gallon glass water bottle is dropped, it can shatter into hundreds of very sharp and dangerous shards. Plastics, on the other hand, are much lighter and easier to handle. If they are dropped, they can certainly rupture. But this usually just results in spilled water and a ruined container—not hundreds of sharp and potentially deadly fragments of glass.

But from the very beginning of the plastic age, there have been concerns about the safety of the various chemicals used to manufacture plastics. For example, vinyl chloride—the gaseous precursor of PVC—is a known carcinogen. But when the molecules of vinyl chloride gas polymerize (combine) into PVC, they become so tightly locked together that the resulting solid is much less reactive. Over the years, dozens of studies have looked for a link between PVC containers (for food and drinks) and the risk of cancer. No such link has ever been established. As far as modern science can tell, PVC is entirely safe to use for food and beverage packaging.

While PVC itself does not seem to be a problem, some of the compounds used along with PVC might be. In particular, compounds known as phthalates are widely used in the plastics industry for a number of applications. In the case of PVC, phthalates are added to make the finished product more flexible, which, in turn, makes PVC better suited for bottles. The ability of phthalates to leach from PVC and other plastics has raised concerns that they may have toxic effects, even at the very low concentrations found in water or food packaged in PVC. Research conducted in both Europe and the United States has not indicated that phthalates are toxic to humans. Nevertheless, the fact that they can leach into food, soft drinks, and bottled water—even though only in very low concentrations—is worrisome to some people.

Other chemicals used to make plastics have also aroused suspicion over the years. Bisphenol-A (BPA), which is used in manufacturing polycarbonate bottles, is one. In 2000, for example, a study in *Consumer Reports* showed that eight of ten water samples drawn from five-gallon polycarbonate bottles contained low concentrations of BPA.[20] Because some studies had suggested that BPA might act as an endocrine disruptor, potentially interfering with developing fetuses, this led *Consumer Reports* to caution pregnant women about drinking water from polycarbonate bottles. In 1997, one study reported that the male offspring of pregnant mice exposed to BPA had slightly enlarged prostate glands.[21] That result, however, could not be duplicated in two subsequent studies, which found no effect of BPA on mice.[22] The majority of studies, but certainly not all, do not show a connection between BPA and adverse health effects.

All this being the case, the level of concern that different people have toward the potential toxicity of plastics is similarly varied. Some people reading about phthalates or BPA prefer to be cautious and have moved away from buying water in PVC or polycarbonate bottles. Just as commonly, people who happen to like those bottles just shake their heads and continue to drink the water as they did before. After all, there is no definitive proof that the plastics are a health risk. Both approaches are reasonable. When there is no clear scientific consensus, it is entirely appropriate for people to make up their own minds about what they will or will not consume. If some people read the reports and find them worrisome, there are other water-packaging materials they might to turn to—glass certainly comes to mind. For people who are not worried, there is no particular reason that they should change their habits.

Today, water packagers have many choices for bottling water. In 1997, about 10% of all bottled water was packaged in PVC, 15% in other plastics such as polycarbonate and HDPE, 25% in glass, and 50% in PET. These days, PET is the material of choice, having captured 70% of the market. Glass is still number two, hanging in there at 20%, with polycarbonate and HDPE accounting for the rest.[23] As of the year 2000, PVC had been largely nudged out of the market, replaced by lighter and more adaptable PET.

Most people, when they purchase bottled-waters, take the packaging very much for granted. It is interesting, however, that the history of water-bottling technology mirrors the history of humankind. From the first crude earthenware pots shaped inside wicker baskets some ten thousand years ago, to the stoneware bottles used to draw water from shallow wells at the Olympic Games, to the urns used in every household to carry and store water, to the miracle of glass, and finally to the invention plastics, the materials used to store and package water have always represented the pinnacle of available technology. When consumers peruse bottled waters on a grocery store shelf, what they see is colorful packaging designed to attract the eye and carefully suggestive of crystal-clear purity. But hidden beneath this obvious exterior are more than ten millennia of human history and progress.

These are not just bottles. They are the modern urns of Cana.

5 HIDDEN LIFE, HIDDEN DEATH
The Microbiology of Bottled Water

As his horse climbed the hill toward Hampstead, England, John Snow thought about the Angel of Death. There had been many deaths in the last week, and Dr. Snow knew each victim by name. This familiarity was no accident. He had visited the Register of Deaths a few days ago and had obtained the names and addresses of each person who had died from cholera in the past week. Since then, he had doggedly visited each house of each person who had died, interviewing the survivors and recording their addresses on his map. This kind of detective work did not come naturally to John Snow. He was a shy, reserved man who disliked speaking with strangers at any time. Having to interview the wives of dead husbands, the mothers of dead children, the children of dead parents, was almost more then he could bear. After a few days of talking with families numbed by grief and by the sheer horror of cholera, his spirits had sunk lower and lower. Perhaps it's me, he thought grimly as his horse plodded along, who is the Angel of Death.

But what he was finding fit a pattern. Since this outbreak of cholera had begun in Soho, London, on August 30, 1854, virtually all of the more than five hundred deaths had occurred in households within a few hundred yards of the Broad Street Pump. This "pump," as it was universally called, was a well equipped with a primitive pitcher pump that supplied water for the local population in Soho Parish. The Broad Street Pump, which was only about thirty feet deep, was particularly popular for its cool, clear, sweet-tasting water. For years, Snow had been investigating the cause of cholera, a disease that had ravaged England since it first appeared in 1823. Most physicians of the day thought that cholera was spread by putrefied, miasmic air. Snow, on the other hand, suspected that cholera was caused by a "poison" generated in the bodies of people suffering from the disease. This poison could then seep into water and spread to healthy people who were unlucky enough to drink it. The names, addresses, and interviews he had so painfully collected over the last few days were powerful evidence that he was right. Virtually all the people who had fallen ill from cholera had drunk water from the Broad Street Pump.

But there were some troubling exceptions to the pattern Snow was seeing. In particular, a widow living in West End, Hampstead—more then five miles from Soho—had died of cholera on September 2. Also, a woman living in Islington, which was even farther from Soho, had died on September 3. This suggested that cholera might indeed spread "through the air" over relatively long distances, which in turn could mean that Snow's hypothesis about waterborne cholera was wrong. He had to find out.

When he reached the house in West End, Snow spoke with the deceased widow's adult son. Exactly what transpired in this interview is obscured by Snow's refusal to identify people by name and by his reluctance to comment on either the son's or his own emotions.[1] Snow clearly considered names and emotions to be irrelevant to the task at hand. No, the son replied, the widow had not visited Soho for many months. Yes, he said, he was sure. But funny you should ask, the widow had lived in Soho years ago and had a great fondness for her old neighborhood. In particular, she liked the water that came from the Broad Street Pump. For years, the widow had sent a servant to fill bottles with water from the Broad Street Pump and deliver them to her house. She said it tasted better than the water of Hampstead. The last bottle had been filled and delivered on August 31, the day the cholera outbreak began. The widow had drunk the water the next day, and she had died the day after that. Even worse, continued the son, the widow's niece had visited Hampstead on September 1, had drunk the Soho water, and had died at her home in Islington the next day. Snow did not comment, carefully maintaining his matter-of-fact demeanor, and continued asking the son questions. After a few more minutes, he closed his notebook, thanked the son, and left him to his grief. After all, it was 1854, and sudden death was no stranger to anyone.

So these deaths fit the pattern too. The Broad Street Pump really was the source of the cholera.

A few days later, Snow persuaded the Soho Parish leaders to remove the handle of the Broad Street Pump, an action that made it impossible for anyone to draw water from the well. This may or may not have helped stop the epidemic, since by then just about everybody had left Soho in fear of the disease. It is entirely possible, though, that Dr. Snow's dogged investigation saved lives. The work of tracking down the source of cholera was not carried out by a grim Angel of Death after all but by a careful, thoughtful physician. Today, John Snow is remembered as the founder of modern epidemiology, the study of how diseases spread in human populations. In his honor, the pump handle has been adopted as the symbol of epidemiology.

But the tragedy of the Hampstead widow and her niece also points out something else. Bottling water, even water from apparently pristine wells or springs, carries a risk of spreading disease-causing microorganisms. Just where these risks come from, however, and how great or small they really are, is not straightforward or obvious. These risks are as hidden, complex, and counterintuitive as the microorganisms themselves. And there is no better example of this than the life cycle of the microorganism that causes cholera.

You might think that, after the epidemic of 1854, the Broad Street Pump would have been abandoned forever. But in fact, only a couple of weeks after the epidemic subsided and the population began to return to Soho, the pump handle was replaced and people began drinking the water again. By this time, however, the water had returned to its previously safe condition. Whatever mysterious waterborne "poison" that John Snow thought was causing cholera was apparently gone. That convinced most of England's medical community that there had never been anything wrong with the water in the first place and that John Snow simply had been wrong about cholera being waterborne. It would not be until 1883, almost thirty years later, that the German physician and microbiologist Robert Koch isolated a bacterium named *Vibrio cholerae* from the intestines of people who had died from cholera.[2] This bacterium, which has a distinctive V shape (hence the name *Vibrio*), had been observed though the microscope as early as 1854 by an Italian named Filippo Pacini.[3] Pacini, like John Snow, thought cholera was spread by water. But it was not until Koch learned to grow the bacterium in the laboratory that it was possible to connect *V. cholerae* directly with people who had contracted the disease. Specifically, Koch was able to culture *V. cholerae* from the intestines of people who had died from cholera and was *not* able to culture *V. cholerae* from the intestines of people who had died from other causes. After the studies of Koch, it was immediately clear that cholera could be spread by drinking water contaminated with *V. cholerae*. John Snow's mysterious "poison" had turned out to be a microorganism.

But if cholera is caused by contaminated water, and if the Broad Street Pump was put back into service after only a few weeks, why didn't the epidemic continue? What happened to the deadly bacteria that had been there only a few days ago? The answers to those questions took more than a hundred years of dogged investigation to work out.

Unraveling this puzzle began with understanding how the Broad Street Pump became infected with *V. cholerae* in the first place. A clergyman by the name of Reverend Henry Whitehead had heard about John Snow's theory that cholera was waterborne and was convinced that Snow was wrong. Whitehead thought that cholera was caused by divine retribution and represented God's wrath toward the sinful ways of humanity. Determined to prove his point, Whitehead undertook a survey similar to the one Snow had done. His investigations led him to a woman who had lost her infant and her husband in the early days of the epidemic. The baby had developed the rice-water diarrhea that is characteristic of cholera in late August, before dying on August 31. The mother, frantic with worry, had rinsed the baby's soiled nappies in water and hurriedly dumped the water into a cesspool on August 30. Incredibly, the cesspool was located only a few feet from the Broad Street Pump. Water contaminated with *V. cholerae* must have seeped from the cesspool to the well, where it immediately infected anyone who drank the water. The Reverend Whitehead was not pleased with his findings—after all, they contradicted his theory of divine retribution—but he was honest enough to accurately report what he had found. Importantly, Whitehead's study provided an explanation for how *V. cholerae* had contaminated the Broad Street Pump.

The next mystery was why, after a few short weeks, the water of the Broad Street Pump became safe again for human consumption. A hint as to why this happened comes from the studies of Robert Koch in 1883. An important part of growing microorganisms in the laboratory is to discover the conditions that they prefer. Koch found that *V. cholerae* grew best in a medium that contained about 15 parts per thousand of salt, which is about half the salinity of seawater, and required a temperature of at least 17°C (63°F). Significantly, Koch found that *V. cholerae* preferred a higher temperature close to 37°C (98.6°F), which just happens to be the normal temperature of the human body. Finally, the bacterium needed a fairly rich nutrient broth in order to grow. These culture conditions necessary to grow *V. cholerae* in the laboratory immediately suggest why the bacteria died out in the Broad Street Pump after a few weeks. The normal ground water temperature of Soho is about 15°C, the water does not contain salt, and there are not enough nutrients in the water to allow the bacterium to grow. Thus, although *V. cholerae* could survive for a few days in the well after being introduced by the ill infant's mother, the bacteria could not reproduce. Without being able to reproduce, they soon died off or became inactive, rendering the water safe again to drink in a couple of weeks.

But where did the *V. cholerae* that started the epidemic come from in the first place? Why are there long periods of time when there is no cholera at all, followed by epidemics that boil up apparently at random? It turns out that cholera epidemics are not quite as random as they seemed in the nineteenth century. In the twentieth century, epidemiological studies such as those that John Snow pioneered, showed that cholera epidemics tended to begin in the spring or summertime. Furthermore, epidemics usually began in cities located (like London) on estuaries, and they often followed torrential rains. By the middle of the twentieth century, microbiologists had learned that *V. cholerae* is a bacterium that lives naturally in seawater. Its life cycle, however, is complicated and took a good deal of time to work out.[4]

It turns out that *V. cholerae* is a highly specialized bacterium that lives symbiotically with certain zooplankton, the single-celled photosynthetic microorganisms that live in the ocean and in estuaries.[5] More specifically, *V. cholerae* naturally inhabits the intestinal tracts of the zooplankton. When the time comes for the zooplankton to reproduce, *V. cholerae* leaves the intestinal tract and grows around the developing egg sacs of the zooplankton. There, the bacterium excretes an enzyme that dissolves the chitinous egg sacs, helping to release a new generation of baby zooplankton into the water. In addition, new copies of *V. cholerae* also are released when the egg sacs break. This is a classic case of symbiosis, wherein the zooplankton and *V. cholerae* work together in order to reproduce more efficiently. But, at least as far as humans are concerned, there is more to this story. The *V. cholerae* that engage in this life cycle are not at all dangerous to their zooplankton hosts. Interestingly, these *V. cholerae* are benign to humans as well. It is at this point that the story takes a truly bizarre twist.

The problem comes in the spring or summer when heavy rains wash large quantities of nutrients into marine estuaries and when the water temperature rises. The warming waters and the presence of nutrients cause zooplankton populations to grow rapidly. As the numbers of zooplankton increase, so do the numbers of *V. cholerae*. The increased numbers of *V. cholerae*, in turn, stimulate the growth of marine viruses that infect bacteria. A certain class of these viruses, called phages, are capable of inserting themselves into the DNA of *V. cholerae*. When *V. cholerae* becomes infected with one particular phage, the virus inserts genes into the bacterium that produce a virulent toxin.[6] It is this toxin that causes the symptoms of cholera in humans. These transformed and now deadly bacteria can then be taken up by filter-feeding marine shellfish such as crabs, clams, or oysters. When people eat these shellfish—particularly if they eat them raw—the transformed *V. cholerae* can be passed to humans. The severe diarrhea caused by the cholera toxin then serves to spread *V. cholerae* even more rapidly in human populations, especially human populations living in unsanitary conditions where drinking water is contaminated by raw sewage. The very same physiological characteristics that make *V. cholerae* a useful symbiont of zooplankton also serve to make it a deadly parasite of humans.

The intricate life cycle of *V. cholerae*—how it lives in nature, how it reproduces and grows, how it is transformed by viruses to cause disease in humans, and how it finds its way into human drinking water—is an incredibly improbable sequence of events. What were the odds that, in 1854, one widow with a taste for drinking water from the Broad Street Pump would find herself at the end of this deadly chain? Nevertheless, it did happen—and that means that it can happen again. The fact that an otherwise innocuous microorganism, making a mundane living floating in the ocean, can spontaneously turn into a deadly waterborne pathogen to humans is an unlikely, uncomfortable, but very real possibility. And this is just one example of the kinds of potential life-and-death issues faced every day by the entire drinking water industry, and by the bottled water industry in particular.

As far as we can tell, life on earth began about 3.9 billion years ago, soon after the planet had cooled to the point that liquid water could accumulate in ocean basins. Just how or when this event or sequence of events occurred is a matter of great interest and debate,[7] but little direct evidence. One idea revolves around the hot springs still found on the ocean floor today, the likes of which certainly existed on the early earth. As hot water moves through basalt on the ocean floor, it picks up reduced solutes such as hydrogen, hydrogen sulfide, ferrous iron, ammonia, and simple organic compounds. As these chemicals discharged from springs on the ocean floor of the early earth, membrane-like bubbles of ferrous sulfide may have formed that arranged the organic molecules into self-replicating configurations. These configurations, in turn, maintained and reproduced themselves by extracting energy from the reduced chemicals present in the hot spring water. Some scientists think that this sequence of events may have happened in hot springs associated with volcanoes on the seafloor. Others think it happened deep in the earth where the emerging microbes were sheltered from solar radiation and meteorite bombardment. Regardless of how it happened, however, the fact is that by 3.5 billion years ago the earth's oceans were teeming with microorganisms. These microorganisms, in turn, would dominate life on the planet for the next 2 billion years.

It seems that primitive microorganisms known as the *Archaea* (ancient life) appeared first, apparently adapted for life in and around hot springs. Somewhat later in earth's history, another class of cells emerged known as the *Prokaryotes* (early nucleus), which are more commonly referred to as the *Bacteria*. Still later, two or more different kinds of prokaryotic microorganisms combined into one symbiotic package with a much more complex cellular architecture. These became the *Eukaryotes* (true nucleus). Later, these eukaryotic microorganisms would begin to combine into multicellular organisms, of which we humans are one example.

The details of this development are hazy, but one thing is fairly certain. For billions of years, life on earth consisted entirely of waterborne microorganisms. During that time, every conceivable ecological niche that was available in the seas, lakes, streams, and springs was filled by particular microorganisms. Some microorganisms became *autotrophs*, or primary producers that used sunlight or chemical energy to grow, maintain, and reproduce themselves. Others specialized as *heterotrophs*, or scavengers that consumed and recycled the deceased bodies of primary producers. Still others specialized as *parasites*, actively infecting and stealing resources from autotrophs and heterotrophs. All these microorganisms competed for the limited resources available for sustaining life. It was this competition, operating over billions of years, that generated the incredibly diverse multitudes of microorganisms we see on earth today.

So, when multicellular macroorganisms first arose about 1.5 billion years ago, they were faced with an aquatic world that was already dominated by single-celled microorganisms. Developing ways of interacting with this sea of microorganisms, therefore, was necessary for survival. It seems likely that many new macroorganisms engaged in *predation,* grazing on the many single-celled bacteria and eukaryotes already there. It would not have taken long, however, for the single-celled microorganisms to turn the tables by parasitizing the macroorganisms. Over the millennia, some of these interactions gradually became *synergistic,* with micro- and macroorganism cooperating to some mutually beneficial end.

By the time the first members of the genus *Homo* came on the scene about 2 million years ago, the ways that micro- and macroorganisms interacted with each other were well established. The most important interactions between humans and microorganisms are synergistic, with large numbers of highly specialized, largely benign bacteria living on our skin and inhabiting our intestinal tract. It is an unsettling thought, but we human beings actually have more bacterial cells living in and on us then the eukaryotic cells we are actually made of. These bacteria, which are known as our *normal flora,* perform a number of useful functions. In particular, bacteria such as *Escherichia coli* and *Enterococcus faecalis* coat the lining of our intestines. This arrangement benefits the microorganisms, since it provides them with a generous living. It also benefits the human host by helping to break down and digest the food we eat. But also, because there are such large numbers of bacteria living in our intestinal tract, it helps us deal with the billions and billions of microorganisms that we ingest every day in our food and water.[8] Our normal flora protect us simply by being better adapted for life in our intestines, effectively outcompeting other, unwelcome microorganisms for available resources.

While synergism with bacteria is a common interaction humans have with microorganisms, parasitism is the interaction that most often gets our attention. Over the last 2 million years of human history, numerous microorganisms including bacteria, viruses, and eukaryotes have developed ways of colonizing and infecting human beings. It is important here to make a distinction between *colonization* and *infection.*[9] Many microorganisms, particularly the ones we ingest on a daily basis, colonize our bodies. This colonization is usually temporary and lasts only until our normal flora gets into gear and excludes the newcomers by outcompeting them. Temporary colonization, therefore, is not injurious to humans. An infection, on the other hand, in which a microorganism begins to actively grow and displace the body's normal flora, is injurious and can make people sick. Human pathogens such as *V. cholerae* have the capability of causing infections that can hurt or even kill the people they infect.

So what distinguishes a member of the normal flora like *E. coli* from a pathogenic parasite like *V. cholerae*? Over the millennia, *E. coli* have adjusted their metabolism to live symbiotically with humans, inhabiting our intestinal tract without producing disease. Over the same millennia, *V. cholerae* have adjusted themselves to live symbiotically with zooplankton. As such, their metabolism and biochemistry are not entirely compatible with humans. Thus, when *V. cholerae* colonizes people, particularly when it has acquired genes that produce deadly toxins, it becomes an infection that injures the host. As a general rule, microorganisms that cause infections have biochemical mechanisms—called *virulence factors*—that enable infection and/or can harm the host. This relationship between infection, microbes, and virulence factors can be thought of in terms of a simple equation.[10]

$$\frac{possibility}{of\ infection} \sim \frac{[number\ of\ microbes] \times [virulence\ factors\ of\ microbes]}{immune\ status\ of\ host},$$

(Equation 5.1)

which states that the chance of a host becoming infected is proportional to the number of microorganisms ingested and the virulence factors they possess, and inversely proportional to the strength of the host's immune system. For example, if a host ingests just a few microbes, or if those microbes lack specific virulence factors, an infection is not a likely outcome. More subtly, proportionally fewer microbes with well-developed virulence factors (*V. cholerae*) might cause quite a serious infection. However, even microbes that do not have strong virulence factors may cause infection if enough of them are ingested. Finally, the better a host's immune status is, the less susceptible it will be to an infection of any kind.

All this goes a long way toward explaining what happened at the Broad Street Pump in Soho in 1854. From the time it was first dug, the water produced from the well contained bacteria that live naturally in soils and routinely get washed into wells and streams alike. However, since soil bacteria seldom interact with humans, they do not have much virulence and so did not produce infections in healthy people very often. Even after the cesspool was dug next to the pump, which certainly immediately began to contaminate the water, the contaminating bacteria were largely members of the normal flora of humans such as *E. coli* or *Enterococcus*. Furthermore, the well water would have diluted the numbers of microorganisms present. The combination of low bacterial numbers, their lack of virulence factors, and the generally high immune status of the local population kept infections at a relatively low rate. With the introduction of the transformed strain of *V. cholerae* from the infected baby's nappies, however, everything changed. Here was a bacterium introduced in fairly large numbers (the rinsed baby nappies), with high virulence factors (the ability to grow in intestines combined with a virus-induced toxin), into a population with little immunity to that particular microorganism. The result was an epidemic of catastrophic proportions.

All this suggests that what constitutes "safe" drinking water is more complicated than simply whether or not water contains microorganisms. In fact, if sterile or near-sterile drinking water were a necessity for human life, then people would have died out long ago. The microbiological "safety" of water is not a fixed entity but is rather a balance between the abundance and kind of microorganisms present and the immunological status of the people drinking it (equation 5.1). Under the carefully controlled conditions maintained by municipal drinking water systems in the United States, this balance provides "safe" drinking water for most people most of the time. Sometimes, however, this balance is upset by particular waterborne microorganisms. Take, for example, the case of Milwaukee, Wisconsin.

In the spring of 1993, people living in Milwaukee began falling ill with a mysterious intestinal ailment. Children and old people were most affected, and the symptoms included severe diarrhea, vomiting, and associated dehydration. The hospitals were almost overwhelmed, and for a while it was the kind of crisis that is the greatest fear of public health officials. Eventually, 400,000 people in all came down with the disease. It only took a couple of days to determine the cause of the epidemic: it was a primitive, waterborne protozoan by the name of *Cryptosporidium* that had contaminated the municipal water supply of the city. More accurately, the water was infected with the oocysts of *Cryptosporidium*. These oocysts are tough, tiny spores, and they represent the inactive part of *Cryptosporidium*'s life cycle. Once ingested by the unsuspecting Milwaukeeans, however, they came to life, multiplied, and caused the epidemic. It took weeks for the epidemic to run its course, and this was probably the most serious, widespread outbreak of waterborne disease the United States has experienced in the last quarter century.

To a microbial ecologist, *Cryptosporidium* is just one more microorganism that has an interesting life cycle involving water. It is a protozoan, which is to say that it is not a bacterium but the same kind of eukaryotic cell that our own bodies are made of. Furthermore, this particular parasite takes advantage of two very common and nurturing environments on earth: the intestinal tracts of mammals and water.

The life cycle of *Cryptosporidium* begins as a tiny oocyst being carried along by water in a stream or a river. These oocysts are only about one to five microns in diameter, and they are covered by a tough chitinous shell. When *Cryptosporidium* is in this cyst form, it is entirely dormant. Furthermore, because of its tough shell, it can remain dormant for years. Just how many years is unclear, largely because not enough time has gone by since *Cryptosporidium* was discovered to really know. Tens of years is a decent guess. These oocysts are also designed to be carried around by water. When a mammal drinks water containing *Cryptosporidium* oocysts, the protozoan has a chance to come out of its dormant state and complete its life cycle. Once it is safely nestled in a mammal's intestinal tract, it takes advantage of the high-nutrient environment to shed its shell and begin metabolizing and reproducing. During the course of this infection, which can last from a few days to several years, millions of oocysts are manufactured and returned to the environment via the mammal's feces. Once out of the mammal, the newly minted oocysts can be washed into nearby streams, rivers, and even ground-water systems, where the life cycle begins all over again.

Since the Milwaukee outbreak of 1993, municipal water treatment plants—and water-bottling plants as well—have modified their water purification philosophy. The problem with *Cryptosporidium* oocysts is that they are extremely tough. Chlorination, which is the mainstay of microbial treatment for municipal water, has little effect on them. Filtration is more effective, but one needs a very fine filter mesh—no larger than 2 microns—to capture a high percentage of the oocysts. Ultraviolet (UV) light treatment also can inactivate oocysts, but the water must be exposed to the light for a sufficient amount of time for the treatment to work. For municipal water treatment plants, filtering large volumes of water though such fine filters and/or using UV treatment is very expensive. Nevertheless, given the fact that *Cryptosporidium* is constantly infecting cows, deer, beaver, and whatever other mammals happen to be around, and given the fact that the feces of these animals provide a source of oocysts to surface water supplies, most water treatment systems have been modified since 1993 to include both filtration and UV irradiation.

Water-bottling plants have an advantage over municipal systems when it comes to treating water for *Cryptosporidium,* since they deal with much lower volumes of water on a daily basis. Furthermore, water-bottling plants more commonly have spring or artesian water sources, which are required by the Food and Drug Administration not to be influenced by surface water and thus are less likely to contain *Cryptosporidium* oocysts in the first place. Those bottled waters that use mountain streams as a source, however, have to pay particular attention to *Cryptosporidium,* since deer commonly inhabit high mountain forests and deer are a major reservoir for oocysts. In addition to filtering, many municipal systems and most water-bottling plants in the United States use some kind of sterilization technology such as ozonation and/or UV treatment.

Cryptosporidium is an example of a true waterborne pathogen,[11] and its life cycle exhibits several characteristics that are shared by other waterborne pathogens. First of all, it is specifically adapted to living in the intestines of its host. This, in turn, enables it to endure the chemical conditions (stomach acid) and the normal flora present in the intestines of all mammals. Secondly, once it has infected the intestines of its host, it immediately begins reproducing copies of itself that are delivered to the environment with the feces of its host. That, incidently, is one reason such diseases commonly cause diarrhea in people and other mammals. The diarrheal response in humans is designed to help expel invading microorganisms, a response that microorganisms like *Cryptosporidium* take advantage of to spread their oocysts around more efficiently. Thirdly, once back in the environment, the pathogen enters the dormant state that allows it to survive for days, months, or years before encountering a new prospective host. Being carried around by water helps, from the pathogen's point of view, since it is free transportation to new potential hosts. *V. cholerae* has basically the same life cycle except that it is designed to use the gut of zooplankton in order to replicate and spread to new hosts. But, under some circumstances, it will do the same thing in the intestines of humans as well. This basic sequence—replication in the intestines, delivery to water, entering a dormant state, finding a new host, and causing a new infection—is the hallmark of waterborne pathogens.

There are many microorganisms in nature that follow this basic ecological strategy. On the other hand, there are many more that do not. The microbiological safety of drinking water, therefore, is not determined by the simple presence or absence of microorganisms.

Rather, it is determined by those kinds of microorganisms with specific virulence factors that enable them to infect, not just colonize, the human intestinal tract. These kinds of microorganisms, in turn, are almost always associated with fecal contamination of water. That was the case in the Soho cholera epidemic of 1854, and it was the case with the *Cryptosporidium* outbreak in Milwaukee in 1993. When considering the microbiological safety of both municipal and bottled water, therefore, fecal contamination is the most important risk factor to look for.

As the quality control and safety manager of the Hawaiian Natural Water Company, Robert Betts knew all about the potential dangers of fecal microorganisms like *Cryptosporidium* and *V. cholerae*. Betts had been trained in the operation and management of municipal water treatment systems and had spent years in the Pacific Northwest working in the water industry. Then, out of the blue, the opportunity to move to Hawaii—known to Hawaiians as the Big Island—arose. The Hawaiian Natural Water Company was growing; in fact it had recently signed a deal to supply bottled water to Thailand, and the company needed an experienced safety manager. This arrangement gave Betts the opportunity to practice his chosen profession—water treatment—while living on the slopes of Mauna Loa, certainly one of the most beautiful places in the United States. But, as he was to soon discover, the enchanting beauty of the tropical rain forests on Mauna Loa provided special challenges as well. Especially when it came to producing bottled water of acceptable microbiological quality.

When he arrived in Hawaii, Betts was well versed in the unending potential for fecal microorganisms to contaminate drinking water. Dealing with them is part and parcel of the water treatment industry. So, it was a given that the most important aspect of his job was ensuring that such microorganisms were entirely absent from the finished water his plant produced. In this respect, the Hawaiian Natural Water Company had some advantages. The source of its water was a deep well (251 feet) drilled into the basaltic rocks that underlie Mauna Loa. The prevailing southeastern wind sweeping off the Pacific Ocean carries large amounts of moisture. As this moist air is forced upward by the slopes of Mauna Loa, it produces lots of rain. The area around Kea'au, Hawaii—where the Hawaiian Natural Water Company is located—has some of the highest annual rainfall (143 inches) in the United States. This rainwater seeps into the porous basalt rock and flows rapidly downward toward the ocean. This set of hydrologic circumstances

produces a relatively unmineralized (TDS about 78 mg/L) ground water that is excellent for drinking. More important, the largely undevel-
oped slopes of Mauna Loa minimize the danger of contamination from
fecal microorganisms. All in all, thought Betts, this pristine source was
going to make his job easier.

But when he first saw the bottling plant, which had begun operations
in 1995, he immediately saw a potential microbiological problem. The
bottling plant was located in a rain forest, surrounded by huge trees
and moldering undergrowth. In particularly, there was a particularly
ancient monkeypod tree located right next to the bottling plant. *Oh no,*
Betts thought to himself, *that tree is going to cause problems.* And
it did. The problem was not the usual kind of fecal microorganisms
that can cause disease in humans. The problem was that, in such a humid environment, the decay of tree leaves and undergrowth produces
molds. Molds, in turn, commonly produce spores in their reproductive
cycle. Most people seeing the monkeypod tree simply saw a pretty tree.
What Betts saw was a mold-spore-producing machine, *right next to his
bottling plant.*

The mold spores did not represent any particular threat to human
health. The types of molds that grew near the bottling plant were
specifically adapted for recycling dead plant matter, and their genetic
machinery lacked the kind of virulence factors that would have allowed
them to infect humans with any efficiency. The problem was that even
a single mold spore in a bottle of finished water could begin reproducing and, in a matter of days, could turn the finished water a milky white
color. If an unsuspecting customer bought a bottle containing cloudy
mold-bearing water, it would be a marketing disaster. Betts knew that,
in addition to ensuring the microbiologic safety of the water, he would
have to engineer a failsafe method for keeping mold spores out of the
finished water as well.

The human body does not depend on just one system to defend itself
against microbial invaders. Rather, it has layer upon layer of systems
that act in concert: skin to block entrance, friendly *E. coli* to outcompete
unwelcome intruders, a complex immune system to attack microbes
that manage to establish infection. Water treatment plants, which have
a problem very similar to the one faced by the human body, have
adopted this same philosophy. Rather than depending on one kind of
treatment, they depend what are called "multiple barrier" systems.
As Betts rolled up his sleeves and got to work, he carefully considered
the kinds of barriers that would be most effective against the spores.

The first barrier was the deep well itself. As rainwater filtered through the basaltic aquifer underlying Mona Loa, particles like mold spores tended to be removed. Betts immediately moved to take advantage of his naturally filtered source, making sure that water pumped from the well never came into contact with air, which, in Kea'au, Hawaii, always contains spores. Once the water was pumped through closed lines to the bottling plant, it was immediately filtered through a 5.0-micron filter. Mold spores are fairly large, often larger than 10-microns in diameter, and so this filtration step probably removed most of whatever spores happened to be present. Next, the filtered water was exposed to UV light, which has the useful property that it can disrupt the genetic material stored in spores, leading to their inactivation. The UV radiation very probably took care of whatever spores had made it through the 5.0-micron filter. Nevertheless, in keeping with the multiple barrier philosophy, the water was then passed through an even finer 1.0-micron filter to remove any remaining spores and most of the bacteria as well. But, since even a few spores getting through the system could be disastrous, the water was once more treated with UV light and then passed though an even smaller 0.2-micron filter. The finished water, which by now had been filtered three times and treated with UV light twice, was treated once again, with ozone. Ozone, which kills bacteria and can also inactive spores, was a "polishing" step designed to back up all the other treatment processes.

A diagram of the basic treatment scheme employed by the Hawaiian Natural Water Company is shown in fig. 5.1. Beginning with a nearly pristine artesian well source, the water goes through multiple treatment steps, or "barriers," each designed to remove potential microbial contaminants. This sequence of water treatment, with variations imposed by local conditions, is used in most bottled water plants in the United States. You might think, given the multiple treatment steps employed, that the finished water produced by such systems would be sterile. After all, filtration physically removes microorganisms, and both UV light and ozone actively kill bacteria. In fact, however, studies have shown that finished water from such treatment systems contains anywhere from 1,000 to 100,000 bacterial cells per milliliter.[12] Those numbers, however, are lower than in most treated municipal waters, and significantly lower than in untreated surface or ground waters (1 million to 1 billion cells per milliliter). Furthermore, since fecal microorganisms are unlikely to pass through the multiple barriers, the possibility of someone with a normal immune system contracting an infection from the water is vanishingly small.

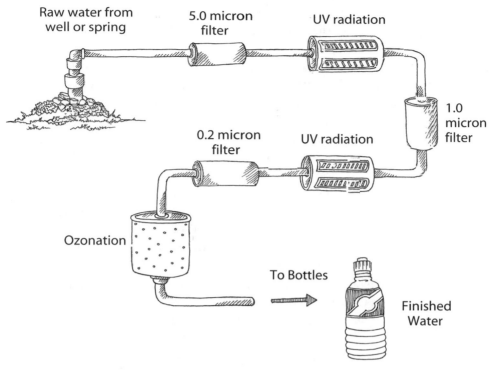

FIGURE 5.1 A typical antimicrobial treatment system used for bottling water.

The reasons American bottled water plants routinely employ such stringent "multiple barrier" treatments are simple. First, it is just a fact of life that waterborne pathogens may be present in water sources, and thus treatment is needed for reasons of health. But secondly, and just as important to the bottled water industry, any hint that microbial contaminants might be present in the finished product—such as molds discoloring the water—would be economically devastating. This confluence between the consumer's expectation that bottled water be microbiologically safe and the economic pressure to provide that safety has shaped the "multiple barrier" philosophy embraced by the bottled water industry.

Just ask Robert Betts.

It is no particular secret that people can be fussy about the water they drink. Entire industries, including municipal water systems, home water purification devices, and the bottled water industry are based on this fussiness. But as stories like those of *V. cholerae* and the Hampstead widow, the Milwaukee *Cryptosporidium* outbreak, and Robert Betts's struggles with mold spores show, this fussiness is grounded in bitter experience. The fact is, water can transmit microorganisms, and it makes perfect sense for people to be careful about what they drink. Over the centuries, the collective experience of humanity has developed, modified, and refined this habit of water fussiness.

Take, for example, the Broad Street Pump. In 1854, nobody thought twice about having a cesspool for human and animal excrement located a few feet from a water-supply well. After all, cholera was thought to be transmitted by miasmatic, putrefied air. Since then, it has become abundantly clear that fecal matter is in fact the source of many waterborne pathogens. Result? Nowadays, human water fussiness includes a huge aversion to fecal contamination of water—a fussiness that was absent in Soho Parish in 1854.

Other components of water fussiness also make microbiological sense. On the whole, people would much rather drink cool water than warm water. Since the growth rate of microorganisms, particularly microorganisms adapted to the intestinal tract, increases as water becomes warmer, it makes perfect sense to prefer cool water. Cloudy water is another example. One reason water can be cloudy is because it contains excessive numbers of microorganisms. Even normally benign bacteria can cause infection if ingested in high enough numbers (equation 5.1), and thus cloudy or discolored water is wisely considered distasteful. Finally, deeply circulating ground waters, which have been isolated from surface sources of fecal matter, are considered preferable to surface waters. This is one reason why the term "spring water" is such a powerful marketing tool for bottled water companies. It is simply part of our collective water fussiness.

If the standard of safety for either bottled water or treated municipal water was sterile water the standard would probably be impossible to meet. Waterborne microorganisms on earth have had 3.9 billion years to figure out various ingenious lifestyles for surviving and thriving in water. Humanity, on the other hand, has only been in the water treatment business for a few hundred years. If you consider all the various ways microorganisms use water to spread themselves around, hide, and reproduce, you can begin to appreciate the problems faced by municipal water treatment systems and water-bottling plants. Nevertheless, it is worth pointing out that, in the eighty years that bottled water in America has been regulated by the FDA, there have been no documented instances of bottled water being associated with an out-break of waterborne disease.[13]

Whether that record will stand indefinitely we shall just have to see. If you consider the virtually infinite ways that microorganisms interact with humans and water, and if you consider their remarkable ability to change and evolve in order to meet new challenges, you have to wonder if this perfect record can be maintained forever. But as long as people maintain their water fussiness, which is just another expression of the "multiple barrier" approach to water treatment, there is hope that it will.

John Snow would be proud.

II   THE BUSINESS
OF BOTTLED WATER

6 THE WINDS OF FASHION
A History of Drinking Water

The sixteen armed men, led by Captain Miles Standish, marched briskly along the shore of the cold ocean. The *Mayflower* had arrived off Cape Cod only a couple of days ago, and the little ship had suffered considerably in the rough crossing of the Atlantic Ocean. The ship's master, Captain Christopher Jones, reckoned that it would take weeks to restore the *Mayflower* to seaworthiness. In the meantime, the Pilgrims were anxious to explore the "hideous and desolate wilderness," as William Bradford described it, that lay before them. Accordingly, on the fifteenth of November, 1620, a small group of men ventured forth to have a look at the land to which, they believed, God had called them.

They had not walked more than a mile when, in the distance, they saw five or six persons accompanied by a dog. The Pilgrims immediately turned toward these people, "who were savages," and tried to get close enough to speak with them. The Native Americans, called "Indians" by the colonists, instantly perceived that they were being chased, melted back into the woods, and disappeared. The sixteen Pilgrims charged after them—which probably did very little to calm the fears of the Indians—hoping to find where they lived. They followed the Indians without success for some miles, and, with night coming on, the Pilgrims set out sentinels and rested overnight.

The next morning, the Pilgrims continued to hunt for the Indians, but it was not long before they were spectacularly lost. They spent the morning stumbling through thickets that "were ready to tear their clothes and armor in pieces," hoping to stumble onto the Indian village they were certain was close by. But torn clothes and bleeding arms were not the worst of their plight. Having gone almost a full day without having anything to drink, the men were suffering terribly from thirst. In the words of William Bradford, they "were most distressed for want of drink. But at length they found water and refreshed themselves, being the first New-England water they drunk of, and was now in their great thirst as pleasant unto them as wine or beer had been in fore-times."[1] To modern ears, these words of William Bradford seem unremarkable enough. After all, if the men were thirsty, of course they would find a stream and drink the water. The North American wilderness they had just arrived in was beautifully pristine, and the water flowing in the small streams and brooks of New England was as pure and healthy as any in the world. To us, to drink such delightfully clear water would be a joy to be savored.

But the Pilgrims did not think so. To them, drinking water—any water—was a sign of desperation, an admission of abject poverty, a last resort. Like all Europeans of the seventeenth century, the Pilgrims disliked, distrusted, and despised drinking water. Only truly poor people, who had absolutely no choice, drank water. The reason was simple enough. For hundreds of years, the waters of Britain and continental Europe had been so fouled with fecal microorganisms emanating from human and animal wastes that to drink them was literally to risk your life. Furthermore, the water the Pilgrims had taken with them on the *Mayflower* stored in wooden barrels had soon soured. It could be used for cooking, but that was about it. To use barrel-stored water for drinking was to risk ingesting the swarms of bacteria, mold, and amoebas that were happily growing in the wooden casks.

Europeans of the sixteenth and seventeen centuries, the years immediately following the Reformation, were an argumentative lot. The very fact that the Pilgrims, who did not approve of the spiritual slackness of their former English and Dutch neighbors, were gently rocking at anchor in Cape Cod Bay attests to this. But there is one thing all Europeans agreed on: drinking water was bad—very bad—for your health. As early as the 1400s, Sir John Fortescue remarked that English peasants never drank water. In his words, "They drink no water unless it be . . . for devotion."[2] A century later, one Andrew Boorde wrote in 1542 that "water is not wholesome, sole by itself, for an Englishman."[3] The Europeans knew nothing about microorganisms, of course. Their prejudice was entirely observational and reflected a lifetime of suffering, and of watching other people suffer, the intestinal maladies caused by bad drinking water. As a consequence, only very poor people actually drank water, a distinction noted, for example, in a 1345 court record of London: "whereas of old a certain conduit was built in the midst of the City of London, so that the rich and middling persons therein might there have water for preparing their food, and the poor for their drink."[4] This association between drinking water and abject poverty, universally held by Europeans prior to about 1700, figures prominently in the history of water drinking in Europe and in North America.

What the seventeenth-century English did drink was beer. Lots of beer. The art of brewing had been brought to England by the Germanic Angles and Saxons in the sixth century A.D., and as the microbiological quality of water supplies deteriorated in the Middle Ages, ale and then beer became the staple drink of the English. Ale was brewed from barley or oats, and the alcoholic content (which often exceeded 5%) helped discourage the growth and transmission of fecal bacteria. Even so, unhopped ale soon became sour, reflecting the growth of alcohol-tolerant microorganisms. Hops, which most people these days think of as a flavor-enhancing additive, were originally used to help preserve ale. Hops, which were introduced as early as the ninth century A.D. in Bavaria, were boiled with beer and then strained off before barreling. Hops contain oils and resins that may or may not retard the growth of bacteria. More important, boiling and leaching the hops helped kill microorganisms, and hopped beer can be stored in wooden barrels for a much longer period of time than ale.

As water supplies became more and more widely polluted during the Middle Ages, beer became the primary drink of middle- and lower-class inhabitants of Britain. This did not mean that water was not consumed. It seems, rather, that the custom was to drink "small beer" as a primary source of fluids. "Small beer" was beer watered down to an alcoholic content of about 1/2 to 1%.[5] This amount of alcohol was sufficient to depress the numbers of fecal bacteria that festered in the water but not so high as to induce dangerous dehydration. The fact that most of Britain had a relatively cool climate, in which the people could actually survive without constant hydration, meant that drinking small beer as a source of fluids was possible. Also, the caloric content of beer made it an important part of their diet.

So when the Pilgrims landed at Plymouth in the fall of 1620, drinking plain water—even the absolutely pristine waters of a virgin continent—was as foreign to them as the wilderness stretching before them. In fact beer, or rather the lack of it, was one reason that the Plymouth Colony was established when and where it was. Captain Jones of the *Mayflower* was much too canny a sailor to attempt a winter crossing of the Atlantic Ocean back to England. This meant that the little ship and its crew would have to spend the winter in Cape Cod Bay. The captain's problem was that, if the Pilgrims and the crew kept drinking beer at their present rate, there would not be enough for the sailors on the return voyage. The only thing the captain and crew could do was to put the Pilgrims ashore and cut off their rations of beer. Accordingly, on December 19, 1620, the Pilgrims struggled ashore, secured their little skiff to Plymouth Rock, and began the laborious and dangerous process of building a life in the wilderness.

None of this hard labor was made any easier by the lack of beer. As William Bradford noted, the Pilgrims "were hastened ashore and made to drink water, that the seamen might have the more beer." But water, even the clean, pleasant water of a pristine New England, was not what the Pilgrims wanted. One Pilgrim named William Wood summed up the feelings of the rest in his *New England Prospects* by remarking that he did not like drinking water. "I dare not prefere it before good beere," he noted grumpily. William Bradford, a man of considerable diplomatic and political skills, did his best to get the *Mayflower's* crew to relent and give the Pilgrims beer. The crew refused outright.

But even the tough, hardened sailors of the *Mayflower* could be moved to Christian compassion upon occasion. On Christmas Day of that first year, some of the Pilgrims came back aboard the *Mayflower* to take refuge from the weather. Once there, William Bradford recorded: "Monday, the 25th, 1620, being Christmas day, we began to drink water aboard. But, at night, the master caused us to have some beer; and so on board we had, divers times now and then, some beer, but on shore none at all."

The Pilgrims who landed at Plymouth, and later the Puritans who founded Boston, never got over their dislike of water. Drinking water, simply was not the fashion of the day. The irony, of course, was that the water the settlers found in New England was for the most part perfectly healthy to drink. But, not knowing anything about the fecal microorganisms that were the real source of waterborne health problems in Europe, they had no way to tell. People in the New World still needed water for cooking, and they needed water for their livestock; they got it from streams, springs, rain barrels, and shallow wells. In Boston, for example, there was a spring on the Boston Common that was a local source of water. But as the population of Boston and the other cities in New England grew, pollution from the ubiquitous privies soon contaminated the shallow aquifers that fed most springs and wells.

For the next century, there was little alteration in the strong preju-dice against drinking water. One of the first buildings constructed by the Pilgrims was a brewhouse,[6] and so the tradition of drinking beer continued. But as time went on, the settlers also tended to drink milk in preference to water. This made considerable sense. After all, when milk is overly contaminated by bacteria, it turns sour, and this can easily be detected by simply sniffing it. Water, on the other hand, can contain dangerous fecal microorganisms with no outward sign at all. Beginning in the eighteenth century, tea became available from China and was a favored drink for the English and the American colonists alike. Because the water used for steeping tea was boiled, tea was much safer to drink than unboiled water. Plain water, in the meantime, was still to be avoided.

This antiwater attitude in the minds of Americans did not change for a long time. Then, in the early years of the eighteenth century, something happened to alter the general attitude toward drinking water. This change can be traced to the European practice of visiting springs to "take the waters." Visiting springs for health reasons had been an established part of medical practice in Europe for some time, but it had always been a luxury reserved for titled gentry. But in the eigh-teenth century, with the rise of trade and the beginnings of industry, newly rich tradesmen and their families began looking for recreational outlets for their substantial incomes. Going to the springs was a way of emulating the nobility—always an important consideration for the nouveaux riches—and the expense involved was a good way of demon-strating their attainment of wealth. With more and more wealthy people showing up at the more fashionable springs, hotels and dining establishments sprang up as well. By the middle of the eighteenth cen-tury, the popularity and elegance of these resorts was such that "taking the waters" was quite the thing to do.

Suddenly, and for the first time in centuries, drinking water was fashionable again.

In England, the most celebrated and fashionable watering place was the town of Bath. The spring waters that issued forth from Bath had a high reputation for eliciting miraculous cures that stretched back be-fore Roman times. One story tells of a young Prince Bladud (who was later to become the father of King Lear) who tragically contracted lep-rosy. Because of this affliction, Bladud was banished from his father's court and was forced to make his living as a swineherd. To make matters worse, the pigs he was taking care of caught leprosy from Bladud, adding to his miseries. But one day in 863 B.C., Bladud happened to watch his sick pigs wallowing in mud generated by a warm spring near what was to become Bath and noticed that they emerged free of the disease. Bladud wasted no time. Wallowing in the mud himself, he cured himself of leprosy.[7]

Over the years, countless stories of miraculous cures accumulated. During the seventeenth and eighteenth centuries, the town of Bath prospered as nobility and commoners of means flocked in to effect cures for diseases ranging from rheumatism to infertility to gout. In fact, Parliament established the Royal Mineral Water Hospital in 1739, which became famous for what we would now call physical therapy. But by the beginning of the nineteenth century, the real significance of Bath was that it was a meeting place for people of means in polite society. It was, in short, *the* place to be seen.

The social significance of spending time at Bath near the end of the eighteenth century was captured in the popular fiction of the day. For instance, Jane Austen's *Northanger Abby* (1803) begins with a late-middle-aged man named Mr. Allen being "ordered to Bath" by his physician "for the benefit of a gouty constitution." But because this was to be a six-week stay (it took time for the curative properties of the water to take hold), Mrs. Allen was to accompany him. In addition, since the couple was childless, Mrs. Allen invited a seventeen-year-old girl, a friend of the family named Catherine Morland, to come along and keep them company. It soon becomes clear that, while having Mr. Allen partake of the healing waters was the excuse for visiting Bath, the real reason was to have fun. In particular, it was fashionable for people to visit "the pump room," where the healing waters bubbled forth and where the health seekers gathered to drink their daily doses of water. But in addition to drinking the water, the custom was for fashionable people to promenade around the room in their best clothes, to gossip, discuss politics, and generally to see and be seen. Jane Austen describes what went on as follows: "They all three [Mr. Allen, Mrs. Allen, and Catherine] set off for the pump room, where the ordinary course of events and conversation took place; Mr. Allen, after drinking his glass of water, joined some gentlemen to talk over the politics of the day, and compare the account of their newspapers; and the ladies walked about together, noticing every new face, and almost every new bonnet." Recall that prior to 1700, drinking water was something done only by people living in extreme poverty, and therefore it was something to be avoided by anyone of even modest means. By 1800, however, thanks to the fashion of "taking the waters" among well-to-do Europeans, drinking water had instead come to be associated with wealth and social position. This was a sea change in people's perceptions, and it led to a striking turnaround in the use of water as a beverage. By the year 1800, drinking water—at least the clean water issuing from a few rare springs—had not only become acceptable but had attained a degree of fashionability that would have shocked the Pilgrims.

Just how much the actual spring waters, and drinking these waters, had to do with this new fashion is an interesting question to consider. In *Northanger Abby,* Jane Austen scarcely devotes two sentences to Mr. Allen and his water drinking in the entire book. The water clearly was not what interested Austen, and this probably reflects the attitude of most of the people who visited Bath in those days. The real point of a visit was to meet people, preferably wealthy and influential people, to go to the theater, to hold polite and clever conversation, and to dally with suitable or unsuitable members of the opposite sex. For most people, "taking the waters" was very much a side issue. The water was simply an excuse to have fun and get into trouble. Jane Austen, who was as sharp an observer of humankind as has ever lived, saw right through the pretense of what was going on and scarcely bothered to describe the waters of Bath at all. Nevertheless, visiting the springs is what brought water drinking out of the ill repute it had suffered for the last eight centuries and made it fashionable again.

Whatever was fashionable in Europe in those days soon became fashionable in the American colonies and later in the newly constituted United States. If Europeans were going to go to the springs, drink the waters, and have fun, then so would Americans. One early example of this phenomenon was Stafford Springs, Connecticut. It seems that in 1765, one Mr. Field of Windsor, Connecticut, contracted a skin infection that caused him great distress. Following the European tradition of seeking cures at healing springs, he visited a spring at Stafford and soon effected a complete cure. Delighted, Mr. Field spread his story far and wide, and Stafford Springs became famous overnight for its "reputation of curing the gout, sterility, pulmonary, hysterics, etc." It soon became "the New England *Bath,* where the sick and rich resort to prolong life and acquire the polite accomplishments," according to one contemporary.[8]

One notable visitor to Stafford Springs in 1771 was a young lawyer named John Adams. Adams was in the process of building up a law practice in Boston, and he was suffering the effects of overwork and anxiety. Worried about him, his friends persuaded him to visit Stafford Springs for a few days. Upon his arrival on June 3, Adams found accommodations, visited the springs the next day, and described what he saw in his diary:

> The spring issues at the foot of a steep high hill, between a cluster of rocks, very near the side of a river. The water is very clear, limpid, and transparent; the rock and stones and earth, at the bottom are tinged with a reddish yellow color, and so is the little wooden gutter, that is placed at the mouth of the spring to carry the water off; indeed the water communicates that color, which resembles that of the rust of iron, to whatever object it washes. Mrs. Child furnished me with a glass mug broken to pieces and puttied together again; and with that I drank plentifully of the waters; it has a taste of fair water with an infusion of some preparation of steel in it, which I have taken heretofore.

This is as accurate a description of spring waters characterized by high concentrations of dissolved iron (known as chalybeate waters) as was ever made prior to the advent of analytical chemistry. When ground water lacks dissolved oxygen, ferrous iron (Fe^{2+}) can be dissolved from the surrounding rocks, accumulating in solution to concentrations as high as 5 or 10 parts per million. Once this high-iron water discharges from a spring, however, the iron is oxidized by oxygen in the atmosphere to ferric iron (Fe^{3+}), which subsequently precipitates out of solution as ferric hydroxides, or "the rust of iron" as Adams calls it. The iron dissolved in the spring waters, as we have seen earlier (chapter 3), can indeed have medicinal benefits for people suffering from simple anemia.

John Adams, however, seems to have lacked the sanguine temperament needed to properly appreciate "taking the waters." He soon got bored and began to miss his family. The next day, he wrote in his diary: "Rode to the spring; drank and plunged; dipped but once; sky cloudy." The day after that he left Stafford Springs and rode home to his farm in Massachusetts to see his wife. Later in his life, Adams commented that "this journey was of use to me, whether the waters were or not."[9]

The fashion of water drinking in America became especially popular in Philadelphia during the years leading up to the Revolutionary War.[10] In particular, some Quakers living in the rural countryside of Chester

County, about thirty miles from Philadelphia, began to tell about the wonderful curative powers of the waters issuing from the Yellow Springs. These waters were heavily impregnated with iron and hydrogen sulfide, and they seem not to have been the most pleasant of drinking waters. Nevertheless, stories of cures wrought by the waters reached the eager ears of Philadelphians, many of whom went to the considerable trouble to visit Yellow Springs personally. Among the Quakers, the spot became such a popular place to visit on Sundays that several meetings, as Quaker churches were called, warned that this practice might not be a suitable activity for keeping the Sabbath. A public road to Yellow Springs from Philadelphia was built in 1750 to accommodate the traffic, and a stone inn was erected to house visitors. Ownership of the Yellow Springs changed hands frequently, and in 1774 a Dr. Samuel Kennedy bought the "noted inn at the Yellow Springs" and began operating the springs as a sanatorium for his patients. One of his advertisements in a Philadelphia newspaper read: "The Advantage of these Baths is well known to the public; an incontestable proof of which is the great concourse of people—from four to six hundred persons have convened there in one day in the summer season." Interestingly, after the battle of Brandywine in September 1777, Dr. Kennedy offered his inn to the Continental Army as a military hospital. Although Dr. Kennedy died in 1778, the inn was used as a hospital throughout the Revolutionary War, and Congress saw fit to appropriate funds for its upkeep.

Another enterprising physician named Dr. John De Normandie was responsible for building up what was to become probably the most popular water spot in the American colonies.[11] Twenty miles northeast of Philadelphia, on the road to Trenton, New Jersey, was a little town called Bristol, which boasted a spring. In 1768, Dr. De Normandie read a paper to the American Philosophical Society in Philadelphia describing his analyses and experiments on the medicinal benefits of Bristol Springs water. Taking his cue from European medical practice, Dr. De Normandie wrote that the waters had "Principles similar to those of the much-celebrated waters of the German Spa with which they likewise agree in the effects which follow immediately upon drinking them; such as quickening of the pulse, exciting an agreeable warmth in the stomach, promoting the appetite, and occasioning a flow of spirits and a greater degree of cheerfulness." In 1768, analytical chemistry was still so crude as to be virtually useless for understanding why the waters seemed to be medicinal. No matter, said Dr. De Normandie; clinical observation of the waters' effects was more useful than chemical analyses. His observations led him to conclude: "But in no cases have their good effects been more evident or remarkable, than in a depraved and debilitated state of the organs of digestion, arising from inactivity and a sedentary life . . . , or from excessive and free living." In other words, the spring waters were good for digestion and could relieve the chronic intestinal discomfort suffered by so many people. Because De Normandie was a prestigious physician and because he garnered the powerful support of the Philosophical Society, which included his "medical papers" in the first volume of its *Transactions* (1771), Bristol grew into a popular and profitable resort. One result of this was the appearance of bottles of various spring waters on the shelves of apothecary shops in Philadelphia. These bottled spring waters were sold as medicines, to ease whatever medical complaint an individual might have, and for more than a century bottled "mineral" waters were thought of as medicines.

No springs in America were more highly sought after for their medicinal properties than those of Saratoga Springs, New York.[12] In particular, High Rock Spring, located near the town of Saratoga Springs, had been visited by Europeans prior to the Revolutionary War and by George Washington in 1783. In 1784, one Mr. Norton built a hostel so that visitors could stay more or less comfortably near High Rock Spring, and a "house of entertainment" was added in 1803. By 1804, rooms catering to "genteel" customers were renting for $4 a week, and those used by "common" boarders were renting for $2 per week.[13]

Over the next fifty years or so, the medicinal properties of Saratoga Springs waters gained a high reputation throughout the world, and the hotels and entertainments steadily improved in quantity and quality. But since not everybody had the means or constitution to visit Saratoga Springs personally, bottling plants began to spring up, and the waters were shipped to paying customers in cities. In 1856, water from Congress Springs—the best known of the springs because it was known to contain iodine—was selling in New York for $1.75 per pint and $2.25 per quart. This price, in 1856 dollars, would exceed $10 per pint in 2003 dollars. By 1900, waters bottled under the labels such as "Vichy," "Sparkling," "Geyser Water," and "Saratoga" were found on the shelves of grocery stores and apothecary shops throughout the Northeast.

The bottled water industry in America had begun, thanks to the shifting sands of time and fashion.

These same shifting sands led to a precipitous decline in the use of bottled water in the early twentieth century. Part of this was due to the invention of chlorinated tap water, and part of it was due to the decline in the perceived virtues of mineral waters as medicine. By the year 1900, the sciences of chemistry and microbiology were fully modern in terms of their understanding of basic principles, and this understanding led to the production of drugs and medical procedures that were much, much more effective then what had been available in 1800. With the fashion of "taking the waters" on the decline, the bottled water industry in America also declined, barely surviving through the 1930s and 1940s.

We need not repeat the reintroduction of bottled water to fashionability, which occurred in the late 1970s, and the subsequent rise of bottled water to its present heights of popularity (chapter 1). But, with that rise in mind, we can clearly see two cycles of water fashion that have occurred since the Pilgrims landed at Plymouth Rock. The cycles began with water being very much out of fashion, which in turn was due to the grossly contaminated condition of most water in Britain and Europe. In 1600, only the poorest of the poor resorted to drinking water, and this served only to make water even less attractive to polite society. Beginning about 1700, however, with the rise of the beginnings of industry and trade that accompanied the Enlightenment, newly prosperous commoners began emulating the nobility by visiting medicinal springs. By 1800, drinking water had entirely lost its association with poverty and was instead a sign of wealth and sophistication. But what goes around comes around, and by 1920 drinking bottled water, at least in the eastern United States, was once again out of fashion. Whereas drinking bottled water had once been a sign of sophistication, by 1940 it just meant you were old-fashioned. This changed again when, beginning in the 1970s, the European tradition of single-serving bottles of water, notably Perrier and Evian from France, was rediscovered by the young urban professionals. In 1960, the idea that people would pay $1 for a 16-ounce bottle of water was laughable. By 1980, a good deal of the appeal of bottled water was that it *was* more expensive than tap water and therefore was meant to be consumed by people of means and taste.

So it goes.

Part of what makes this history interesting is the similarity between what made water drinking popular and fashionable in 1800 and what makes it popular today. First and foremost, there was and is a large component of health consciousness involved. In 1800, "taking the waters" was considered to be a healthy practice, largely because of the real or purported medicinal effects of certain spring or well waters. Now, in the early twenty-first century, drinking water is also closely associated with health. There are, however, some interesting differences between the attitudes of today and those of two hundred years ago.

For one thing, bottled waters are no longer widely considered to be "medicinal" in the sense that they are supposed to cure specific diseases. Rather, drinking water is considered to be an essential part of a lifestyle that *leads* to better health. An important part of this lifestyle includes eating a healthy diet, which means not consuming too much in the way of animal fats and refined sugars. But just as important, this healthy lifestyle includes regular exercise. Numerous studies have shown that simply walking a mile or two a few times a week can lead to improved aerobic capacity, better flexibility, and better muscle tone. But also, moderate exercise makes people feel better. The human body is designed to be used, and when it is used regularly and judiciously, this not only improves physical function but also gives people a better and more positive outlook on life.

The definition of "moderate" exercise varies widely from person to person and can range from walking around the block a time or two to running twenty or more miles per week. When people engage in physical exercise they get thirsty. It is just a given, therefore, that drinking fluids is part and parcel of a lifestyle that includes regular exercise. There are a variety of sports drinks designed to replace carbohydrates and salts for people engaged in sports, and these are very popular. For many people, however, the preferred drink is water. When you are really, really thirsty, there is nothing quite like a cool drink of crystal clear water. The popularity of exercise as part of a healthy lifestyle has contributed significantly to the increased popularity of drinking water. That was a dynamic that was not around in 1800.

The idea that drinking fluids and staying properly hydrated is good for people engaged in sports and exercise is a fairly recent development, at least in the United States. In the 1960s, for example, high school athletes were regularly forbidden to drink any kind of fluids (especially water) during football, basketball, or wrestling practice. Wrestlers probably suffered the most in this regard, since they were constantly trying to lose weight, especially water weight. Incredibly, the idea that a two-hundred-pound football player should practice for two hours in the hot sun without drinking anything at all was actually considered to be wisdom. Water, it was thought, would cause nausea and cramps if drunk during practice.

It is now known that proper and optimal hydration is crucial for maximizing athletic performance. This is particularly important in endurance sports such as long-distance biking or running. The reason is fairly basic. As you exercise, you loose fluids and begin to dehydrate. The human body responds to dehydration by producing stress hormones that cause muscle tissues to swell, which in turn causes painful aching. It is the body's way of saying "enough, it's time to stop." In cases of extreme dehydration, this pain can become unbelievably intense.

One person who learned about the pain of dehydration the hard way was the astronaut John Glenn, who later became the first American to orbit the earth. During the early 1960s, when the American space program was ramping up, the astronauts were trained in various survival techniques just in case their spacecraft happened to land somewhere unexpected. Part of this training involved survival in desert environments. The instructors responsible for the training were careful to explain to the astronauts just how dangerous dehydration could be in the desert. Glenn listened with interest. But, since he had never spent much time in a desert and since he had no experience with dehydration, he was curious as to just how right the instructors were.

Being a rationalist, Glenn resolved to do an experiment. As part of their training, all the astronauts had to complete a three-day survival test in the desert. He told one of his instructors he would not drink water for an entire day to begin the exercise and would see what happened. The instructor just shook his head and said he would check in on Glenn regularly. After the first twenty-four hours were over, the instructor came to see how Glenn was faring. By that time, however, Glenn was almost beyond responding. In his own words:

I had dug out a little area under some sagebrush, as we had been taught to do—the subsurface temperature was a little lower, and the sagebrush with parachute fabric over it provided shade—and I was lying there as debilitated as I have ever been. When Bill showed up again, I didn't even want to raise my hand and shade my eyes to look at him as he came walking up. Bill had brought plenty of water, and told me to drink as much as I wanted. I drank fifteen pints over the next nine hours without passing a drop. I could not believe how quickly my body had dried out, and to this day I still carry extra water if I have to drive across the desert.[14]

As John Glenn found out on this day in July 1960, the most prominent effect of dehydration is that it hurts. A lot. It saps strength, endurance, and most of all the will to keep going. Modern endurance athletes—be they bikers, runners, swimmers, hikers, or whatever—are familiar with the effects of dehydration and go to great lengths to avoid it. Very simply, this involves drinking fluids constantly during exercise, even during cold-weather exercise. Some people prefer sports drinks; others prefer water. Most use a judicious combination of the two.

The bottled water industry was quick to appreciate the sales potential of providing water to the millions of people who joined the exercise boom of the 1970s and 1980s. One early believer in this approach was Hinckley Springs Water of Chicago. Hinckley Springs had been founded by Otis Hinckley and a pharmacist named George Schmidt in 1888. Schmidt had noticed that many of his customers were buying bottled water as a way of avoiding disease-ridden municipal water taken from Lake Michigan, and he decided to go into the water delivery business. In time, Hinckley Springs became one of the most popular brands of bottled water in the Midwest.

In the 1980s, someone at Hinckley Springs got the idea of providing free bottled water for those participating in local road races. This did not provide any profits up front, but it was a great way to build name recognition. In long races such as marathons, the effects of dehydration typically build up gradually as the race goes on. You can just imagine how grateful a thirsty marathoner would be for a bottle of cool, clear water at the end of the run. These days, having bottled water companies be sponsors of sporting events is so common that it is seldom even noticed. In the 1980s, however, bottled water was still unusual enough to be considered exotic, and having it available during and after road races caught on. The association of bottled water with health-enhancing exercise, an association the bottled water industry was careful to cultivate, is one factor that contributed to the growth of the bottled water industry in the late twentieth century.

Now, in the early twenty-first century, bottled water has opened numerous niche markets—high-priced "designer" waters served in single-serving glass bottles, more widely available "drinking" waters in PET bottles, and five-gallon watercoolers for home or office use, to name a few. And, if you look deeply enough, you will find a good bit of health consciousness at the root of each of them. It is just a fact that drinking water is both a necessity and a pleasure for people engaging in recreational sports. It is little wonder that drinking water has become so closely associated with health and fitness.

It really does help.

By the standards of today's clothing industry, the cycles of water's popularity have been so slow as to be barely noticeable. Today's chic outfit, for men and women alike, can expect a fashion life of a couple of years. On the other hand, the fashion cycles of water drinking seem to be measured in centuries. The real point, however, is that these cycles have occurred in the past and will doubtless occur in the future. It would be interesting to be around in the year 2100 to see if the popularity of bottled water has once again reversed itself. No one knows what will happen in the future, of course, but it is entirely possible that bottled water will cycle out of popularity once again. New beverages, new tastes, new people will combine to make new fashions. And these fashions may or may not include drinking water.

It has happened before.

7 PAYING DUES
The Bottled Water Business

From the kitchen window, Linda Adams could watch Blue Springs Creek as it tumbled down the canyon and past the corral. Over the last few years, she had given Blue Springs, the source of the creek, a lot of thought. The springs seeped out at the floor of the canyon in a dozen or more places near her house, and they were noted for producing particularly cool, clear drinking water. This water, she had always thought, was an opportunity. She was well aware of how popular bottled water had become in the last few years, and the idea of bottling Blue Springs water intrigued her. The Blue Springs produced what had long been considered to be the best drinking water in this part of Idaho. This was not just Linda's opinion; the Blackfoot Indians had come to the same conclusion several hundred years before.

Winters in this part of Idaho, in the foothills of the Beaverhead Mountains overlooking the Snake River plain, are long and cold. Since the Blackfoot first moved into this country, they preferred to spend their winters in a low-lying area near modern-day Pocatello where the weather was relatively moderate. But over the winter, when travel was difficult or impossible, human and horse wastes tended to accumulate, delivering a variety of fecal microorganisms to the nearby streams, which were the principal source of water. By the end of winter, this contamination caused many people of the tribe to suffer from a variety of intestinal ailments. Once winter broke, the different bands dispersed and headed for whatever summer range appealed to them. Every year, a few bands would travel north across the Snake River Plain to a canyon running up into the Beaverhead Mountains. There, drinking water from what white settlers would later name Blue Springs, the Blackfoot noticed that their intestinal upsets disappeared and that everybody felt better. Just what they called the springs is obscured by time and translation. But one name remembered to this day is something akin to "waters of health."

Linda knew that Blue Springs water was excellent for drinking—it was what she used on their own table—but she also knew that bottling water could be financially dangerous. A previous owner of Blue Springs Ranch also had had dreams of bottling the water. He had spent years and thousands of dollars drilling boreholes trying to locate the underground source of the springs. In the end he found the source, but it had cost so much money to do the drilling that he had to delay starting the bottling business. Then disaster struck. His wife was diagnosed with cancer, and, buried under an avalanche of troubles, he sold the ranch. The next owner of Blue Springs Ranch did not have the same interest in the springs and also was not a particularly good businessman. When Linda and her husband, Jim Tarpley, bought the ranch, it was on the verge of being taken over by the bankruptcy court.

Jim, who had been a cowboy and rancher most of his life, intended to use the spring water for irrigation. The canyon in which the two-thousand-acre ranch was located offered some of the most sheltered range in the area. This was good for raising cattle and horses because it gave a measure of protection during the cold windy winters. The Blue Springs provided a steady source of water for their stock as well as water for irrigating and growing hay. The combination of water, feed, and shelter was a good one for raising horses and cattle, which is what Jim wanted to do.

Linda, in the meantime, quietly began looking into the business of bottling water.

The bottled water industry in America, at the beginning of the twenty-first century, is really two distinct businesses. These businesses had different beginnings, developed in different ways, and today serve very different markets. One way to illustrate this split in the bottled water industry is to begin with some numbers. In the year 2000, the top-selling brands of bottled water, in terms of both sales and market share, were those listed in table 7.1. The first thing to notice about this list is that, in terms of sales, four large multinational companies—Perrier, Pepsi, Groupe Danone, and Coca-Cola—dominate the market. This is not unlike the carbonated beverage industry, in which just three large companies (Coca-Cola, Pepsi, and Cadbury/Schweppes [Seven-Up and RC Cola]) also dominate the market. What is different between carbonated beverages and bottled water, however, is the percentage of sales produced by the really big companies. In carbonated beverages, the top three companies control more than 90% of total sales. In bottled

TABLE 7.1 Top-10-selling bottled waters in the United States, 2000

Rank	Brand (parent company)	Sales (millions of $)	Market Share (%)
1	Poland Spring (Perrier Group)	450.7	7.9
2	Aquafina (Pepsi)	444.8	7.8
3	Arrowhead (Perrier Group)	333.2	5.9
4	Sparkletts (Groupe Danone)	322.9	5.7
5	Evian (Groupe Danone)	220.0	3.9
6	Dasani (Coca-Cola)	210.0	3.7
7	Deer Park (Perrier Group)	202.0	3.5
8	Alpine Spring (Crystal Geyser)	185.0	3.2
9	Crystal Springs (Suntory Water Group)	170.0	3.0
10	Zephyrhills (Perrier Group)	164.4	2.9
	Subtotal	2,703.0	47.5
	All others	2,992.7	52.5
	Total	5,695.7	100.0

Source: Beverage Marketing Corporation, Bottled Waters in the U.S., 2000 Edition (New York, 2000).

water, however, the top four control less then 50% (table 7.1). In other words, while a few companies control the top-selling brands of bottled water, at least half of the sales are made by smaller—often much smaller—bottled water companies. That split between large and small companies is not a statistical fluke. Rather, it has deep roots in the history of how the bottled water industry developed first in Europe and then in America.

In Europe, the bottled water industry began two or three hundred years ago by providing medicinal waters to apothecary shops. In those days, drinking certain mineral waters was considered an important part of established medical practice. Only a few people, however, had the means to be able to travel to and stay at the various springs and spas. So, over the years, various enterprising individuals began bottling the waters, transporting them to the cities, and selling them as medicines. Packaging water in single-serving bottles, which were once thought of as "doses," is still the norm in Europe and has been for many, many years.

The bottled water industry in America began in the same way, with "medicinal waters" from places like Saratoga Springs being bottled as medicines in the early nineteenth century. But as bottle-making technology improved and bottles became less expensive, Americans, particularly Americans living in dirty, crowded northeastern cites, began to have "drinking water" delivered to their homes. Municipal water supplies in the late nineteenth century were seldom very clean and often actually dangerous. So, over time, the concept of having "bulk" water, or water delivered in relatively large two-, three-, or five-gallon bottles, became common in the United States. The "companies" that delivered bulk water were usually one- or two-person operations that catered to a few dozen clients. The difficulties inherent in transporting and delivering water necessarily limited the size of such delivery businesses.

After chlorinated tap water was introduced in the United States, most of these water delivery businesses—especially those in the Northeast—went out of operation. After the 1920s, only a few companies managed to stay in the water business, often serving local businesses with watercoolers. This was the state of the art in America in the 1960s, with most of the bottled water companies being very small and serving a limited clientele with five-gallon watercoolers. The bottled water boom began in the late 1970s when Americans discovered—or, more accurately, rediscovered—the European concept of single-serving bottles. Not everybody liked sweet soda pop, many people were tired of chlorinated tap water, and bottled water became stylish. Instead of having a martini at a cocktail party, having a glass of European bottled water (Perrier, Evian) with a twist of lime was not only acceptable; it was considered chic.

American bulk water companies that had managed to survive into 1970s were quick to appreciate the potential of this new market, and many of these small companies scrambled to get into the single-serving business. But selling bulk water for coolers is much different than selling single-serving water. Bulk water in five-gallon bottles is delivered by trucks, usually to homes and businesses once or twice a week. The distributor drives to the customer, says hello, unloads the bottles from his truck, and installs them in the watercoolers. This is often a very personal relationship, with genuine rapport developing between distributor and customer. In this kind of business, it pays to be friendly and personable and to know your customers as well as possible.

But the size of any particular bulk water business is inherently limited. Distribution by truck means that it is not really practical to serve customers more than a few hundred miles away from the water source. It also means that the size to which the business can grow is limited by the number of "routes," or individual territories for distributors, that the local economy will bear. By 1975 there were more than three hundred different bottled water companies operating in the United States. Most of them employed fewer then ten people and delivered water by truck along well-defined "routes," some of which had been operated for fifty years or more.

The single-serving market is much different. Here, the product is sold in individual bottles that can be put right on a grocery store or convenience store shelf. Marketing this water involves a salesperson making a pitch to a stock manager for a grocery store chain. The water can then be delivered in various small packages, ranging is size from a gallon or two down to six ounces. Because there is no need to reinstall bottles in individual watercoolers and because there is no personal relationship involved, there is much less limitation on the amount of water that can be delivered to individual stores. Once at the store, the bottled water becomes exactly like every other product. It is kept in stock and moved to the shelves as previous stock is sold. Notice that the personal touch, so necessary in selling bulk water for coolers, is largely absent.

All of this means that economies of scale do not limit the sale of individual serving packages in the same way they limit bulk water sales for coolers. If you can get a big enough bottling plant capable of filling tens of thousands of handheld bottles per day, it now becomes possible to ship water as much as a thousand miles away. There is still a delivery-radius limitation, and the cost of the water will go up with distance transported, but it is much less of a limitation than in the bulk water business.

One effect of these economic factors was that, beginning in the late 1970s, the rush among American bottled water companies to get into the single-serving market began a long process of industry consolidation. At first, many companies simply tried to piggyback the new single-serving business on top of the bulk water business that was still their bread and butter. But it soon became apparent that when it came to selling single-serving bottled water, large companies had a huge competitive advantage over small companies. Large companies could ship more water, they could ship it farther, and they could afford advertising to develop their markets. This started a frenzied series of mergers and buyouts as small companies grew, frantically seeking the safety of size.

The fact that, by the year 2000, the single-serving water business was dominated by four very large companies (table 7.1) testifies to this industry consolidation, which had gone on for thirty years. Since 2000, Groupe Danone has merged with the Suntory Water Group, creating DS Waters of America. This merger, presumably, was designed so that DS Waters could compete more effectively with its main rival, the Perrier Group of America. The Perrier Group had been acquired earlier by the Nestlé Corporation, this to take advantage of the very deep marketing pockets provided by a multinational corporation. Coca-Cola, stung by its lower status than Pepsi's Aquafina, has made a strategic alliance with DS Waters to promote mutual marketing of their products. In other words, consolidation of the bottled water industry continues apace.

But interestingly, this consolidation has left many small to medium companies still in the bulk water business. As single-serving bottled water has increased in popularity, the popularity of bulk water delivered directly to homes and businesses has also increased. But again, because of the economies of scale, the size to which companies specializing in bulk water delivery can grow is inherently limited. Many of the most successful of these companies have a very defined territory and very defined local markets.

Kepwel Spring of Ocean, New Jersey, is a good example of the bulk water business model. Three hundred years ago, the site of Kepwel Spring was a summer camping ground for the local Lenape Indians. The springs were purchased from the Lenape by one Benjamin Woolley for a single barrel of whiskey in the mid-1700s. The land was then bought by "Quaker Billy" Layton, and Layton's descendants began bottling and selling the spring water in 1872. Early in the twentieth century, the Cold Indian Springs, as they were then known, were bought by one William Morrell, who developed a private bathing area that he called Kepwel Park. Because of Kepwel Park's popularity—and because of its name recognition—Morrell changed the name of the bottled water to Kepwel Spring. "Get well with Kepwel" was the company's motto. Nowadays, Kepwel serves a very limited area of just three counties in New Jersey (Monmouth, Middlesex, and Ocean), selling the water to homes and businesses in three- and five-gallon bottles. As is the case with many small bottlers, Kepwel's business is based largely on long-standing personal relationships and a local following built up over more than a century.

This fundamental split between the single-serving and bulk water businesses is one thing that distinguishes the bottled water industry in the United States from those in Europe or Asia. In Europe and Asia, there is much less emphasis on the bulk water side of the business, and the single-serving model predominates. Once again, this simply reflects the history of how the industry has developed in different places.

This split also defines the difference between large and small bottled water companies. The large U.S. companies that bottle water, including Nestlé, DS Waters, Pepsi Cola, and Coca-Cola, tend to concentrate on the single-serving model. The small companies—examples include Kepwel Spring in New Jersey, Camp Holly Springs in Virginia, and dozens of others—concentrate on the delivery of bulk water to coolers in homes and businesses. While both single-serving and bulk water products fully qualify as "bottled water," they are provided, in reality, by two entirely different businesses. Furthermore, the single-serving business is a relative latecomer to the table in the United States: it really did not get started until the late 1970s. Prior to 1980, virtually all the bottled water consumed in the United States was delivered in bulk by very small companies.

When Linda Adams began researching the bottled water business, the first thing she noticed was that bottled water is not regulated as water but as a food. Under the Federal Food, Drug, and Cosmetic Act (FFDCA), a food is defined as "articles used for food and drink for man or other animals." Because of this, bottled water is regulated by the Food and Drug Administration (FDA), not, as she had assumed, by the Environmental Protection Agency (EPA). The EPA does regulate the quality of municipal tap water but not bottled water. The difference, it seems, is that municipal water is deemed a *commodity* pursuant to the Safe Drinking Water Act. Bottled water, on the other hand, because of the language in the FFDCA, is deemed a *food*.

The next thing she learned was that there are many different *kinds* of bottled water on the market. Right up front, the FDA "Standard of Identity" outlined in 21 CFR§165.110a (CFR stands for Code of Federal Regulations) draws a basic distinction between *natural waters* and *processed waters*. Natural waters are, well, natural—in the sense that they come from naturally occurring sources and that their chemical composition has not been fundamentally changed by the bottling process. Natural waters include spring water, well water, and surface water (table 7.2). Processed waters, on the other hand, have been chemically changed in order to make them purer (by removing chlorine or dissolved solids) or more palatable (with added flavorings) or to fortify them with minerals deemed desirable (fluoride). Two of the largest-selling bottled waters in the United States in 2003, Pepsi's Aquafina brand and Coca-Cola's Dasani brand, are not spring waters at all. Rather, they are usually municipal waters that are processed in various ways.

By FDA's classification, both Aquafina and Dasani qualify as *purified* waters. This is to say that the raw water they begin with is usually municipal water. The chlorine and most of the dissolved solids are then removed using reverse osmosis technology. In the case of Dasani, dissolved solids are then added back to the water (according to a proprietary formula) in order to produce a better taste. The formula used reflects the work of taste-testing panels, whose members probably worked very hard to select a "flavor" that would appeal most broadly to the American palette. Coca-Cola makes a great fuss of keeping this formulation secret, just like it keeps the formula for Coke secret. In the case of water, however, this is a bit silly. Anyone can take a bottle of Dasani to a local analytical laboratory and, for less than $100, learn exactly the kinds and proportions of dissolved solids that it contains.

One interesting fact about Aquafina and Dasani is that they are such latecomers to the bottled water business. Aquafina was not even market tested until 1994, and it took until 1997 to attain national distribution. Nevertheless, Aquafina has enjoyed great success, eventually becoming the number-one-selling brand in the United States by 2003. The reasons for Aquafina's success have to do with Pepsi's vast marketing network, which was already in place, and the fact that by 1997 single-serving bottled waters had become so popular. Coca-Cola followed with Dasani in 1999 in order to compete with Pepsi. But, although Coke has always outsold Pepsi in the carbonated beverage market, Pepsi's Aquafina currently has the lead in the bottled processed water business. This does not particularly please the folks at Coca-Cola. One of their more interesting marketing stratagems for catching Aquafina has been to form alliances with natural water bottlers, such as DS Waters, and market their products alongside Dasani.

At first, the many different classes of bottled water seemed confusing. As Linda studied them, however, there were some obvious

TABLE 7.2 The different classes of bottled water

NATURAL WATERS

Class	Definition
Spring water	Water derived from an underground formation from which water flows naturally to the surface of the earth
Ground water	Water derived from an underground formation that is not under the direct influence of surface water
Well water	Water derived from an underground formation tapped by a bored well
Artesian water	Water from a bored well tapping a confined aquifer
Surface water	Water derived from a surface water body such as a stream, river, or lake.
Mineral water	Water from a protected underground formation that has a total dissolved solids (TDS) content greater than 250 mg/L and contains no added minerals

PROCESSED WATERS

Class	Definition
Purified	Waters whose chemical composition has been modified by artificial means that include deionization, distillation, and reverse osmosis
Enhanced	Waters whose chemical composition has been modified by artificial means that include deionization, distillation, and reverse osmosis, and to which artificial minerals or flavors have been added
Fluoridated	Waters to which fluoride has been added
Minimally treated municipal waters	Municipal waters that have been subjected to treatment such as chlorine removal, filtration, or ozonation

Source: International Bottled Water Association

ambiguities built into the definitions. For example, there was no requirement that spring waters be collected at a naturally occurring spring orifice. Rather, spring waters could be "collected through a borehole tapping the underground formation feeding the spring." In other words, it was possible to collect spring waters from drilled boreholes. That seemed odd. How, then, were "spring" waters different from plain ordinary "well" water? Reading further, Linda discovered this had been the subject of a long and bitter controversy in the United States. Naturally occurring spring orifices are often subject to contamination from land surface. Because of this, many state health departments actually *require* that boreholes be used to collect spring waters simply because they are more sanitary.

Purists, however, often refused to concede this point. To this day, many small bottlers of spring waters insist that their waters be collected from natural orifices, a characteristic that they proudly proclaim in their marketing. In the end, the consensus of most state regulators is that boreholes, or other constructed orifices designed to prevent surface contamination, are the best way to collect spring waters for bottling. In any case, whatever designation is claimed on a bottle's label (spring, artesian, mountain stream, etc.) has to be documented. Furthermore, the records demonstrating such designations have to be maintained at the bottling plant for inspection by state regulators or to be available for responding to requests for information by the public.

This brings up the issue of regulation. Although the federal government through the FDA has regulatory responsibility over bottled water, the actual regulation is delegated to the different states. The FDA provides standards of identity (CFR§165.110a), standards of water quality (CFR§165.110b), and good manufacturing practices (CFR§165.110 and 129), but the grassroots business of licensing and inspecting bottled water plants is actually performed by various state agencies. Most states regulate bottled water based on FDA's designation of bottled water as a food. A few, Pennsylvania being one, regulate bottled water containers of more than one gallon (bulk water) in the same way they regulate municipal water supplies. In both cases, the foundation of the regulatory system is licensing, record keeping, and unannounced plant inspections one or more times per year. Nevertheless, because individual states differ in their approaches to regulation, the level of oversight also varies. Many water bottlers belong to industry organizations, the largest being the International

Bottled Water Association (IBWA), which assist members in meeting the FDA and state identity, water quality, and manufacturing standards.

As Linda accumulated a basic understanding of the bottled water business, and as she researched the regulatory requirements needed to begin, she became more and convinced that Blue Springs water could be a moneymaking operation. Jim, however, remained skeptical. He had never bought a bottle of water in his life. Why, he wondered, would anybody spend money for water? For her part, Linda worried about other technical issues. Were there hidden chemical contaminants they did not know about? Was there microbial contamination of the water they could not see? These were all questions that needed to be resolved, and neither Jim or Linda knew how to do it.

Then, out of the blue, three scientists from the U.S. Geological Survey drove up to their house one day and asked to sample Blue Springs water for a project they were working on. Jim, thinking that this was a chance to learn more about the springs and their water quality, agreed to show them one of the larger springs, one that had been tapped with a borehole years before by the previous owner. The scientists were delighted. This part of Idaho is dotted with both hot and cold springs. Just a mile away from Blue Springs, for example, are the Lidy Hot Springs, which produce highly mineralized water with a temperature of 152°F. Blue Springs, on the other hand, produced low-mineralized waters that were a mere 46°F. The scientists, who were interested in the chemical differences between the hot and cold spring waters, had been looking for a representative cold spring. Blue Springs was perfect.

With Jim's interested permission, the scientists deployed their equipment and proceeded to collect water samples in a variety of bottles and vials. A number of the water chemistry parameters, such as dissolved oxygen, iron, and sulfide, had to be measured right there in the field. Within half an hour, the scientists knew that Blue Springs water was saturated with dissolved oxygen ($\sim$8 mg/L) and did not contain any measurable iron or sulfide. This, in turn, suggested that the water was entirely pure, lacked large populations of microorganisms, and was certainly safe to drink. Since it was hot in the canyon, and since they had not brought any other drinking water, one of the scientists filled a spare bottle and took a drink. It was delicious. "You know Jim," one of them mentioned casually, "this water is good enough to bottle and sell."

After a few hours, the scientists were finished sampling and drove off, promising to send Jim a copy of the water's chemical analysis. When the analysis arrived a few weeks later, it simply confirmed what Jim and Linda had always suspected. The water contained only about 100 mg/L of total dissolved solids (TDS), most of which were calcium, magnesium, and bicarbonate. More important, there were no organic contaminants, no fecal bacteria, and incredibly low concentrations of heterotrophic bacteria that grow naturally in soils. The water was, as one of the scientists had surmised from his initial field analyses, absolutely pristine. The relatively low concentrations of dissolved solids, the proportions of dissolved solids, and the relative lack of microorganisms were why the water tasted so good and was so pleasing to drink.

"Jim," Linda said with sudden conviction, "I think we should go into the bottled water business."

Jim sighed. He had been a cowboy all his life, with one brief interlude as a navy frogman. Now it looked as if he was going to change professions. "I'll plumb the spring so that it's up to code, I'll build the bottling plant, and once it's built I'll run it," Jim told Linda. "You'll have to do everything else."

Linda nodded her agreement.

Jim could only shake his head, wondering just how much they did not know about the bottled water business. He doubted that their learning was going to be quick or easy. Or cheap. They would have to pay dues, Jim though grimly, lots of dues.

The first order of business was to engineer a system for collecting the spring water in a sanitary fashion and to construct a pipeline to carry water to the yet-to-be-built bottling plant. All this would be subject to inspection and approval by the state health department, so it was important to do it right. Fortunately, financing was not a problem. Jim had owned some ranch land in nearby Medicine Lodge that he sold for a reasonable profit. With money in the bank, Jim and Linda were ready to start work.

Like most springs, Blue Springs is not one spring issuing from a single, well-defined orifice. Rather, the spring waters seep to the surface in numerous places along the floor of the canyon. This is simply a reflection of the hydrology of the Beaverhead Mountains, and it is typical of many mountainous terrains in the western United States. Because mountain slopes are so steep at high elevations, rainfall and snowmelt quickly run off and wash away any loose sediment or cobbles. This rocky debris, which has been washed free of clay and silt-size particles, then accumulates around the base of the mountains, forming a mantle of sediments ranging is size from gravel to boulders. These *talus* sediments, as they are called, are highly porous and quickly soak up snowmelt running off the highlands. As this recharging water percolates into the ground, it continues sinking until it encounters the relatively impermeable bedrock. At this point, the water turns laterally and moves toward lower elevations under the pull of gravity. At lower elevations, usually in canyons, the water can emerge as springs. In most cases, the recharge area feeding such springs is fairly small, and the spring discharge is correspondingly small and often flows only seasonally. In the case of Blue Springs, however, the recharge area is fairly large—probably more than hundred square miles—and so the flow of water to the springs is also relatively large. Furthermore, because the spring waters have been in the ground for a relatively short time—twenty to thirty years is a good guess—they have not had time to accumulate high concentrations of dissolved solids. This is just the kind of low-TDS water that Americans like for drinking.

But while these geologic and hydrologic circumstances produce good drinking water, they also make it difficult to collect the water in a sanitary fashion. As the spring waters seep upward through the soil of the canyon, they can pick up whatever organic matter or microorganisms happen to be there. The obvious solution to that problem would be to excavate four or five feet downward, below the soil zone, and lay a bed of permeable gravel to collect the spring water. Next, a length of perforated plastic pipe would be laid on top of the gravel. Because of FDA regulations, this pipe would have to be made of food-grade plastic. The pipes would then be covered with three or four feet of gravel that would direct the upwelling waters into the collection pipes. The collection pipes would be plumbed to carry the waters downhill to where the bottling plant would be built. Finally, the gravel would have to be covered by an impermeable barrier that would keep surface contaminants out of the spring waters, and this barrier covered by soil. All this would have to be inspected and approved by the Idaho Department of Environmental Quality.

From the beginning, questions kept coming up that Jim did not expect, questions that took a fair amount of thought to answer. What size gravel should they use? Should the gravel be crushed rock or washed stream gravel? Crushed rock was cheaper, but it was more likely to partially dissolve and change the chemistry of the spring water. Finally, how many cubic feet of gravel would they need? In the end, Jim and Linda decided to use washed river gravel and excavate an area 20 feet wide and 150 feet long. Fortunately, Jim's son-in-law was an experienced trackhoe operator who could manage this kind of tricky excavation.

The spring flow from the part of the canyon they wanted to excavate was hard to measure, but it looked to be in excess of two hundred gallons per minute. Using the trackhoe, the area was excavated below the soil zone—which was about four feet thick—and the floor of the excavation covered with two feet of washed river gravel. The pipe was laid and the area immediately backfilled with more washed gravel. In the end, Jim used more than four hundred cubic yards of "inch and a half minus" gravel, which is to say gravel that has been passed through a one-and-a-half-inch mesh sieve. Four hundred cubic yards of gravel is a lot of truckloads, and it took two full weeks to finish the backfilling.

With the gravel laid over the collection pipes, it was time to install the impermeable barrier. For this, Jim chose a single sheet of what is known as "water saver fabric," a plastic material eight millimeters thick used in road construction to keep out unwanted water. This barrier was laid horizontally over the gravel, carefully stretched, and then covered by three or four feet of soil. By the time they had finished, Jim and Linda had constructed a sealed spring-water collection system shielded from surface contaminants that flowed at more than five hundred gallons per minute.

The final hurdle was for Jim and Linda to get approval from the Idaho Department of Environmental Quality (DEQ), the state agency responsible for inspecting water collection systems in Idaho. The inspector who arrived on site in late 2001 had seen home-built bottled water operations before, and he expected the worst. Such bottling operations were often started without enough capital and did not include proper safeguards for the sanitary collection of raw water. Having read the permit application from Jim and Linda, the inspector was prepared to see just one more undercapitalized, poorly engineered, and therefore unsafe operation.

But when the inspector arrived, Jim and Linda showed him photos of how the water collection system had been built, and they had receipts for all the food-grade materials used in construction. Later, the inspector admitted to Jim that he had fully expected to shut down Blue Springs before they had even built the bottling plant. The inspection, however, showed that the spring source had been properly protected, and the source was up to modern standards. The permits were approved.

With the water collection system approved by DEQ, the next step was to build the bottling plant. Jim was an experienced builder, and so constructing the shell of the building, which was to be about five thousand square feet, was fairly straightforward. What proved more of a challenge was finding, buying, and assembling the water treatment and bottling equipment. Linda had been able to locate a secondhand bottling system from a company that had recently gone out of business and was able to buy it at a good price. Jim paid for these cost savings, however, by having to figure out how to assemble the hundreds of parts that arrived in unlabeled crates. More dues, Jim thought grimly, as he laid out and sorted through the parts. Fortunately for Jim, the equipment's original manufacturer, Norland International, was willing to walk him through the assembly procedure. All this had to be done over the phone, of course, which made it an agonizingly slow process.

An important part of the bottling procedure would involve final treatment of the raw spring water. Even though Blue Springs water is as pristine as any water in North America, the performance standards mandated by FDA mean that systems have to be in place to exclude particulate and microbial contaminants. To this end, FDA has formulated what are called good management practices (GMPs) to ensure production of a safe product. In response to these GMPs, the bottled water industry has evolved what it calls "multibarrier" treatment systems. In other words, rather then relying on a single disinfection step, several are used that target different kinds of possible microbial contaminants (chapter 5).

In Jim and Linda's case, a series of progressively finer filters were used to remove particulate matter, UV treatment, and finally ozonation. After one final filtration step, the water was ready for bottling. Because they were planning to sell both single-serving PET bottles and five-gallon watercooler bottles, Jim and Linda ended up building two separate bottling lines for the different products. All in all, it took two full years to build the spring water collection system, install and troubleshoot the water treatment equipment, and build the PET and five-gallon bottle-filling lines. The final step was to obtain the necessary permits from the Idaho Health Department Division, which was responsible for seeing that FDA's GMPs were being followed. The permits were approved.

Now all they had to do was sell the water.

Selling Blue Springs water, Jim and Linda thought, was going to be the easy part. The springs had a local reputation, and, in their opinion anyway, Blue Springs water tasted a lot better then most of the bottled water available in local grocery stores and convenience stores. They were confident that their product could compete. Blue Springs's first customer was the Ashton General Store, located about sixty miles away, where 24-ounce bottles of Blue Springs water were put on the shelf in direct competition with Dasani. Evidently, the local population preferred Blue Springs water to Dasani, because sales boomed, and it was difficult to keep the cooler stocked. Soon, Jim had a dozen customers and was being kept busy running the bottling plant and making deliveries.

But as sales of Blue Springs water increased, Jim and Linda found that the other water vendors were not going to let them go unopposed. It turned out that Coca-Cola actually owned the coolers in many convenience stores where bottled water was sold. At first, the Coca-Cola representative servicing the Ashton General Store was content merely to move the bottles of Blue Springs water to the bottom shelf. Then, citing the fact that he owned the cooler, he demanded that the store owner remove Blue Springs water altogether. Fine, the store owner replied. He removed the Blue Springs water from the Coca-Cola cooler, but he also bought his own cooler just for Jim's water. For good measure, and possibly out of irritation with Coca-Cola, the store owner moved his new cooler containing Blue Springs water to the front of the store where everybody could see it.

The reaction of Ashton's General Store owner, however, proved to be the exception rather than the rule. Even though Blue Springs water was selling well, most convenience store owners were not willing to risk a fight with Coca-Cola to keep it in stock. Pepsi Cola had an even tighter hold on its distribution of Aquafina. It turned out that Pepsi's standard cooler contract had an "exclusive" clause, forbidding store owners to sell both Aquafina and other brands of bottled water at the same time. These incidents of competitive exclusion, which are entirely legal and simply part of the business, became more and more common as sales of Blue Springs water increased. Also, Jim and Linda were being squeezed on price. Because they had to purchase their 24-ounce PET bottles, for example, they could not put water on the shelves at the same price as Aquafina or Dasani, both of which came from facilities that had the capacity to blow their own bottles. Coca-Cola and Pepsi were well aware of how the economies of scale were on their side, and they used them as effectively as they could.

Two things saved Jim and Linda at this crucial, early stage. First of all, they had not had to borrow money to build and operate their bottling plant. If they had, they would have been far more vulnerable to the marketing warfare that they quickly encountered. Second, they had also entered the bulk water business. Linda knew that the water cooler business would avoid direct competition with Coca-Cola and Pepsi—a competition that over time Blue Springs just could not hope to win— so Jim and Linda began concentrating on placing watercoolers in various local businesses. To this end, they found some local distributors who were more than willing to market Blue Springs water. With the help of these distributors, sales of bulk water soon outpaced sales of handheld bottles. As long as Blue Springs concentrated on bulk water, avoiding direct competition with the likes of Coca-Cola and Pepsi, they had a chance.

But Jim, who had been an frogman in the navy (the precursors of the elite SEALs), was not one to shy entirely from a good fight. At one local outdoor expo at Mountain River Ranch, Jim brought a load of 24-ounce bottles with the intention of selling his water to the thirsty patrons. Predictably, however, Aquafina had an exclusive contract for the event, and the organizers informed Jim he could not sell his water. Fine, Jim replied, and he proceeded to give away Blue Springs Pure H_2O for free. Jim and Linda did not make any money that day, but lots of people found out about the new bottled water company in the neighborhood.

Aquafina did not sell much water that day either.

From the time Linda first conceived the idea of selling Blue Springs water, sometime about 1995, it had taken a full six years before a single bottle of water was ready to be sold. Jim and Linda had to learn about the regulations, they had to learn about GMPs, they had to learn about marketing. Jim had to engineer his spring in accordance with state health regulations, build a bottling plant, install a treatment system, and have the whole thing approved by two different sets of state regulators. Then Jim and Linda had to go head to head with two of the most powerful international companies in the world in order to sell their product. All along the way, they had to pay dues. The more they paid, the more they learned. As anybody who tries to go into the bottled water business has found, there is a lot more to it than just filling bottles with water. The mortality rate for new bottled water businesses, as you might imagine, is appallingly high.

But after the initial rush of problems, accomplishments, setbacks, reassessments, changes in strategy, minor victories, and uncomfortable defeats, things began to settle down. Jim and Linda shifted from the flush of excitement surrounding their new business to a phase of routine daily work. Jim spent mornings in the bottling plant fixing machinery, changing filters, troubleshooting the lines, and filling bottles. Endless hours of filling bottles. Linda worked the phones, did the paperwork, kept the accounts, stayed in touch with established customers, and contacted new ones. In the afternoons, both Jim and Linda made deliveries and dealt with their customers. As the business settled into more of a routine, Jim and Linda could see that it was succeeding and that they were beginning to turn a profit.

But it was a hard, tough daily grind.

There is a story in Greek mythology that illustrates the work inherent in bottling and delivering water. It seems that one King Danaus of Argos had fifty daughters. Danaus' brother Aegyptus, on the other hand, had fifty sons. Sensing the opportunity to swallow up his brother's lands, Aegyptus proposed that his fifty sons marry Danaus' fifty daughters. Danaus knew that this arrangement would be the end of his kingdom, but, unable to resist his brother militarily, Danaus agreed. Secretly, however, he ordered each of his daughters hide a dagger in her gown and to kill her new husband as he slept on their wedding night. All but one of the daughters dutifully obeyed their father. As punishment for these crimes, the gods condemned the forty-nine guilty daughters to an afterlife of unending labor. Specifically, they were charged with filling a large bronze vessel with water drawn from the river Styx, which separated the land of the living from Hades. The gods made sure, however, that the vessel leaked. This meant that the daughters were doomed to an eternity of drawing water in bottles, carrying it from the river, and pouring it into a vessel that could never be filled. This grueling punishment is the subject of John William Waterhouse's painting The Danaïdes (1904), which is reproduced on the jacket of this book.

The endless, difficult, repetitive work involved in running a bottling plant is not what most people associate with the bottled water business. What could be easier, you might think, than filling bottles with spring water and selling it? The reality, however, is much, much different. Jim and Linda had no illusions that the bottled water business would be easy. But even they were not quite prepared for what they found. Nobody really is. There are few labors as difficult and demanding as bottling, carrying, and delivering water.

The daughters of Danaus would probably agree.

8 THE BATTLE OF ICE MOUNTAIN
Bottled Water and the Law

The young woman, who looked to be eighteen or twenty years old, planted herself firmly in front of Dave Dowdy. Anger sparkled in her eyes as she addressed him sternly. "How dare you sell something that nature gives us for free?" she demanded.

Dave, who was weighed down by a five-gallon water bottle he was delivering to one of his customers in Richmond, Virginia, stopped in his tracks. This was the early 1970s, long before bottled water began its meteoric rise to popularity. Still, however, some people—especially members of the egalitarian counterculture known as hippies—were philosophically unhappy with the capitalistic nature of American society. Many of them believed that selling anything for a profit was inherently wrong. Selling natural resources, of which spring water was an obvious example, was particularly wrong.

"You didn't make the spring, did you?" she said sternly. "You don't make the water, do you? What's more, you don't purify it either. Nature does. All you do is fill up your bottles with something that nature is giving to us. That water belongs to everybody, not just you. It should be free!"

The young woman was standing directly in front of Dave, her hands on her hips, and she was a picture of righteous indignation. Dave was taken aback. His mind flashed over the thousands of hours he, his father, and his wife spent at the bottling plant, washing bottles, sterilizing them (a rare amenity in 1970), filling them with spring water, and loading them onto trucks. He thought of the interminable driving in the delivery truck, and the effort and danger of lugging glass water bottles up and down steps. All this to be lectured about the evils of selling Mother Nature's bounty. The irony would have been amusing if the woman hadn't seemed to be on the verge of decking him.

Actually it was the irony that came to Dave's rescue.

"Ma'am," Dave said with unconscious southern politeness, "I sell the time it takes to wash these bottles and sterilize them. I sell the equipment it takes to rinse the bottles out and fill them with spring water. I sell loading the bottles onto my truck and driving all over the countryside to deliver them."

Dave paused a second for effect.

"But the water's free."

The question as to who actually owns water, who has the right to use it, and who has the right to sell it is as old as humanity itself. This chance encounter between Dave Dowdy and the young woman in the early 1970s was just one manifestation of a timeless conflict in human society. Simply stated, the question is one of private versus collective ownership. Does a landowner like Dave Dowdy have absolute ownership of spring waters that discharge on his property? On the other hand, since the ground water feeding the springs ultimately comes from rainfall, and since ground water in the subsurface moves constantly across property lines, is it owned collectively by everybody? In either case, who decides whether the water is used or not and what it is used for? These questions are particularly important because water is a basic necessity of life, and whoever controls water or allocates water use becomes very powerful. Now that the bottled water industry has become such a big business, the issue as to who actually owns spring waters—individual landowners or the public at large—has become increasingly contentious in recent years.

One of the real problems about deciding who owns spring waters is that the law concerning water ownership and water rights is, to put it delicately, a muddle. In the United States today, there are not one but three legal frameworks for deciding water ownership and use.[1] The first of these is called "riparian" rights. Riparian rights evolved from the idea that landowners bordering surface water bodies have a special right to use the water. However, they are expected to use the water in "reasonable" ways that do not adversely affect other riparian water users. In the eastern part of the United States, where from early colonial times most land was privately owned, riparian rights govern how water use is allocated. In the western United States, however, where most of the land was initially publicly owned, water law is based on the idea of prior appropriation. In other words, whoever began using the water first in a "beneficial" way has the right to continue using it in that way. "First in time, first in right" is the basic idea of prior appropriation. But, since this is the USA and nothing is ever simple, some states, for instance California, use a combination or "hybrid" system of riparian rights and prior appropriation.

These water law frameworks, which are derived from European law, were originally designed primarily to deal with the use of surface water—streams, rivers, lakes, and artificial impoundments. The law concerning ground water, springs, and wells, on the other hand, is a more recent development. For most of human history, the occurrence and movements of subsurface water were considered to be so uncertain and so mysterious that ground water was held to be outside the purview of the law.[2] This lack of regulation allowed landowners to use ground water and springs in any way they pleased. And this led to what came to be known as the "absolute ownership doctrine." Under this doctrine, a landowner has an unlimited right to withdraw any water found beneath the land. The legal thinking was that ground water was similar to the soils or mineral deposits underlying the land, which are owned solely by the landowner. Because this doctrine was first set forth legally in England in 1843, it is sometimes referred to as the "English Rule."

The English Rule of absolute ownership was widely adopted in the United States prior to 1850. However, with the advent of the new drilling technologies that developed after 1850, technologies that enabled wells to capture large amounts of ground water, it soon became apparent that the English Rule was impractical. Minerals could not move from beneath one parcel of land to another. Ground water, however, did move. In fact, if one landowner drilled several wells and pumped them heavily, that owner could draw water from neighboring properties. Because of this movable nature of ground water, the right of landowners to absolute ownership of ground-water has been moderated over the years by means of the "reasonable use" doctrine in riparian rights. This concept, that landowners have the right to the reasonable use of ground water under their land, was so widely adopted in the United States that it is sometimes referred to as the "American Rule." The term "reasonable" is usually interpreted as meaning that landowners have ownership rights to ground water underlying their property as long as the use does not adversely affect the rights of other landowners.

The question of who actually owns ground water varies depending on what state you live in. In Texas, for example, surface water is considered to be the property of the state, whereas ground water is considered to be the property of the landowner (i.e., the English Rule applies). That distinction has, in recent years, led to an interesting situation in West Texas. Taking advantage of the English Rule, onetime oilman T. Boone Pickens has been buying up the water rights of ranches overlying the Ogallala aquifer. His plan is to pipe the water to cities such as El Paso, Lubbock, San Antonio, and Dallas and sell it for municipal water supply. Considering that this would lead to substantial depletion of the Ogallala aquifer, and considering that such depletion is already adversely affecting people in Texas, it is hard to defend this sort of scheme on grounds of "reasonable use." Nevertheless, as long as Texas law subscribes to the English Rule of absolute ownership for ground water, people like T. Boone will happily try to take advantage of it.

In other states such as Colorado, ground water is not considered to be owned by the landowner at all. In 1983, the Colorado Supreme Court held that ground water is not subject to the right of citizens to appropriate water, nor is it owned by the owner of the overlying land.[3] Rather, the state through its natural resource agencies has the responsibility to decide how to manage and allocate ground-water resources.

The law in Colorado is more the rule than the exception in this matter. In general, most states assert some measure of control over the use of ground water, considering it subject to management by the state. In some cases, particularly in states east of the Mississippi, states require that people get permits to use ground water. Such permits are viewed as a manifestation of the "reasonable use" doctrine. In Maryland, for example, anyone using more than ten thousand gallons of ground water per day is required to obtain a permit from the state. Because wells owned by individual home owners generally pump less than thousand gallons per day, they do not need pumping permits. But anyone wanting to start a new water-bottling plant in Maryland, which would certainly use more than ten thousand gallons per day, would need a pumping permit from the Department of Natural Resources, the state agency that regulates ground water use.

What is interesting about this legal mishmash is that it shows that both Dave Dowdy and the young woman held perfectly reasonable points of view, even though they were diametrically opposed. For her part, the woman was perfectly correct in saying that the spring waters "belonged" to everybody, at least in the sense that many states regulate how the resource is used. Dave, on the other hand, was correct in thinking he "owned" the water because as a landowner he had a special right to use the water in "beneficial" ways. Such terms, however, are so legalistic that they conceal the cost and effort involved in using water in a way that is truly "beneficial." The story of Dave Dowdy and Camp Holly Springs is a good example of this.

Camp Holly Springs, which is located just outside of Richmond, Virginia, got the name because it is indeed a natural campsite. Humans first arrived in North America about twelve thousand years ago, and it took them only two thousand to discover Camp Holly Springs. Of the thousands of artifacts found near the springs, some are beautiful spearheads characteristic of what archaeologists call the Clovis industry (named after Clovis, New Mexico). These large, symmetrical spearheads were apparently used by hunters who were pursuing very large game, such as mammoths. Between that time and the time that Europeans arrived on the scene, Native Americans lived continuously near the springs.

The attraction, of course, was the spring water. Camp Holly Springs is located in the Atlantic Coastal Plain, and the hydrology is similar to that of the Healing Springs (chapter 2) in South Carolina. A sandy aquifer is recharged by rainfall in topographically high areas, the water percolates vertically till it is blocked by a clay bed, and then it moves laterally to where it discharges on the slopes of hills.[4] This spring water, which essentially is just rainwater filtered and buffered by the sandy aquifer, is delightful drinking water. It has very low concentrations of dissolved solids (only about 30 mg/L), it is naturally oxygenated, and it is delightfully cool and clear. It is no wonder that Native Americans wanted to live nearby.

The same was true when Europeans arrived. Over the years, troops camped near the springs during the American Revolution, the War of 1812, and the Civil War. It was because of these various military camps that the locals came to refer to the springs by the name Camp Holly Springs.

As in many springs characteristic of the coastal plain, there is not one surface outlet but many. In fact, water seeps out of the ground in fairly broad areas where the fine-grained clays crop out along the hillsides. It was possible, however, to excavate into these seeps and direct the water to a single outlet. This was first done in the 1800s by various landowners. In 1923, a local preacher named Rev. Thurborne Clark began bottling the water from one of these constructed spring outlets and selling it under the name of Camp Holly Water Company. This operation consisted of Clark and his son filling bottles one at a time on the back of a flatbed truck. Later, after the death of the son, the business was taken over by Clark's son-in-law. It was a small, modest operation, but in the 1960s it drew the attention of Dave Dowdy's father, who owned about a hundred acres adjoining the spring used by the Camp Holly Water Company. There were several springs on the Dowdy property, one of which was known as Diamond Springs.

The elder Dowdy ran a grocery store near the springs and, being a merchant by trade, was fascinated by the idea of selling this wonderfully pure drinking water. Dave Dowdy, however, had his doubts. Why, he wondered, would anybody in this day and age of 1967 be willing to pay money for water when there was essentially free municipal water available everywhere? But the elder Dowdy had been paying attention to the Camp Holly Water Company over the years, and he had an answer. Many small businesses in and near Richmond—warehouses, auto repair shops, manufacturing facilities, and department stores—rented commercial space for their enterprises. As such, none of these businesses had much need or desire to install anything but the most basic plumbing. Just to install a water fountain, for example, was a fairly expensive undertaking. It was actually cheaper and easier to rent watercoolers as a source of drinking water for employees. Thus, there was a ready market for installing watercoolers and keeping them stocked with five-gallon bottles of water.

By 1967, there were at least three water-bottling "companies" that collected water from the various springs in the Camp Holly area, filled five-gallon bottles, and sold them as drinking water to various businesses all over southern Virginia. These companies were a far cry from the corporate image of the bottled water industry today. In each case, they consisted of one man, with one truck, who installed watercoolers and kept them stocked with spring water. The procedure, such as it was, was to back the truck up to the spring outlet, wash and rinse the bottles by hand, fill them with fresh spring water, and haul them off to customers. This was heartbreakingly difficult work, and some of the individuals in the business did not seem inclined to work particularly hard at it. Dave Dowdy's father thought he and Dave could do better. In 1968, Dave Dowdy bought one of these companies—the Broad Rock Water Company—for $1,000 and went into business as the Diamond Springs Water Company. On Monday through Thursday, Dave filled water bottles and delivered them to his customers. On Friday and Saturday, Dave helped his dad in the grocery store. After all there were bills to pay, and there was no guarantee that the water business would work out.

The Dowdys knew that if the water business was to be successful, they would have to make it more efficient so that they could increase their customer base. The elder Dowdy had already erected a cinder-block building around the spring outlet, and they went about improving the plumbing and the bottle-filling operations. They rigged the plumbing so that they had two spring outlets, one of which was reserved for washing and rinsing bottles. The other outlet was equipped with food-grade Teflon hoses and steel nozzles for filling the cleaned bottles with water. In these early days of the business, washing the bottles was the real chore. The Dowdys knew that their customers wanted clean water, and the only way to provide this was to thoroughly clean the bottles before refilling them with water. In addition to washing and rinsing the bottles, Dave began sterilizing the bottles using a solution designed for washing dishes in restaurants. When Dave had the luxury of two helpers—sometimes his dad, sometime just local kids—they could wash, sterilize, and fill about thirty-five-gallon bottles per hour. In the meantime, Dave's wife, Pat, worked the phones, handled the accounts, and did the paperwork.

One modern innovation that the Dowdys instituted was the use of plastic caps. In earlier years, the technique had been to cover the mouth of a newly filled bottle with a square of waxed paper, push in a cork, and cover the cork with another square of waxed paper tied down with a string. The corks, incidently, could not really be cleaned, and they were used over and over again. From the very beginning of their operation, the Dowdys invested in reusable, sterilizable plastic caps that would protect the water more reliably then the corks. These quality-control measures, which were state of the art in the late 1960s, impressed Dave's customers, and the business began to grow.

As with any business, growth was both a necessity and a problem. It took about two years of water deliveries for the Dowdys to make back the investment of installing a new watercooler. So it was essential to constantly add new customers. The problem was that washing bottles by hand meant that their production capacity was inherently limited. Dave and his dad solved this problem by buying a bottle cleaner, which used pressurized water to clean, rinse, and sterilize the bottles. Working by hand, 40 bottles an hour was the fastest they could clean bottles. The automatic washer, on the other hand, could clean 160 bottles an hour, and the work was far easier. Other innovations followed. The

Dowdys bought a system to automatically fill bottles, and they also installed an ozone generator to keep unwelcome microorganisms from growing in the water lines. By the time the 1980s rolled around, Dave had a thriving, productive, profitable business. After the Perrier boom hit the marketplace and bottled water suddenly become fashionable, the Dowdys and their Diamond Springs Water Company were perfectly placed to take advantage of this new trend. And they did.

In 1990, Dave sold the water distribution side of Diamond Springs and began custom bottling under the name Camp Holly Springs, Inc. This meant he could spend his time tinkering in the bottling plant making it operate more efficiently and more hygienically. This was more to his taste then driving around the countryside in a delivery truck, and now he had the means to indulge himself. Today, Camp Holly Springs is a scrupulously clean, fully automated, productive water-bottling plant run by Dave's son Dusty. Looking at the gleaming pipes, the conveyor belts carrying hundreds of bottles per hour, and the high-tech sterilization procedures, it is easy for a casual observer to see this as just one more cog of corporate America. But a walk through the plant today gives no hint of the humble beginnings, the grinding sixteen-hour days, the endless drives on the delivery truck that it took to build the business to where it is now.

When the young woman confronted Dave Dowdy in 1970 with her strongly held opinion that it was wrong to sell spring waters that Mother Nature provided for free, you can imagine just how stunned Dave was. Nature did provide a rainwater-gathering aquifer and a clayey confining bed that directed ground water toward the springs. This indeed was a free gift of nature. But collecting the water hygienically, filling the damnably heavy glass bottles, and transporting them to paying customers was not free at all. For Dave Dowdy and his family, the right to use the springs in a "beneficial" way was dearly won indeed.

In cases like Camp Holly Springs, where there is a clear history of prior and beneficial use, the rights of spring owners to bottle and sell spring water are fairly straightforward. But what happens when a new bottling operation wants to move into a new area in order to bottle water? Is it wrong in these instances for a public resource to be used for private profit? For many people—the philosophical descendants of the young woman who confronted Dave Dowdy—the answer is that it is wrong. For others, such an enterprise is just one more "reasonable use" and, given the assent of the local community, is perfectly OK.

There is no better example of this difference of opinion than the battle of Ice Mountain.

When it comes to high-quality spring waters suitable for bottling, the midwestern United States is less well endowed then much of the rest of the country. The principal geologic and hydrologic reason for this is that the much of the Midwest lacks moisture-trapping mountains, which are the source of many spring waters. Furthermore, as Dave Dowdy discovered very early on in his bottled water business, the actual cost of the water is trivial compared with the cost of treating it and distributing it. Whether you consider municipal water, bottled water, or even water from private wells, a good bit of the real expense is in distribution. Whether this involves laying water lines, plumbing a well, or buying fuel for delivery trucks, getting the water from its source to where it is actually consumed is the real cost.

In the late 1990s, this economic reality became more and more of a problem for Perrier of North America, Inc. As the largest bottled water company in America, and with plans to become even larger, Perrier needed to have a presence in the northern Midwest. The problem was that it did not have a good source of water in this part of the country. Although it could ship water from other bottling operations in other parts of the country, this would drastically increase costs and lower profit margins. The obvious solution to the problem was to identify and develop a source of water as near to the midwestern markets as possible.

The first place Perrier looked was in Wisconsin. Wisconsin, after all, has an abundance of water, and springs that produce high-quality drinking water are fairly common. In 1999, Perrier found a site near Big Springs, in Adams County, and began the process of obtaining the necessary zoning and water use permits. The idea was to drill a well on state-owned land, where the recharge area would have a better chance of remaining pristine over the years. This water would then be piped a mile or so to a bottling plant that would be built on private land. This plant would eventually be a 250,000-square-foot facility and would employ 250 people. The water would be marketed under the name Ice Mountain Natural Spring Water.

At first, Perrier was welcomed by local officials and politicians and even obtained a conditional permit from the Wisconsin Department of Natural Resources (DNR) to withdraw water from wells. After all, bringing 500 million of investment into a rural part of Wisconsin seemed to be a good thing. Furthermore, the amount of water that would be withdrawn, about 500,000 gallons per day, was fairly modest in the context of this particular aquifer system. By the standards of "reasonable use," this amount of water seemed reasonable to Wisconsin DNR.

But all this, and particularly the definition of "reasonable use," soon changed. One characteristic of the glacial topography of Wisconsin and Michigan is that rainwater recharges the underlying aquifers on hilltops and springs discharge at the base of the hills. Such waters are effectively filtered of silt and clay particles, providing a perfect habitat for the brook trout native to these ecosystems. Soon after Perrier began the process of permitting the proposed bottling plants, local residents began expressing concern that withdrawing water would affect trout fishing in the Mecan River. They also did not like the idea of water trucks bouncing along their country roads. But even more, they did not like the idea of a large corporation waltzing in to take advantage of a local resource, particularly a corporation like Perrier, which, for better or worse, exuded a certain arrogance in dealing with the local population.

As the debate heated up, it began to morph. Although it began with concern about possible adverse impacts on the environment, it soon changed into a debate about corporate America using public resources for private profit. A local group called Waterkeepers of Wisconsin (WOW) got involved and began a campaign against Perrier. Petitions opposing the bottling plant were circulated, citizens organized meetings, and local politicians were lobbied. Finally, in November of 2000, the Adams County Board of Supervisors passed a resolution opposing Perrier's plan to bottle water. Legally, such local government agencies do not have jurisdiction to decide issues of "reasonable use" for ground water. This board could, however, deny zoning changes needed to build the bottling plant or other infrastructure.

Perrier was, to say the least, stunned by what happened in Wisconsin. But the company also learned a lesson. Since ground water was a resource with multiple uses and functions (both economic and ecological) that affected entire communities, it was first necessary to convince local residents that bottling would be a "reasonable use." In part, this involved demonstrating that withdrawing water would not adversely impact other users. But more than anything, it meant convincing communities that they would be better off if local water supplies were used for bottling. With this lesson etched in its corporate consciousness, Perrier began looking for other water sources in neighboring Michigan.

Soon, Perrier had two possible sites to consider in Michigan, one in Osceola County and another in Mecosta County. From the beginning, Perrier went out of its way sell the idea of a water-bottling plant to the local residents. It also cagily turned the selection process into a competition between the two counties. Perrier had seen what could happen if it just picked a site and tried to move in. The key was to be invited. So Perrier representatives met with citizens, met with local politicians. The company initiated a "preservation" fund to protect and restore the local Muskegon River Watershed. Importantly, it also cultivated a favorable relationship with the local newspapers. Billing itself as "Your Natural Neighbor," it went about convincing Mecosta County residents that bottling this water was really in their interests. While Perrier still managed to ruffle some local feathers with its goal-oriented philosophy, it did better than it had in Wisconsin.

The reaction from local environmental groups, however, was not far behind. A group called Michigan Citizens for Water Conservation (MCWC) began organizing to oppose the plant, at one point raising nearly $20,000 in a month in donations. By 2001, MCWC began circulating petitions against bottling the water, again making the case that withdrawing water would hurt local wetlands. It also made the case that water-rich Michigan should reserve the water for local use, not bottle it and ship it out of state. In fact, the issue of bottled water escalated into a debate about diverting water from the Great Lakes Basin, which was claimed by MCWC to violate the Federal Water Resources Development Act of 1986. In June of 2001, MCWC filed a lawsuit to block the Perrier project.

In this lawsuit, the arguments soon gravitated back to the age-old principles of riparian rights, reasonable use, and beneficial use. Attorneys for MCWC argued that the nearest surface-water body, locally known as Dead Stream, received its recharge from ground water. Thus, pumping ground water would deprive people who owned land adjacent to Dead Stream of their riparian rights. Michigan, like all states east of the Mississippi, governs water use by riparian principles. These principles grant the owners of land adjacent to surface-water bodies the right to use that water. "The company (Perrier) is a non-riparian intercepting water from a riparian system resulting in the diminishment in the flow of the stream," MCWC's attorney said. "It is illogical to contend that a non-riparian has rights which a riparian does not. Perrier, a non-riparian, is prohibited from diverting (water) for sale or use on riparian land."

That is an interesting argument, since it contends that pumping ground water intercepts water that would eventually discharge into an adjacent stream or lake. Thus, anyone using ground water is, in effect, co-opting the riparian rights of people who own property adjacent to those surface water bodies. If the courts accepted this argument, then theoretically any use of ground water at all could be banned as an infringement of someone else's riparian rights.

Perrier's attorney tried to steer away from riparian rights and replied, "Riparian law does not apply to the ground water withdrawals of Perrier simply because there is a hydrologic connection between the ground water and surface water." He went on to argue that Michigan's ground-water law, not surface-water riparian law, applied to this case. Michigan law allows landowners to pump ground water as long at its removal is not "injurious" to other landowners, including people with riparian rights to surface water. This is based on the "reasonable use" doctrine, which, paradoxically, comes from riparian law.

At this point, it is worth considering the hydrology of what's going on here. In the humid eastern part of the United States, including Michigan, ground-water systems are recharged by precipitation in topographically high areas, the water percolates to the water table, and ground water flows downward under the pull of gravity.[5] At topographically low points, this ground water reemerges as springs or seepage into streams or lakes (fig. 2.1). If a well is drilled into the aquifer adjacent to a stream, a portion of the water that otherwise would have discharged into the stream is intercepted and pumped out of the ground.

So, pumping wells can in fact affect the amount of water flowing in streams, just as MCWC claimed. The more important question, however, is whether ground-water pumping affects stream flow enough to cause *injury* to riparian users or wildlife. The answer is that sometimes it does and sometimes it does not, depending entirely on the hydrology of the ground-water system in question. One factor is the proportion of water delivered to a stream from surface sources (direct rainfall and surface runoff) and from ground-water seepage (sometimes called "base flow"). In the humid eastern United States, stream flow is usually a combination of ground- and surface-water sources, although the proportion can vary considerably depending on weather conditions. Some portion of the flow in Dead Stream, the direct recharge by surface water components, would not be affected at all by intercepting ground-water flow with a pumping well. So right off the bat, one component of the water in Dead Stream would not be affected by ground water pumpage.

But the ground-water seepage component to streams *can* be affected by pumping wells, and the magnitude of this effect is related to a number of factors. One important factor is the size of the recharge area feeding the ground-water system. Consider, for example, a hypothetical recharge area overlying a ground-water system that has an area of one square mile. Michigan receives about sixty inches of rain per year, and in the sandy glacial soils about twelve inches of this rainfall typically percolates downward and recharges the water table aquifer. The rest either runs off (entering local streams directly), evaporates, or is transpired back to the atmosphere by plants. Given a one-mile-square basin, and one foot of net recharge, there is a total of 27,878,400 cubic feet of water recharging the underlying aquifer each year. The total flow in the stream, therefore, is the sum of this 27,878,400 cubic feet of ground-water seepage per year plus whatever surface runoff also enters the stream.

For argument's sake, let us focus just on the ground-water seepage to a stream. Units of "cubic feet per year" for surface-water flow are inconvenient, since the numbers tend to be so large. Because of this, hydrologists prefer to quantify stream flow in units of cubic feet per second (cfs). Our hypothetical aquifer-fed stream, therefore, with a one-mile square recharge area, will *on average* have a stream flow of 0.88 cfs. Since one cubic foot of water equals 7.49 gallons, the stream flow is only 6.62 gallons per second, or 397 gallons per minute. This hypothetical stream, in other words, is a very small stream indeed. If a well was drilled in the center of this small basin and pumped hundred gallons per minute, the well could capture about 25% of the total flow through the basin, which would certainly measurably affect stream flow. This assumes the recharge rate would not go up (it probably would), but in any case that much pumping would certainly cause a noticeable decrease in the flow of the stream. That, in turn, could affect the survival of fish in the stream and could damage the riparian rights of people owning land adjacent to the stream.

But a drainage area of one square mile (one mile by one mile) is a very small recharge area for a ground-water system. If the recharge area goes up to 10 square miles (3.16 miles by 3.16 miles, which is still a pretty small recharge area), a well pumping 100 gallons a minute would capture 2.5% of the total flow in the basin. This might have a measurable affect on stream flow, but it certainly would not be noticeable to a casual observer. Finally, if an aquifer has a recharge area of 100 square miles, which is typical of small basins in Michigan, the well would capture 0.25% of the total flow in the basin, which would be neither noticeable nor measurable. If the effect of pumping a well produces an effect on stream flow that is not measurable, it is pretty hard to argue that it will "injure" either the biota associated with the stream or people with riparian rights to the stream.

The question, therefore, was not whether pumping Perrier's well would affect the flow of water to Dead Stream in Michigan. It would. The real question was whether the well would be capturing a high enough percentage of the total flow in the basin stream, which includes both a ground- and surface water component, so that Dead Stream would be *adversely* affected. That, in turn, depends on the size of the recharge area, the amount of potential recharge (rainfall) available, and the hydrologic properties of the underlying rocks or sediments. These are general principles that apply not only to Dead Stream but to all groundwater systems. *If the available recharge is large relative to the amount of pumping, then the effects of pumping on adjacent surface-water bodies will be small, and the pumping will be sustainable over time. Conversely, if the available recharge is small relative to the amount of pumping, then the effects of pumping on surface-water bodies will be more profound, and the pumping will not be sustainable over time.*[6]

But hydrology was not the only thing at issue, and MCWC's attorney went on to open another front of argument. "To alienate or subordinate public trust waters, the legislature must give its consent and it must serve a public purpose." In other words, surface water rights cannot be infringed upon by the use of ground water. "No one has directly raised the fundamental question regarding the nature of the ownership of the ground water," MCWC's attorney continued. "That question has been raised now before this Court by the Plaintiffs."

That was the heart of the matter. Who owns ground water? MCWC was taking the position that the public trust doctrine for *surface water* also applies to *ground water,* and therefore any private appropriation of ground water (i.e., bottling it) is inherently wrong. Whether the bottling operation would have a measurable adverse impact on Dead Stream was not really the point.

That argument, in effect, would preclude any private utilization of ground water.

But it was not to be. In October of 2002, a Mecosta County circuit judge ruled against MCWC and for Perrier, allowing the sale of water.

Ground-water usage in this case, he ruled, did not constitute "injury" to other riparians. Furthermore, since Perrier had obtained permits from the Michigan Department of Environmental Quality to pump ground water, the state had exercised its responsibility to ensure that the Perrier pumping was "reasonable" use. Soon after, Ice Mountain Water was being bottled and sold throughout the Midwest. MCWC, however, was not going to give up. More lawsuits followed, and lawsuits continue to this day.

The Battle of Ice Mountain is far from over.[7]

Is ground water public or private property? That issue, not hydrology, is the real source of the Perrier-MCWC dispute. One side argues that ground water is a resource that is wholly owned by the public and therefore should not be used for generating private profit. The other side argues that private ownership of land gives the landowner the right to use underlying ground water for private enterprise as long as it constitutes "beneficial use" and does not harm other property owners. By now you might recognize this as a continuation of the absolute ownership doctrine (the English Rule) versus the reasonable use doctrine (the American Rule). You might also notice the split between an essentially capitalistic and socialist philosophy. It is this ideological split, incidently, that makes these disagreements so heated. In each case, the argument is partly about the water, of course, it is partly about the environmental impacts of using water, and it is partly about who controls water. But it is really an argument about public versus private control of natural resources.

This conflict would be unresolvable if there was no other interest at work. But there is, and that interest is the consumer. Remember that virtually all water law turns on the crux of "beneficial use." One of the jobs a court has in adjudicating public-versus-private water disputes is to balance the interests of the public at large. You might think that this would bring the scales down on the side of public ownership of water resources. Sometimes it does, but not always. Consider, for example, a much more economically important utilization of ground water than bottled water—the irrigation of food-producing crops.

In the year 2000, the United States used 83.3 billion gallons per day of fresh ground water.[8] Of this impressive total, 56.9 billion gallons per day, or 68.3% of all the ground water used in America, was used to irrigate croplands. In the same year, incidently, bottled water accounted for 0.015 billion gallons per day, or just 0.018% of all ground water consumed.[9] Clearly, farmers are by far the largest users of ground water in the United States, and virtually all farmland in the United States is privately held. If the ground water that is being so vigorously pumped is a publicly owned resource, how is it that so much of it is used by private farmers?

The answer is that there is a compelling public interest in the production of food. Without irrigation, food production in the United States would decline, food costs would soar, and people could go hungry. Another effect would be a decline in the *variety* of available food. California's Central Valley, which is a natural desert, produces much of the fresh vegetable crop available in the wintertime in the United States. Without irrigation by ground water, a good bit of that production would cease. This, in turn, would dramatically decrease the food choices available to consumers. A good bit of the public interest in ground-water pumping and irrigation resides in maintaining consumer choice.

The same reasoning can be applied to bottled water. The comparison is milder, since if bottled water were to disappear tomorrow nobody in America would die of thirst. What would happen is that consumer choice in available drinking waters would immediately decline. Municipal waters in each hydrologic region of the United States usually come from a single source. It may be a river or a reservoir or an aquifer, but it is still just one source. Bottled water gives consumers the choice of drinking waters from different sources, just as irrigation in California gives consumers in the Northeast the choice of eating fresh vegetables throughout the winter. If consumer choice is deemed to be in the public interest, then so is bottled water.

The public interest in having choices in the kinds of water available for drinking goes deeper than simply the availability of rare or unusual bottled waters. Anyone who has ever dealt with publicly or privately owned municipal water companies knows they tend to be monopolistic. The reason is simple enough. Tap water is the only choice most consumers of water have, particularly low-income consumers. If the tap water happens to be of poor quality, or is more expensive than people like, or if the they simply dislike the way it tastes, that's just too bad. Without choices, there is no alternative. Monopolies, whether they are public or private, inevitably gravitate toward serving the interests of the monopolists to the detriment of their customers.

Bottled water, therefore, provides a public benefit that extends further than just the luxury or convenience it offers to consumers. By giving people a choice in the kinds and quality of drinking water available to them, it discourages the establishment of water monopolies. Bottled water is not the only option for providing consumer choice in this regard. Home-based water treatment systems, which have improved dramatically in technology and cost in recent years, produce additional alternatives for drinking water. In many parts of the United States there are also "water stores" that treat municipal waters to individual or local tastes. All of this choice, this competition between different sources of drinking water, is the surest defense against the establishment of water monopolies of any ilk.

That, in turn, is very much in the public interest.

When Dave Dowdy and the young woman squared off in the early 1970s, they were engaging in a human debate that was already several thousand years old. It is unlikely, therefore, that this controversy will be resolved any time soon. But as long as ordinary people have a choice in how, when, and where their water is delivered, and as long as competition between different water providers is never eliminated, our prospects are reasonably good. We can only hope that the battle of Ice Mountain will continue forever. As long as neither side of the debate between public and private ownership of water ever wins entirely, the water might not be free.

But at least we'll have a choice.

III AN ENDLESS SEA

9 AN ENDLESS SEA
Regional Geology and the Variety of Spring Waters

The Boeing 767 lifted off smoothly from Runway 8 Right of Atlanta's Hartsfield International Airport. This morning, Delta's Flight 159 was on its way from Atlanta to Seattle-Tacoma Airport, a four-and-a-half-hour flight that would take it diagonally across North America.

For most of the sleepy business travelers on Flight 159, the aisle seats were generally preferred. After all, on such a long flight, it was a given that you would have to visit the lavatory a time or two, and sitting next to the aisle makes it easier to get back and forth. Also, the flight attendants have an easier time delivering coffee and snacks. All in all, a majority of frequent fliers prefer to sit by the aisles, and most will not even consider occupying a middle seat. Avoiding middle seats is understandable. Avoiding window seats, however, has pitfalls. On this spectacularly clear winter day, there was going to be a magnificent show unfolding outside the airliner's windows. Those passengers lucky enough to have window seats, and those with the time and interest to watch, would witness the endless sea that is America.

Most people take it for granted that most of the fresh water available for human use in North America resides in the rivers, streams, ponds, and lakes that dot the countryside. That perception could not be less true. If you add up the volume of all of the surface-water bodies in North America, which includes the watery vastness of the Mississippi River, the Great Lakes, and the mighty Columbia River, the total comes to a mere 2% of all the fresh, usable water that is actually there. By far the largest portion of water in North America, fully one quintillion gallons (that's 1,000,000,000,000,000,000 gallons), is hidden away as ground water. But while these vast quantities of water are invisible, effectively shielded from the prying eyes of humans, the aquifers that contain them are not. After all, fresh water ultimately comes from rain and snowfall, and this water can permeate and saturate only the rocks and sediments occurring at land surface. When you stand on the sur-

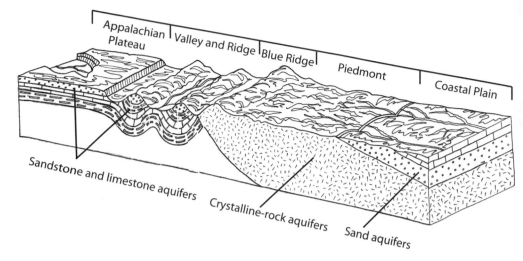

FIGURE 9.1 The surface expression and underlying structure of the Coastal Plain, Piedmont, Valley and Ridge, and Appalachian Plateau physiologic regions. Source: U.S. Geological Survey.

face, however, your perspective is usually too narrow to see just how this happens. A better vantage point is several miles overhead. For this reason, there is no better way to see how geologic formations intersect land surface, connecting them with the hidden sea below, than from the window of a jetliner.

The 767 banked into the flight pattern around Atlanta's airport and leveled off at about five thousand feet. Below, you could clearly see the red Georgia clay that Scarlett O'Hara held so dear. This "clay," as it is locally called, is actually a weathering product of the underlying metamorphic rocks that make up the Piedmont Physiographic Province of the eastern United States (fig. 9.1). These rocks were originally deposited as sediments on the bottom of the Atlantic Ocean some 600 million years ago. Over time, repeated collisions between North America and Africa squeezed and heated these sediments, eventually turning them into crystalline metamorphic rocks. In addition, these tectonic forces lifted the entire landscape above sea level.

Georgia is blessed with a warm, humid climate, and typically receives about fifty inches of rainfall per year. Rainwater, even perfectly pristine rainwater, is fairly acidic and will dissolve the silica that makes up metamorphic rocks. Over the millennia, rainwater falling on the rocks of Georgia's Piedmont has dissolved out a good bit of silica, leaving behind a soft, porous, crumbly residue that geologists call *saprolite*. In addition, because the parent metamorphic rocks are relatively iron-rich, these saprolites turn red as they weather, giving the Georgia soils their characteristic deep red color. This red saprolite mantles the underlying fractured bedrock and can be as thick as one hundred feet in places. Because it is so porous, saprolite acts like a gigantic sponge, storing vast quantities of rainwater as it seeps into the earth. This saprolite is an excellent filter and serves to cleanse rainwater of surface contaminants and microorganisms as it percolates downward. Eventually, this saprolite-cleansed water seeps into the network of fractures present in the underlying metamorphic rocks. These fractures serve as conduits, moving ground water rapidly through the subsurface. Where the water-bearing fractures intersect the land surface in valleys, springs develop. These saprolite-filtered springs often produce water that is cool, clear, and excellent for drinking. Native Americans used these springs for thousands of years as sources of drinking water, and the Scotch-Irish settlers who arrived in the eighteenth century followed suit. A few of these springs, such as Pleasant Springs of Tiger, Georgia, serve as sources of bottled water.

With its nose pointed to the northwest, the jetliner once again began accelerating and climbing out of Atlanta's airspace. The Piedmont of Georgia was soon left behind, and the scene below changed as the 767 approached its cruising altitude of thirty-five thousand feet. The landscape of eastern Tennessee is dominated by a series of valleys and ridges that look like waves in the earth. These "waves" are made of folded limestones and sandstones that are about 500 million years old. The limestones, which are readily dissolved by acidic rainfall, form the valleys. The sandstones, which are made of more resistant quartz, form the ridges. This is what geologists call the Valley and Ridge Physiographic Province (fig. 9.1), and it extends northward through the Shenendoah Valley of Virginia, through Maryland, and into Pennsylvania and New Jersey. Rainwater falling on the ridges recharges the ground water in underlying rocks, which have been extensively fractured and faulted by the compressive forces that folded the rocks in the first place, and this water moves toward lower elevations in the valleys. At these lower elevations, particularly where permeable rocks contact less permeable rocks, cold springs often form that produce excellent drinking water. In places, however, steeply dipping fractures carry water as much as a mile into the earth. There, the water is heated, expands and is forced to land surface under pressure, and produces hot springs.

During the nineteenth century, the hot springs of Virginia were the favorite "watering" spots of the South. Even today, people come to soak in the warm waters at places like Warm Springs, Virginia.

After only a few minutes, the wavelike folds in the earth were left behind as the airliner moved over central Tennessee. Here, the appearance of the individual beds of sandstones, limestones, and coals changed again. Whereas the rocks of the Valley and Ridge Province had been conspicuously bent and folded, here they were entirely horizontal. In the wintertime, when the foliage is off of the trees, these horizontal beds of sedimentary rocks—the hallmark of the Appalachian Plateau Physiographic Province—are readily seen. Unlike the folded rocks of the Valley and Ridge, the entire Appalachian Plateau has been lifted as a block (fig. 9.1), preserving the original flat-lying orientation of the sedimentary rocks. The limestones in particular tend to be dissolved by rainfall, forming conduits and partings for water flowing in the subsurface. The term "underground river" is seldom an accurate description of ground water, but in parts of the Appalachian Plateau it actually applies. Mammoth Cave in Kentucky, located just a few miles north of the airliner's course, was carved out of the St. Louis Limestone over millions of years by ground water flowing in the subsurface. Mammoth Cave, part of the largest single system of caverns in the world, is a spectacular exception to the more modest partings and bedding planes that carry groundwater in the limestone aquifers of the Appalachian Plateau. Where these partings and solution cavities discharge on the slopes of hills, springs develop. Some of these springs, actually very few of them, carry ground water that is suitable for drinking. Surface runoff containing excessive amounts of microorganisms and organic matter drains easily into these limestone aquifers, often rendering the water unsuitable for human consumption. In places, however, such as in the Tennessee mountains near Collinwood, the springs tap deeper aquifers. These deeper-circulating waters are naturally cleansed, and are excellent for drinking. An example of such waters is bottled under the name Tennessee Mountain Pure.

Soon, however, just forty-five minutes into the flight, the Appalachian Plateau was left behind. Ahead and to the south lay the broad expanse of the Mississippi River Valley. There are few sights more awe-inspiring than the Mississippi River from thirty-five thousand feet. The great sweep of the river bends and meanders gracefully, and huge barges, linked together like sausages, plow doggedly into the current. Understandably, the river itself dominates the view. However, if you look closely at the freshly plowed fields on either side of the river, you will see faint scars of meanders sweeping as broadly as the river itself. The Mississippi is one of the most restless rivers in the world, and it is constantly changing, or at least trying to change, its banks and channels. This happens less in these days of the Army Corps of Engineers, who carefully control—or at least attempt to control—the river. But in times past, the meanders, loops, and cutoffs of the Mississippi were constantly changing.

In *Life on the Mississippi,* Mark Twain tells the story of the little town of Delta, which used to be three miles downstream of Vicksburg. However, a massive cutoff caused by a flood changed the course of the river, and the little town found itself two miles *upstream* of Vicksburg. Mark Twain also mentions that, in the days before the Civil War, such a cutoff could take slaves in the state of Missouri and transfer them overnight to Illinois, where they would be free.

These scars, loops, and cutoffs, which are clearly visible from the air, are a living testament to the shifting channels of the Mississippi River. But there is more to their legacy than just their surface impressions visible from the air. The Mississippi River carries millions of tons of sand, silt, and clay to the sea every year. As the river sweeps back and forth over its floodplain, it lays down layer after layer of clean, water-washed sands and gravels. These sands and gravels contain far more ground water than resides in the river itself, and they are commonly referred to as the Mississippi River Alluvial Aquifer (MRAA). The aquifer itself is not visible from the air, of course, but it is no secret to the farmers of Mississippi, Louisiana, and western Tennessee who use it extensively to irrigate their crops. In places, the aquifer produces drinking water of exceptional quality. The Mississippi Bottled Water Company headquartered in Jackson, Mississippi, which has been in business since 1937, draws water from the MRAA.

The airliner crossed the Mississippi River just to the south of St. Louis. On the left side of the plane, the highlands that mark the beginnings of the Ozark Mountains could be seen in the distance. The Ozark Plateau, as it is more properly called, is a geologic oddity, placed as it is between the Mississippi River Embayment to the south and the Illinois Basin to the north. The core of the St. Francis Mountains in southern Missouri is where ancient igneous and metamorphic rocks—locally known as "basement" rocks—were lifted up and exposed about 600 million years ago. On the flanks of these basement rocks are a series of limestones and dolomites that were deposited about 500 million years ago. For much of geologic time, the interior of North America was submerged beneath shallow seas, which, like the Caribbean Sea today, produced great quantities of shellfish and thus great quantities of carbonate shell material. When these shells are broken and ground up by wave action in the sea, they produce carbonate sands and muds, which are then deposited as limestones, which consist mainly of calcium carbonate—$CaCO_3$. Some of these limestones contain enough organic matter to support very active populations of microorganisms, and the metabolism of these microorganisms can convert limestone to dolomite, which is mainly calcium-magnesium carbonate—$CaMg(CO_3)_2$. In the rocks that make up the Ozark Mountains, much of the carbonate has been converted to dolomite. Rain that falls on the plateau seeps into vertical fractures and crevices of the limestones and dolomites, dissolving and enlarging them over time, and recharges the underlying ground-water system. The downward movement of this water is impeded by the underlying basement rocks, and ground-water flow is directed sideways toward the foot of the plateau. There, the water collected by the mountains discharges from hundreds of springs. Many of these springs, such as Big Springs in Arkansas, have spectacularly large flows that emerge from openings enlarged by the dissolving effects of water on the limestones and dolomites. Not surprisingly, these springs have been used as water supply as long as humans have been around.

One such spring in Arkansas, called Eureka Springs, has a particularly interesting history attached to it. According to legend, sometime around 1800 the Sioux Indians brought the daughter of one of their chiefs to the spring. She was suffering from an eye affliction that had rendered her blind. When she bathed her eyes in the spring waters, however, her sight was miraculously restored. This story was picked up by a gentleman calling himself Dr. Jackson (whether he was really a medical man or not is subject to some doubt), who began bottling the water under the name "Dr. Jackson's Eye Water" in the 1870s. By 1905, and before the advent of chlorinated municipal water, this business became known as Ozarka Spring Water and the product was sold as "table water," or drinking water, meant to be served with meals. The Ozarka label is now part of Nestlé and is one of the more popular waters bottled in Arkansas, Texas, and the rest of the Southwest.

After crossing the Mississippi River, the airliner followed the Missouri River to the west and north. Below, the beginnings of the central Great Plains stretched from horizon to horizon. This part of Missouri is underlain by ancient sandstones, shales, and limestones deposited by the great inner seas that covered North America for most of its history. To the north, these ancient rocks are mantled by glacial sediments formed during the ice ages. Because of the flatness of the plains, however, springs, are rarer than in the Ozark Mountains to the south. As the airliner crossed over western Iowa and into Nebraska, the landscape below changed again. The trees gradually disappeared and were replaced by a vast, rolling plain. These are the High Plains, and they are underlain by one of the most remarkable and productive aquifers in the world.

The High Plains aquifer consists of several geologic formations, the most extensive of which is known as the Ogallala Formation. The Ogallala aquifer, as it is often called, consists of sands and gravels deposited by streams and rivers flowing out of the Rocky Mountains to the west. As the Rocky Mountains were pushed up by tectonic forces about 10 million years ago, coarse-grained sediments choking what must have been huge rivers spread out over the plains to the east. Even today, the High Plains slope from an elevation of about 4,500 feet above sea level at the base of the Rocky Mountains to about 600 feet in eastern Nebraska. In places, these sediments accumulated to a thickness of several hundred feet, and they stretch from South Dakota in the north to Texas and New Mexico in the south. It has been estimated that the Ogallala aquifer contains more water than Lake Huron, and it produces more water—about 5 trillion gallons per year—than any other aquifer in North America.[1] That, incidently, is about the average flow of the Missouri River at Kansas City. Almost all of this water, more then 90% of it, is used to irrigate crops. By itself, the Ogallala aquifer supports the production of more than $20 billion worth of food and fiber crops. Human consumption, in contrast, accounts for barely a tenth of the water drawn from the Ogallala. Even so, the Ogallala aquifer is an important source of water for municipal water systems as well as for countless private wells.

From the air, the most striking evidence of this vast underground reservoir is the giant polka-dot effect of green circular fields that stand out vividly from the surrounding brown plains. These circular fields are the result of the center-pivot irrigation systems that were developed specifically to utilize the Ogallala aquifer to support agriculture on the High Plains. Originally, the idea was to drill a well in the center of a forty-acre field, pump the water to irrigation lines that were equipped with wheels, and slowly rotate the lines in a huge circle. This allowed water to be spread over the rolling plains more efficiently than with conventional flood irrigation. Over the years, this technology has become increasingly complex in order to make the best use of the available land and water. Nowadays, as you fly over the Ogallala aquifer, you can see circular green fields characteristic of center-pivot irrigation systems for hundreds of miles in all directions.

But while the Ogallala aquifer excels in terms of water quantity, it is not always the most desirable water qualitywise for bottling. It is actually debatable whether the problem is the water itself or whether the problem is just the American taste for bottled water. In the United States, premium bottled waters have relatively low concentrations of dissolved solids. You might remember that the water produced from Camp Holly Springs in Virginia has a total dissolved solids concentration of just 30 mg/L. That is only about three times higher then rainwater. Ogallala aquifer water, on the other hand, has TDS concentrations that range from 250 to as high as 1,000 mg/L. That, in turn, does not translate to a bottled water that most Americans are willing to buy.

The American taste for low-TDS drinking water vastly amuses Europeans. In Europe, there is a long tradition of drinking mineral waters with relatively high TDS concentrations (more than 250 mg/L), largely because these minerals are considered to be good for the health. The fact that Americans do not share this taste is puzzling to most Europeans. The joke is that Europeans drink water for what it contains (dissolved minerals), whereas Americans drink water for what it does not contain (dissolved minerals). In any case, the Ogallala aquifer, by virtue of its relatively high concentrations of dissolved solids, is not widely bottled for human consumption. Some companies do bottle it, but many of these waters are reprocessed by reverse osmosis in order to lower their dissolved solids and thus make them more palatable to American tastes. One bottled water that is not treated is Lakota Water, which is produced by Sioux Indians on the Rosebud Reservation of Nebraska.

As the airliner continued west, the South Platte River became visible, flowing eastward from the distant Rocky Mountains. It is interesting to watch the distinctive shallow, gravel-choked channel of the South Platte from seven miles up. You cannot see the gravel, of course, but you can see that there is often not one but several main channels, bending and twisting together like braided hair. Not surprisingly, these kinds of gravel-bed streams are referred to as *braided streams*. The transportation of gravel, which is being carried out of the Rocky Mountains to the west, to be deposited on the High Plains of Nebraska and Kansas, is how the Ogallala aquifer was formed in the first place. The South Platte

River that we see today is a remnant of the aquifer-building processes that created the Ogallala aquifer beginning about 10 million years ago.

The airliner cruised on over South Dakota. Gradually, the green circles that indicate center-pivot irrigation and the Ogallala aquifer became rarer and were replaced by dusty-looking brown fields characteristic of dryland farming (farmers here eke out an existence without irrigation). To the north, the brightly colored red beds of South Dakota's Badlands came into view. As the airliner passed south of Rapid City, the landscape below changed abruptly. What had been dry, brown plains from horizon to horizon was now interrupted by strikingly green hills. These are the Black Hills. The path of the airliner just clipped northeastern Wyoming, and the gleaming Teton Range could be seen to the south. Just to the north of the airliner's path, Devils Tower could be seen rising from the surrounding plains. The airliner cruised smoothly over Montana. In the distance, the shield of the snow-covered Rocky Mountains came into view.

The Rocky Mountains have a long history, going back at least 200 million years. Over that time, the convergence of the North American Plate with the Pacific Plate has pushed the Rocky Mountains upward over and over again. In places, whole blocks of rock the size of two states have been lifted; in other places the rocks have been folded and faulted more locally. As they were lifted, the forces of erosion—water, ice, and chemical dissolution—carved the rocks. The spectacular alpine scenery visible from a jetliner represents a long and complicated history of uplift and erosion that has been going on for a very, very long time. In addition, the climatic conditions created by the uplift of these mountains produce ground and surface waters that have many desirable qualities.

It is common to divide the climatic conditions found in alpine mountains into three distinct zones. The first of these, corresponding to the highest elevation, is called the *upper mountain zone* and includes the steepest slopes. Because of its elevation and steepness, sediments and rock fragments generated here by weathering bedrock are washed away faster than they can be formed. Consequently, the land surface tends to be barren, devoid of well-developed soils, and often covered by snow and ice. From an airliner window, the upper mountain zone is the most visible and most striking part of the mountains. Hydrologically, the upper mountain zone is where snow and ice accumulate during the long, cold winters. In the spring and summer, meltwater from this snow and ice fills the steep valleys and gullies with cold, clear streams. Because this water begins as snow and has so little time to react with the underlying rocks, it tends to be very cold and have very low concentrations of dissolved solids—just the way Americans like their drinking water.

The problem, however, is that this water is so transient (spring and summer) and moves so fast that very few, other than hikers, climbers, and other committed outdoor enthusiasts, can enjoy it direct from the source. It is here that the next hydrologic zone comes into play. The *middle mountain zone* is characterized by extensive weathering caused by freeze-thaw cycles. Because water expands when it freezes, water efficiently cracks open rock fractures and crevices, eventually shattering the rock. These large rock fragments then accumulate along the bases of valleys, forming thick wedges of sediments consisting of boulders and gravels. Such sediments, which geologists call *colluvium* or *talus*, are extremely porous and very permeable. They soak up waters transported from the upper mountain zone and direct them into the subsurface, where their rate of downward movement is slowed. Once stored in the colluvial sediments, the waters can also seep downward into the underlying fractured rocks of the mountains themselves. From there, the water is directed toward lower elevations where it often emerges as springs. It is these springs and seeps, rather than the higher streams, that are more easily utilized as sources of water. Furthermore, because the spring waters are still cold and relatively unmineralized, they are often used as sources of bottled water. The Rocky Mountains, stretching from New Mexico to the Arctic Circle, produce some of the best bottled waters in the world.

One company that takes advantage of the Rocky Mountains' unique hydrology is Deep Rock Water of Denver, Colorado. Like virtually all regional bottled water companies in America, Deep Rock Water has its own fabled history. It seems that in 1896 the city of Denver refused to provide city water to a druggist named Stephen Kostitch, because his property was too far outside the city. Miffed, Kostitch began drilling his own well, which eventually reached a depth of 852 feet where it tapped the underlying Arapohoe Sandstone. The artesian water produced by this well had a TDS of 180 mg/L, which is high by the standards of American bottled water, but it also had a fresh, pleasing flavor. Soon, so many of Kostitch's neighbors were requesting his drinking water that he gave up the apothecary business and started the Deep Rock Water company. This company is still bottling water from Kostitch's original well to this day, exploiting both the bulk water delivery and handheld PET businesses. Like many regional bottlers, Deep Rock Water has a loyal local following in and near the Rocky Mountains.

Clouds began to shroud the mountains as the airliner continued to the west over eastern Washington State. The landscape below changed once again to flat-lying brown plains. In a few minutes, Mount Rainier came into sight away in the south, its perfectly symmetrical volcanic cone towering above the clouds and other peaks in a north-south range. These are the Cascade Mountains. The Cascades are considered part of the western mountain ranges but differ from the Rocky Mountains because, in the state of Washington, anyway, they are largely composed of volcanic rocks. As North America grinds past and over the Pacific Plate to the west, the rocks at depth partially melt, and molten rock rises closer to land surface under the Cascades, where it occasionally erupts as volcanoes. Because these melted rocks—magmas as geologists call them—are relatively viscous, the volcanoes of the Cascades tend to erupt explosively. When Mount St. Helens exploded in 1980, approximately one cubic kilometer of lava and ash blew out of the crater into the air in just a few seconds. That seems impressive until you consider that, in the not-so-distant past, some of the explosive volcanoes of the Cascade Mountains had eruptions that were ten or a hundred times larger.

Because the Cascades capture so much of the moisture coming off the Pacific Ocean, a great deal of rainfall and snowmelt flows from the upper mountain zone into the colluvium mantling the middle and lower mountain zones. This, in turn, recharges the aquifers around the base of the mountains feeding hundreds of seeps and springs. Farther south, in California at the foot of Mount Shasta, springs flow from a series of volcanic tubes, or cooling features, associated with lavas. These tubes carry snowmelt from the high altitudes directly to the base of the mountain, and this water is cold, clear, and relatively free of minerals. One set of springs, known as Mossbrae Springs, was once the source of Vasa bottled water, a brand sold in California.

Finally, the airliner began its decent into Seattle-Tacoma Airport. Any passenger who had paid attention for the last four hours had been treated to a front-row view of several different aquifer systems that underlie much of North America. Surface-water bodies come in a vast variety of forms—fast-running mountain streams, stagnant swamps, vast lakes, and sweeping rivers. Ground-water systems have just as much variability and variety. The hydrologic differences between the aquifers of the Ozark Mountains and the Ogallala aquifer are just as vivid and striking as the differences between a Louisiana bijou and Lake Superior.

But while a trip across the United States in a 767 gives the casual observer a sense of how hydrologic systems vary from place to place, it tends to give the impression that their distribution is entirely random. For a long time, geologists thought that the distribution of the rock types, mountain ranges, and basins that control the availability of water *was* random. But since about 1970, it has become clear that there is a central theme to the hydrologic organization of North America. Furthermore, it has become clear that this organization reflects a geologic history that goes back almost to the very beginning of the earth.

The earth is about 4.5 billion years old. This is to say that, by 4.5 billion years ago, the earth had largely finished condensing out of the clouds of dust, debris, and gas circling the newly formed sun. A combination of heat generated from the radioactive materials present in the rocks and heat generated by gravitational and frictional forces soon melted most of the early earth. The densest material, largely liquid iron and nickel, sank and accumulated at the center of the earth, forming its core. This core was surrounded by a larger mantle of somewhat lighter material made up largely of silica and iron. The very lightest materials, made up mostly of silica, aluminum, and oxygen—as well as gases and water vapor—were left to accumulate on the surface of the new planet. This material cooled, forming a thin outer crust made up largely of black rock called basalt that probably looked similar to the basaltic rocks that now form the Hawaiian Islands. At some point, the planet cooled enough for liquid water to condense, eventually covering most of the surface of the earth with deep oceans.

But then as now, the earth was a very active place. Periodically, plumes of molten rock from the mantle punched through the solidified crust and erupted into huge volcanoes. These volcanoes, in turn, formed mountains that rose out of the surrounding seas. Once out of the sea and exposed to the elements, the volcanic rocks began to erode. As they eroded, the more soluble components of the rock were dissolved away, leaving behind minerals composed largely of insoluble silica and aluminum. These residual sediments were less dense than the surrounding basaltic rocks and tended to "float" on top of them. Over hundreds of millions and billions of years, these lighter rocks accumulated into what were to become continents.

The accumulation, or accretion, of continents on the early earth began a long cycle of violent collisions. By now, the solid crust had segregated itself into discrete plates floating on the semimolten mantle below, and convection currents in the underlying mantle moved the plates. The continents, which were embedded in these plates, moved as well. As the crustal plates and continents moved they collided with each other, causing more mountains and volcanoes to develop. These collisions, in turn, partially melted the lighter continental material deep in the earth, leading to the production of the granites and causing the continents to grow even more. North America, Europe, Africa, and the rest of the continents that we know today are the products of these plate movements and resulting cycles of volcanic activity, mountain building, and erosion over billions of years.

Although the history of these collisions and cycles of mountain building and erosion is complicated, there is a certain order to what happened. In particular, because the collisions necessarily occurred at the margins of the continents—what geologists call mobile belts—the continents tended to grow from the inside out. This is clearly recorded in the ages of bedrock underlying North America.[2] The oldest rocks, known as Algoman-Saganagan, are found in the center of the continent. These rocks are anywhere from 2.3 to 3.3 billion years (BY) old and represent the ancient core of the North American continent. Because these rocks are exposed in central Canada, they are often referred to as the *Canadian Shield*. This ancient core of continental rock is surrounded by rocks that are progressively younger. If you start at the Agoman-Saganagan core (3.3–2.3 BY) and travel southeast, you first encounter Penokean rocks (1.6–1.9 BY), Mazatal (1.2–1.5 BY), Grenville (0.8–1.0 BY), and finally Appalachian (0.4–0.18 BY). Each of these rock belts represents the accumulation of sediments at the continental margins followed by collisions with other continents or ocean basins. The Appalachian Belt, for example, represents a collision between North America and Africa that began 400,000 years ago. More recently, the Cordilleran Belt in the West reflects North America overriding the Pacific Ocean Basin beginning about 300,000 years ago, a process that is still going on today.

The distribution of rocks and aquifers in North America, and thus your view from an airliner window flying coast to coast, is complicated but not random. The Cascade Mountains are the result of North America grinding over the Pacific Ocean Basin, melting the crustal rocks at depth, and forming the dozen or so active volcanoes you see today. As you might expect, this same compression has caused the uplift of the Rocky Mountains farther to the east. You might not know, however, that this compression has also lifted up the Ozark Mountains of Arkansas, two thousand miles from the Pacific Ocean. Incredibly,

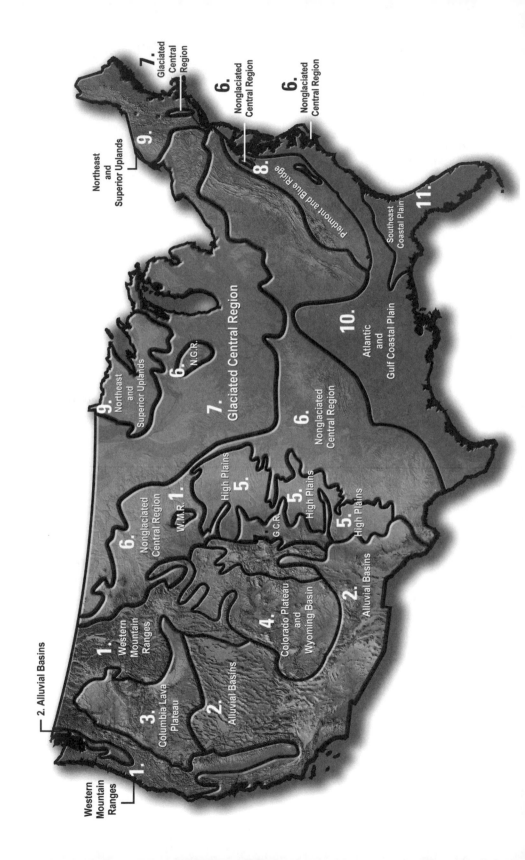

this same continental compression is translated as far east as the Carolinas, where it unleashed the Charleston earthquake of 1883, the strongest earthquake ever recorded east of the Mississippi River.

Oscar Edward Meinzer (1876–1948) never had the opportunity to fly across the United States in a jetliner. If he had, however, you can bet he would have been sitting in a window seat with his eyes glued to the panorama below. In 1923, Meinzer published a landmark book that recognized the different ground-water regions in the United States.[3] A few years later he published another book documenting the occurrence of large springs in the United States, and related them to the geology of the different ground-water regions.[4] In those days, most people still viewed ground water as something so hidden and mysterious that it was outside the realm of scientific inquiry. Meinzer was determined to change this attitude, and he systematically went about showing how the availability of ground water depended on such mundane and unremarkable things such as the lithology of the underlying rocks (limestones, sandstones, granites, etc.) or sediments (fine-grained clays or course-grained sands and gravels, etc.), the structure of the rocks (folded, faulted, or flat-lying), their elevation (mountains or plains), and the climate of the surrounding area (wet or dry).

What Meinzer did not have was the organizing principle of plate tectonics, and so his approach was entirely observational. From his experience, however, he could see the similarities and differences between different parts of the country. Taking these factors into account, he divided the United States into twenty-one distinct regions, or "provinces" as he called them, in which the characteristics of the underlying ground-water systems were similar. This method of classification, which Meinzer attributed to earlier work,[5] identified the most common kinds of ground-water systems in the country. It was exactly analogous to someone pointing out the fact that surface-water bodies in Louisiana were fundamentally different from those in Arizona. This approach of focusing on ground-water provinces has been refined and expanded over time, largely because it has proved to be so useful.[6] The ground-water regions recognized by Ralph Heath[7] are particularly easy to follow and are shown in figure 9.2.

FIGURE 9.2 *(opposite)* Hydrologic regions of the United States. Source: U.S. Geological Survey

The distribution of these ground-water regions is of great economic significance. It is no particular secret, for example, that agriculture is important to the economy of California. Less well known is the fact that this agriculture largely depends on the ground water underlying the San Joaquin and Sacramento valleys (Region 2, Alluvial Basins) and ground- and surface water derived from the Sierra Nevada (Region 1, Western Mountain Ranges). Similarly, agriculture in many western states would be impossible without ground water derived from the Ogallala aquifer (Region 5, High Plains). The booming economy of Florida could never have happened without the underlying water resources of the Floridan aquifer (Region 11, Southeast Coastal Plain). Finally, the seaside hotels and casinos of Atlantic City, New Jersey, would never have be built without groundwater from the underlying coastal plain aquifers (Region 10, Atlantic and Gulf Coastal Plain).

But there is another, admittedly less grandiose, significance to the hydrologic regions of the United States. The kinds of aquifers present in a particular area determine the kinds of springs that develop. They control the distribution of artesian and nonartesian well waters. And most important, they control the chemical characteristics of the ground water. In other words, given the preferences and tastes of the water-drinking American, these hydrologic regions control the availability of waters suitable for bottling—which is to say, waters that people are willing to buy even though there is no lack of virtually free tap water. That standard, that bar, is higher than the casual observer might think. And given the economic reality that the real cost of water is largely the cost of transporting it, the distribution of hydrologic regions affects the variety and cost of bottled waters available in different parts of the country. Some places, notably the Northeast and California, because of the proximity of mountain ranges and sources of moisture, have enormous choice in the kinds of bottled waters available. Other places such as Kansas and Nebraska, where springs and artesian waters of suitable chemical quality are rare, have less choice in the kinds of bottled waters that are available.

One logical way to think about the natural history of bottled waters, therefore, is to consider the hydrologic regions from which they come. This approach has the advantage of immediately showing why springs are either abundant or rare in any given area, why spring discharge tends to be high or low, and whether the waters circulate deeply into the earth or not. It also goes a long way toward explaining the chemical differences—both good and bad—between different waters. After all, aquifers consisting of limestones and dolomites (the Ozark Mountains) produce water that is chemically distinct from aquifers comprised of fractured granites (the Sierra Nevada). Finally, this approach makes it easier to blend the hydrologic characteristics of a particular area with its human history.

There is a definite chicken-or-egg interplay between the availability of water, the chemical characteristics of that water, and the history of the United States. This history always begins with occupation by Native Americans, continues with the tentative arrival of European or American pioneers, and eventually includes the following flood of farmers, artisans, speculators, bankers, and preachers. The relationship between water and this history, which is evident practically everywhere in the country, is strongly reflected in how bottled waters are marketed even today. One thing that makes bottled waters interesting, therefore, is that their natural history and their present-day utilization are so intertwined as to be inseparable.

Let's begin in the Northeast.

10 GRANITES AND GLACIERS
The Northeast

In 1827, Wentworth Ricker was a man with a plan. His father, Jabez, had died that year, and now Wentworth was the head of the family business near the little town of Poland, Maine. Thirty years earlier, when Jabez, his wife Molly, and their ten children had just arrived on the farm, a weary coachman asked for a night's lodging. As it happened, the new Ricker farm was on a hill overlooking a road frequented by coaches traveling from Montreal to Portland. With plain, straightforward country hospitality, they gave the tired man a meal and a place to sleep. Impressed, the coachman told others in his trade about the friendly new people living near Poland, and more coaches began stopping for overnight accommodations. Sensing opportunity, Jabez and his sons built an inn, and in 1797 they went into the hostelry business. The inn was an immediate success and became a regular stopping place for coaches and teamsters. One of its attractions was a small spring on the side of the hill, which produced unusually good drinking water. In addition to having a place to rest, tired and thirsty travelers, and their horses as well, could also count on having a drink of cool refreshing water. The Ricker family's business thrived.[1]

But business is never so good that it cannot get better. In 1827, when Wentworth took over, he decided to build a road connecting Portland and Paris, a town located just west of Poland. This road had the potential to significantly increase traffic and thus the profitability of his hostelry. But then disaster struck. Wentworth, who by then was in his forties, fell ill with what was described as "gravel," as kidney stones were called in those days.[2] The doctors who attended Wentworth, such as they were, despaired of his recovery. But Wentworth remembered that, years ago, his younger brother Joseph had recovered from a fever after drinking water from the spring. Lacking any better medical help, Wentworth decided to try using the water as a cure. His family, afraid that Wentworth was dying, moved his sickbed to the spring, where he consciously drank as much water as he could. After a few days, just as suddenly as his pains had appeared, they vanished.

It is certainly true that drinking water can be beneficial to people suffering from kidney ailments. In the case of infections, simply drinking large amounts of water can help flush out the harmful bacteria. Similarly, drinking large amounts of water can also help pass kidney stones. Regardless of how it happened, though, Wentworth recovered and built his road (now Route 26 going through Poland Spring to what is now South Paris), and business prospered. Meanwhile, the water bubbling out of the little spring began to gain a local reputation for its healing powers.

Things went along fine for the next few years until Wentworth died. The family business passed to Wentworth's son Hiram, who soon began to run into trouble. In 1844, a Canadian rail line known as the Grand Trunk Railroad began operating in both Maine and New Hampshire. This led to a decline in stagecoach travel and thus a decrease in the hostelry business. The unlucky turn of events weighed heavily on Hiram, who became increasingly moody and depressed. To make matters worse, he began to suffer from stomach pains, which became more and more troublesome. As his health deteriorated, Hiram, like his father before him, turned to drinking water from the spring as a cure. To his relief, and possibly to his surprise, Hiram soon got better.

This turn of events greatly interested Dr. Eliphalet Clark, a physician of Hiram's acquaintance. At this point in the nineteenth century, "healing" waters were all the rage in the serious practice of medicine. Saratoga Springs had already come to prominence as a source of medicinal waters. In this context, the term "prominence" is synonymous with "profitable." Many physicians had built up lucrative practices by prescribing the various kinds of spring waters found near Saratoga Springs. Dr. Clark wondered if the water that had apparently helped Hiram could help other patients as well. Could Hiram please send him a barrel of this "elixer"? Dr. Clark inquired. Hiram obliged, and a month later the results were in. According to Dr. Clark, every patient he had given the spring water to had made a "remarkable" recovery.

That, apparently, was all the proof Dr. Clark required. Would it be possible, Dr. Clark wondered, for Hiram to sell him water for use in his medical practice? Since 1845, Hiram had been selling three-gallon demijohns, or clay jugs, of the spring water in local grocery stores for fifteen cents each. Selling water to Dr. Clark was a natural extension of this new business, and soon physicians from Boston, New York, and even Philadelphia were buying the water and prescribing it to their patients. Also, the captains of clipper ships and whaling fleets—which were major businesses in New England at that time—began to purchase barrels of water for use on their ships. The theory seems to have been that if the water could heal sick people, then maybe it could also prevent sickness among crews on long voyages. Hiram Ricker had stumbled into a new and profitable business. Water from Poland Spring has been bottled and sold ever since.

In the United States, any history that goes back two or even three hundred years is considered to be of impressive antiquity. As such, the story of Poland Spring and the Ricker family—who emigrated from Germany to America about 1650—qualifies as being ancient indeed. But the story of the geologic and hydrologic circumstances that led to the "healing" waters of Poland Spring go back much further than Ricker family history, or even human history. At a minimum, this geologic history of can be traced back to when the igneous and metamorphic rocks now underlying much of New England were formed. You can perhaps argue that this history goes back 3.7 billion years, when the continent that was to become North America first emerged from the primeval oceans. But, at least as far as age is concerned, the rocks that now underlie Maine and most of the Northeast can be dated to a series of geologic events that began in Ordovician time (500–405 million years ago) at the margins of the North American continent.

Ordovician time in what is now New England began quietly enough, with a stable but low-lying landmass (North America) to the west surrounded by shallow seas that teemed with marine invertebrate life, which is to say organisms that had not yet developed backbones. This life included snails, clamlike organisms known as brachiopods, and swimming creatures with spiral shells called ammonites that are related to the modern nautilus. The shells of these marine organisms, which were made mostly of calcium carbonate, accumulated on the seafloor over millions of years and were laid down as thick beds of limestones. These limestones now underlie much of the eastern United States and are especially visible in the Shenandoah Valley of Virginia.

But beginning about 430 million years ago, the quiet, settled life of North America began to change. A range of largely volcanic mountains emerged on the edge of the continent, and these mountains began dumping sediments onto the carbonate-covered seafloor. This mountain-building event is known as the Taconic Orogeny and was the first of several events that eventually formed what we now call the Appalachian Mountains. (Orogeny is the geologic term for mountain-building events, and this particular orogeny named after the Taconic Hills of southeastern New York, where the rocks are exposed.) Exactly what caused the Taconic Orogeny is a matter of debate, but it seems to have resulted from the North American continent moving east and grinding over the oceanic crust it encountered.

By about 400 million years ago, things settled down again on the eastern margin of North America. But the relative eastward drift was bringing North America close to two other continents, one that was to become Europe and another that was to become Africa. Beginning in Devonian time, about 360 million years ago, North America, Europe, and Africa collided, causing a massive mountain-building event that is called the Acadian Orogeny. In Europe, this collision became evident a few million years earlier than in North America and is called the Caledonian Orogeny. In other words, the same series of events that led to the formation of the Appalachian Mountains in North America also contributed to the formation of the Caledonian Highlands of Scotland.[3]

The *Acadian Orogeny*, named after the old French term for southeastern Canada and New England, thrust up mountain ranges that probably reached as high as the modern Himalayas. As North America, Europe, and Africa welded themselves together, they formed a huge landmass that we now call Pangaea. The heat and pressure caused by these collisions served to partially melt rocks at depth, which led to the formation of the granites that underlie much of New England. In addition, the huge volumes of sediment washing off of the upthrusting mountain ranges formed thick beds of red sandstones and shales in both North America and in Great Britain. These Devonian sandstones now form the Catskill Mountains of New York and the Old Red Sandstone of England. The Old Red Sandstone, incidently, is what numerous English castles are built of. In any case, the rocks formed by this intercontinental collision 400 million years ago comprise the backbone of what is now the northeastern United States.

The metamorphic rocks and granites that underlie most of New England and give it a distinctive rocky appearance are due to events that can be traced back at least 430 million years ago. Today, Poland Spring discharges from fractures in these metamorphic and granitic rocks that, by coincidence, happen to intersect land surface on the side of Ricker hill.

When Hiram Ricker began selling demijohns of Poland Spring water in 1845, he probably did not foresee just how big the bottled water business was going to become during the nineteenth century. In fact, a number of events fortuitously converged to make the water business profitable. One obvious factor was the relatively primitive state of medical practice in those days. Physicians did not have much of a repertoire of useful drugs, and they knew it. The observation that drinking water from certain springs sometimes helped sick people feel better, and sometimes even seemed to cure them, was seized on as a panacea. These "healing" waters were used to treat everything from the common cold to cancer but in most cases were no more therapeutic then any other reasonably clean drinking water. Nevertheless, such spring water was better than nothing, or so people thought, and drinking it was fashionable as well.

But economics also played a role. In the early nineteenth century, the United States was growing rapidly. And as it grew, many people were becoming comfortably well-to-do, and a few were getting seriously wealthy. The industrialists of the North were busy building textile mills, factories, and foundries. The foundries poured out the iron rails needed to build railroads, and the factories made household goods and farm implements that were wanted and needed by farming families. In the South, agriculture had matured, producing an abundance of cash crops such as rice, tobacco, and cotton that had become very valuable on world markets. The fact that railroads now existed to bring this agricultural bounty to port cities like Charleston made these crops even more valuable. By 1850, there was a good bit of disposable income around, and people were looking for ways to spend it.

One way to spend it was to go to the springs for extended holidays. Saratoga Springs was one of the first places in the North that developed as a resort and playground, and Hiram Ricker was quick to see the potential of developing Poland Spring in the same way. Hiram was making a good bit of money selling his spring water, and in 1860 he went to the expense of building a springhouse. But to really cash in on the springs mania sweeping the United States and Europe, he would need to build a hotel. And not just any hotel. To attract the newly rich members of American society, he would need to build a hotel that was not only comfortable but luxurious. The Civil War, and the hard economic times that followed, delayed his plans somewhat. But in 1876, his grand hundred-room hotel opened. This hotel included the first antifire sprinkler system ever installed in a public building in the United States, which is appropriate considering that water was the motivation for building the hotel in the first place.

One of Hiram Ricker's more interesting innovations was also on display in 1876. Hiram knew that many more people were interested in drinking Poland Spring water than could actually come to his resort. He had been selling bottles of water for some time, but he knew that if the waters were deemed truly special, they would sell even more. Remember that when Moses had been leading the Hebrews through the Wilderness of Sin after escaping from Egypt, he had twice produced spring water by striking rocks with his rod. Moses, in other words, was strongly connected to springs and spring water in Bible-conscious America. Hiram decided to capitalize on this story and began making bottles molded into an image of Moses. These "Moses" bottles, which were about a foot tall, were prominently displayed when the hotel opened in 1876 and eventually found their way all over the world. Slick, stylish packaging is part and parcel of the bottled water business today. But no modern packaging scheme has quite surpassed Hiram Ricker's Moses bottles for sheer marketing brilliance. These bottles remain treasured collector's pieces to this day. All this clever marketing worked spectacularly well, and soon the rich and famous of America and the world were flocking to the water resort of Poland Spring.

By the 1890s, Poland Spring bottled water was enough of a fixture in Maine that it was included in the Maine exhibit at the Columbian Exposition in Chicago, where it was awarded a Medal of Excellence. A few years later, at the 1904 World's Fair in St. Louis, Poland Spring water was declared "the best spring water in the country." This tribute is highly significant for what it says about the development of bottled water in the United States. In both Europe and the United States during most of the nineteenth century, the preferred drinking waters for health purposes were mineral waters. By present-day standards, this means water that contains more than 250 mg/L of total dissolved solids (TDS). Saratoga Springs, one of the first waters bottled for health purposes in the United States, was also mineral water.

Poland Spring water, however, is different. On average, Poland Spring water has a TDS of only about 40 mg/L. This is not much more mineralized then rainwater, which has a TDS ranging from 4 to 22 mg/L depending on where you are. The fact that relatively unmineralized

Poland Spring water caught the fancy of American water drinkers is important in the history of bottled water. The popularity of this water was the first predominantly American water fashion, and it stands in stark contrast to the European custom of preferring mineral waters. This new fashion seems to have caught on at about the turn of the twentieth century and is recorded in the various honors accorded to Poland Spring water at the Columbian Exposition in Chicago (1893) and the St. Louis World's fair (1904).

The development of a preference for low-TDS drinking waters among Americans is significant for a number of reasons. One reason is that it still defines the difference between American and European tastes in bottled water. Another is that the American preference for low-TDS drinking water helped preserve what was left of the bottled water industry after the introduction of chlorinated municipal water in 1913. Chlorinated surface waters, which dominate municipal waters to this day, seldom have a TDS under 100 mg/L. Thus, even in the brave new world of chlorinated tap water, there remained a niche for Poland Spring water. It is worth considering, therefore, just why Poland Spring produces water characterized by such a low TDS.

The geologic history of the Northeast, as it pertains to the availability and character of spring waters, does not quite end with the formation of granites and metamorphic rocks 330 million years ago. This overall geologic framework has been carved and sculpted over succeeding millennia by a variety of erosive forces, the most recent of which began 2 million years ago. This geologic event was the repeated advance and retreat of glaciers that, at times, covered much of North America and all of New England. The sediments left behind by these glaciers, in turn, form a veneer that greatly affects the availability of both ground and surface water.

The "ice ages," as they are popularly known, were a series of glacial advances that covered northern Europe and North America beginning about 2 million years ago, a time known as the Pleistocene epoch. The contrast between the warm, tropical seas that characterized North America for most of its history and the thick masses of ice that formed during the Pleistocene is notable. In part, this reflects the northern migration of both Europe and North America over geologic time. During Devonian time, when the backbone of New England was forming, North America was located astride the equator, and the tropical seas typical of these latitudes generated thick beds of limestone and dolomite. Over the last 350 million years, however, North America has moved progressively northward.[4] Now the ancient core of the continent resides in Canada, well above a latitude of 50 degrees north. This northerly drift is part of the reason why North America's climate is cooler now than it was in the distant geologic past.

The root causes of the Pleistocene ice ages are still argued about vociferously, especially now that global warming has become such a contentious political topic. Most scientists, however, feel that the ice ages reflect a combination of geographical causes (which control circulation patterns in the oceans and thus the transport of heat from low to high latitudes), astronomical causes (the wobble of the earth on its rotational axes changes the angle of the sun over a cycle of about twenty-thousand years), and solar effects (the solar output of the sun seems to vary over time). What actually caused the ice ages may never be fully known. Nevertheless, the unarguable fact is that, over the last 2 million years, there have been at least six major ice advances over North America. And these are just the "major" ice advances. In all, geologists can see evidence for at least fourteen "ice ages," or glacial advances and retreats, in the last million years alone. The most recent, known as the Greatlakean advance in America, occurred between eleven-thousand and eight-thousand years ago.

These thick continental glaciers have had a profound affect on the topography and hydrology of the northeastern United States and Canada. They carved deep gouges in the underlying bedrock, which now direct the drainage of streams and rivers as well as providing basins for the lakes and ponds that dot the New England landscape. The weight of glaciers has alternately pressed the continent downward several hundred feet into the underlying mantle, only to let it spring back up again as the glaciers melted. This process, known as *isostasy*, has helped to thoroughly fracture the bedrock, forming conduits for groundwater to seep through. In addition, the retreat of the glaciers has blanketed much of the landscape with a veneer of glacial sediments that form the most productive aquifers in this part of the country.

The term "glacial sediments" is a convenient one, but it tends to obscure the variety of sediment types that glaciers produce. Of all the flowing media that are capable of moving sediments (wind, water, ice), ice obviously is the most viscous. Advancing glaciers will move boulders the size of a house just as readily as they will move the tiniest speck of clay. In other words, glaciers do not discriminate very well between very large sediment grains (boulders) and very small sediment grains (clays). The hallmark of ice-borne sediments, therefore, is that they tend to be poorly sorted, with clay-, silt-, sand-, and boulder-size cobbles all mixed together. These poorly sorted, ice-transported mixtures of boulders, cobbles, and silt are called *glacial till*. As glaciers advance, they push sediment ahead of them like bulldozers. When a glacier ceases advancing, this sediment gets unceremoniously dumped, often forming fairly substantial hills. These hills are call *moraines*. Sometimes, glaciers regather their forward momentum and readvance over moraines. In this case, the moving ice has the effect of "smearing" the moraines in the direction of flow, forming distinctive long ridges of glacial sediment called *drumlins*. In many cases, these ice-transported sediments are so poorly sorted—that is, the cobbles and boulders are imbedded in a matrix of fine-grained silts and clays—that they often tend to restrict the flow of ground water and thus make fairly poor aquifers.

But once a glacier stops moving forward and starts to melt, water immediately comes into play. Because water is much less viscous than ice, it is much better at sorting coarse from fine-grained sediments. Fine-grained clays and silts tend to be washed away by rapidly flowing waters, leaving the coarser-grained gravels and sands behind. Such "glacial outwash" sediments most commonly form in streams at the toe of a retreating glacier. But it takes a long time to melt a glacier, especially a thousand-foot-thick continental glacier, and streams and channels often form underneath retreating glaciers. Because they are so tightly channeled, these outwash sediments sometimes formed oddly shaped hills and rises known as *eskers*.

All of which brings us back to Poland Spring. The hill that came to be occupied by Jabez Ricker and his family is underlain by fractured metamorphic bedrock formed 350 million years ago in the Acadian Orogeny. This bedrock, in turn, is overlain by washed glacial sediments formed during the last retreat of the glaciers eight-thousand years ago. These glacial sediments act as a trap for surface water, allowing rainfall and snowmelt to percolate into the ground. Because these sediments are so permeable, this new ground water moves rapidly downward and feeds water to the underlying fractured bedrock. In one place on the side of Ricker Hill, the glacial sediments have been eroded away, exposing the fractured bedrock. Because the glacial sediments so efficiently trap water on top of the hill, the water pressure in the fractured bedrock at this spot is higher than at land surface, and water bubbles out as a spring.

Hydrologically, Poland Spring is fairly simple, and the water discharging from it probably has not traveled much more then a few hundred yards in the subsurface. During its underground journey, which probably takes less than five years, the water encounters only clean, washed glacial sediments and hard crystalline rocks. None of these sediments or rocks are particularly soluble, and thus the water that percolates through them remains relatively free of dissolved solids. Also, the fact that the water has only a few years to react with the rocks (as opposed to the thousands of years that Saratoga Springs mineral water has) helps keep the TDS low. The water's low TDS, which is the defining characteristic of Poland Spring water and which has contributed significantly to the American ideal of "good" drinking water, is a direct result of the hard bedrock and the washed glacial sediments that combine to form Ricker Hill.

In many ways, the years 1900 to 1913 were the high-water mark of Poland Spring, as well as being the heyday of the new American bottled water industry. This period of time was one of relative economic prosperity, meaning that people had disposable income available for amenities such as bottled water. Furthermore, bottling technology had advanced to the point where it was economical to package drinking water in glass bottles. Glass bottles had been used for medicines and drinking water since before the Civil War. But the invention of a fully automatic glass-bottle-making machine in 1903 brought bottled water into a price range that was affordable for just about everybody. Even more important, waterborne diseases were still rampant in the years leading up to the chlorination revolution of 1913. The dangers of unclean water, virtually forgotten today, were still very real. One tragic illustration of these dangers was the death in 1912 of Wilbur Wright, coinventer of the first powered airplane, from typhoid fever. Although the source of the *Salmonella typhi* that killed Wilber Wright has never been settled, the fact is that typhoid fever was killing thousands of people a year. And by 1900, people were fully aware that this disease was spread by drinking contaminated water. The fear of typhoid fever alone led many people to prefer relatively clean drinking water that came in a bottle.

All this led the sons of Hiram Ricker to invest in a major upgrade of their bottling operations between 1906 and 1907. A new, permanent springhouse was built that clearly reflected the economic prosperity of Poland Spring and the bottled water industry at the time. This springhouse, which was built with a Spanish motif, had marble floors and walls and columns made of Italian marble. The spring itself was encased in marble and plate glass, and a bronze grille laid over it. The water was diverted from the spring into glass and silver pipes that carried it to holding tanks made of granite and lined with glass. Business was brisk. Life was good.

But, alas, in 1913 the chlorination revolution struck. Chicago, Philadelphia, and numerous other cities and towns had been tinkering with various solid chlorine compounds for years. When engineers finally figured out a way of adding liquid chlorine to water, the chlorination revolution took off. This dramatic innovation has probably saved more human lives than any other technological advance in public health history. *Salmonella typhi* might be a dangerous pathogen and one that is efficiently transported and spread by water. But it is also very sensitive to and easily killed by chlorine. As long as municipal systems maintain a low "chlorine residual" in the water being distributed, *S. typhi* cannot survive very long. In the years prior to 1920, typhoid fever killed thousands of people a year in the United States alone. After 1920, with the widespread introduction of chlorination, the frequency and severity of these typhoid epidemics decreased substantially. By 1950, typhoid fever in the United States had been virtually wiped out.

While all this was very good for public health in the United States, it was not good for the business of selling bottled water. Because Poland Spring was known as a "drinking water," which people would have at the dinner table, its business took a significant hit. But Poland Spring had luckily developed a distribution system in Europe, where it was sold in many upscale hotels. The bottled water business in Europe, which by now was firmly established, was less impacted by the chlorination revolution than it was in the United States. The combination of selling water to hotels in both the United States and Europe is what allowed Poland Spring to survive through the 1930s.

But more contributed to the decline of Poland Spring's businesses after the turn of the century than just the decreased popularity of bottled water. By 1910, Poland Spring was a very big business indeed, and only part of it involved bottling and selling water. There were, for example, three hotels serving hundreds of guests that employed as many as two-thousand workers at a time. Managing these many different businesses, and dealing with the problems of so many employees, was a difficult and daunting task. Gradually, the three sons of Hiram Ricker were drawn further and further away from the water business. The Depression hit in the 1930s, only to be followed by the start of World

War II. The beginning of the war meant, among other things, that exporting bottled water to European hotels was no longer possible. Also, the war itself drew many of the younger Rickers away from the family business. By the late 1940s, creditors had taken over what was left of the hotel and water businesses. In a cruel twist of fate, Charles Ricker, the great grandson of Jabez, who had originally settled Ricker Hill, became an employee of the various owners who halfheartedly attempted to make the businesses work again.

By the end of World War II, both the water-bottling and the hotel facilities had fallen into disuse and disrepair. In 1962, a hotel businessman from Boston named Saul Feldman bought the property and began to revive the resort. Feldman, who apparently was a pretty sharp fellow, made sure to keep a steady stream of celebrities coming to the resort including Jack Paar, Joan Crawford, Robert Goulet, and Jimmy Durante. The fact that Poland Spring had a golf course helped. In fact, the golf course at Poland Spring was one of the first to be built (1896) in the United States.

But in 1967, a new disaster struck. This time the trouble came from Washington, D.C., and President Lyndon Johnson's Job Corps. For whatever unfathomable reason, Poland Spring was chosen as the site for training young people to become hairdressers, barbers, seamstresses, and carpenters. Within months, over two thousand young people moved into old hotels and buildings. And, as young people are wont to do, they inflicted massive amounts of damage to the delicate infrastructure. Even worse, funds for the Job Corps were cut off a few years later and everybody left, leaving the Poland Spring resort a shambles. The resort hit rock bottom in 1975, when the Poland Spring House was destroyed by fire.

Amazingly, Poland Spring managed a comeback. The fire drew the attention of a local TV news director named Jim Aikman, who publicized the former glory and subsequent decline of the resort. Aikman, concerned that Maine was losing a valuable part of its history, was instrumental in forming the Poland Spring Preservation Society. Since that time, much of Poland Spring has been restored, partly by funds generated by Mel and Cyndi Robbins, who have been operating the Presidential Inn on Ricker Hill since 1972, and partly by the individual efforts of the Preservation Society. But part of this renaissance can also be traced to the pluck of an entrepreneur named Paul Haene, who was attempting to revive the Poland Spring bottled water business.

Haene was one of those businessmen who understood the psychology of other businessmen. In 1978, the Perrier Company of France decided to reintroduce the concept of single-serving bottled water in the United States. At that time there were several hundred different bottled water companies in the United States, but they focused mostly on bulk water, selling the five-gallon watercoolers that had carried the industry through the Depression, World War II, and the years thereafter. In contrast, Perrier began to advertise the idea of buying high-quality drinking water in smaller, handheld bottles. The idea caught on, especially among the yuppies who were flooding Manhattan in search of fame and fortune. Suddenly there was a brand-new market for "packaged" water, as single-serving bottles are called in the industry. Seeing the success of Perrier's advertising campaign and sensing opportunity, Haene began airing radio commercials suggesting that Poland Spring water was as good as or better than Perrier. "Try a little Poland Water on the rocks," the commercials suggested, taking direct aim at the market opened up by Perrier. Furthermore, Haene began to appeal in a not-so-subtle fashion to American patriotism. "For an American to be healthy, is it necessary to get water from Europe?" one advertisement asked, "That's like sending your laundry to Europe."

In the end, Haene's strategy worked brilliantly, and sales of Poland Spring water began to increase. To accommodate the increased demand for water, Haene built a new bottling plant at the foot of Ricker Hill. Also, since Poland Spring itself produces only about six gallons of water per minute, Haene decided to drill a series of boreholes into the glacial outwash sediments at the base of the hill. The theory was that the bedrock fractures discharging at Poland Spring were also discharging into the glacial sediments at the base of the hill. At the time this seemed to be a logical way to grow the business, particularly since the water produced from the boreholes was virtually identical (in terms of its chemistry) to the water of Poland Spring itself.

All this brought Poland Spring to the attention of Perrier. Perrier had grown as a business since the 1920s by marketing itself as a high-quality drinking water, playing up the hydrologic circumstances that make the water unique, and wrapping itself in the local spring's long human history, which some say goes back to Hannibal's invasion of Italy in 218 B.C. When Perrier's executives looked at Poland Spring, they saw a small company that, left on its own, would be a weak competitor and a minor irritant. However, if brought under the umbrella of Perrier's marketing, it could be an asset. Why not use Poland Spring's history in the United States the way they used Perrier's history in Europe? The business logic was inescapable, and in 1980 Perrier bought Poland Spring. Perrier then proceeded to market Poland Spring water as a premium "designer" water in precisely the same way that Paul Haene had envisioned.

This acquisition of Poland Spring began a long-term business strategy for Perrier Waters of North America, as the company was then called. This was to identify good-quality, regionally famous, historically interesting bottled spring waters, buy out the owners, and apply Perrier's considerable marketing expertise and distribution network to increase sales. At Poland Spring, this marketing strategy included helping to restore the 1907 springhouse and building a museum on Ricker Hill cataloging the history of the business. After all, if the history to be part of the marketing strategy, it was necessary to document and display it. In addition, the local amateur historians of the Poland Spring Preservation Society took up the task of restoring and maintaining the various other buildings left by the Rickers. These include the Maine House, which displayed Poland Spring Water at the 1893 Columbian Exposition in St. Louis and which Hiram Ricker had shipped to and reassembled at Poland Spring in 1895. It also includes the All Souls Chapel, a masterpiece of Gothic masonry built in the early twentieth century. Today, Poland Spring on Ricker Hill is a combination hotel, golf resort, and historical attraction. In many ways, it has simply returned to Hiram Ricker's vision of an opulent resort and all-around playground he originally conceived of in 1860.

In the 1990s, Perrier itself was acquired by the Swiss-based food conglomerate Nestlé, which has continued Perrier's basic marketing strategy. If you look at Nestlé's present-day product line—including Zephyrhills bottled water in Florida, Ozarka in the Midwest and Southwest, and Arrowhead and Calistoga in the West—they all have followed a pattern similar to what happened at Poland Spring. First and foremost, Poland Spring has geologic and hydrologic circumstances that produce desirable drinking water. Second, it has a history that includes rumors of medicinal benefits that were actively exploited by early purveyors and that led to commercial bottling operations. Third, it managed to survive the chlorination crash of the early 1900s.

The acquisition of Poland Spring first by Perrier and then Nestlé has, on one hand, probably saved the Poland Spring water business from economic oblivion. On the other hand, it took what had been a family operation and transformed it into part of a multinational corporation. It would be interesting to see what would have happened had Paul Haene's David decided not to take on Perrier's Goliath, thereby waking the sleeping giant. But he did, and history often seems to turn on such small occurrences. Not all or even most bottled water companies in America are associated with corporate giants like Nestlé, but most of them have a similar history.

And as the story of Poland Spring shows, history matters.

11 THE LAND OF SPRINGS
Florida

The legend goes something like this: For years, Juan Ponce de León, an adventurer who had accompanied Columbus to the New World in 1493, had heard stories from local Indians about a magic fountain. The fountain, which could be found in a land that lay over the horizon, could restore old men to vigorous youth. With age creeping up on him, Ponce de León resolved to find this magic fountain and restore his own failing youth. Accordingly, in March of 1513, he sailed from what is now Puerto Rico to find this fabled land, which in those days was called "Tera Bimini." He did find a land that he named "La Florida," but, tragically, he never found the fabled fountain of youth. After years of fruitless searching, he died a disappointed and defeated man.

Like most legends, the story of Ponce de León and the Fountain of Youth is part history and part fable. In the case of Ponce de León, however, it is actually possible to get beyond the fable and concentrate on the history. That history, as it turns out, is more interesting then the fable.[1]

Ponce de León was a born adventurer who, as a penniless eighteen-year-old, managed to talk his way into Christopher Columbus's second expedition to the New World in 1493. When Columbus arrived for the second time on the island of Española (now Haiti and the Dominican Republic), he found that the small settlement he had left behind had been destroyed by the native population. This precipitated a long series of wars to "pacify" the local Indians, a process that consisted mostly of killing or enslaving them. Ponce de León was an able soldier and soon proved to be an effective field commander, a commodity always in demand during military operations. As payment for his service, he was given a grant of land on Española in 1504, which he promptly turned into a profitable farm. It seems that bread made from the yuca plant (cassava) has a particularly long shelf life, and this bread was an important part of the diet for ship crews returning to Europe. Taking advantage of the demand for this uniquely Caribbean product, Ponce de

León got rich by growing the yuca plant and selling bread to departing ships.

By 1508, however, the adventurous Ponce de León was getting restless. Christopher Columbus had died 1506, and the politics of Española were complicated, messy, and favored Columbus's heirs. As a result, Ponce de León applied for and received permission from King Ferdinand of Spain to lead an expedition to the neighboring island of San Juan Bautista, now known as Puerto Rico. In August of 1508, Ponce de León led fifty men on one ship to Puerto Rico and established a colony. But even this was too close for Diego Columbus, Christopher Columbus's son, who considered Ponce de León to be a rival. At first, Ponce de León was named governor of Puerto Rico, but Diego Columbus, who was the viceroy of Española, soon had him removed. After much political maneuvering, King Ferdinand of Spain—a great admirer of Ponce de León—suggested that he ought leave Puerto Rico and find some other place to colonize. This apparently suited Ponce de León, who promptly poured his personal fortune into an expedition to find and explore "Tera Bimini," a land that was rumored to lie over the horizon to the north and west. In March of 1513, Ponce de León, three ships, and about sixty-five men left Puerto Rico and sailed northwest, where they were to find and name "La Florida."

Just where the Fountain of Youth comes into this otherwise straightforward narative is difficult to say. It is worth noting that Alexander the Great had searched for a fabled rejuvenating river in India as early as 325 B.C. Since the Spaniards were keen to find a passage to India— that is why Columbus made his 1492 voyage in the first place—it is possible that they may have connected the ancient tales of a rejuvenating spring with their own hoped-for discovery of a new route to India. That hope, after all, is why Europeans gave Native Americans the confusing and inappropriate name "Indians" in the first place.

The stories told by Española's natives, however, have their origins in the fact that Florida, of all places on earth, is indeed a land of springs. Of the seventy-eight first-magnitude springs in the United States, that is, springs having a discharge of more than hundred cubic feet per second (which equals a tad less than 65 million gallons per day), thirty-three are found in Florida.[2] It has been estimated that the daily discharge from the more than six hundred springs in Florida is about 8 billion gallons, which is greater than the output of any similar-size area on earth.[3] This being the case, it is no wonder that Native American stories about Florida included tales of springs. Furthermore, because discharging spring waters in Florida are so much cleaner than the local surface waters, which typically are laden with dissolved organic carbon, it is no mystery as to why spring waters would be considered healthy if not actually rejuvenating.

Juan Ponce de León himself was only thirty-eight at the time of his first voyage to Florida, hardly someone in immediate need of rejuvenation. Furthermore, his main motivations seem to have been, first, a love of adventure and discovery, second, a desire to escape the political intrigues of Diego Columbus, and third, the hope of getting even richer than he was. The only surviving record of Ponce de León's 1513 expedition, written many years after the fact from original sources by one Antonio de Herrera y Tordesillas, does mention, very much in passing, that "he [Ponce de León] had an account of the wealth of this Island [Florida] and especially that singular fountain that the Indians spoke of, that turned men from old men to boys. He had not been able to find it because of shoals and currents and contrary weather."[4] This suggests that Ponce de León had indeed heard the story of the Fountain of Youth and that he may well have kept an eye open for it. But it is clear that finding it was not his top priority. After all, the "shoals and currents and contrary weather" did not stop him from exploring most of Florida's coast over a six-month period, checking out likely spots for future settlements as he went. So, while Ponce de León knew about the fabled Fountain of Youth, and while he might have been perfectly happy to find it, it was not the primary motivation for his voyage of discovery.

Unlike Ponce de León, finding a suitable spring was very much on top of Bob Hirst's agenda when he visited Florida in the mid-1990s. The bottled water company Hirst worked for, AquaPenn, had carved out a thriving business in its home state of Pennsylvania and was actively moving into the Midwest and the Northeast. The next logical market for AquaPenn to target was Florida and the Southeast. As always, transportation costs limited just how far it was feasible to ship finished bottled water to market. So if AquaPenn was going to expand into Florida, it would need to have a spring source suitable for bottling. It was Bob Hirst's job to find one.

AquaPenn is a good example of the many companies that emerged in the 1980s to take advantage of the burgeoning demand for bottled water. AquaPenn was started in 1984 by one Ed Lauth, who soon proved to be one of the shrewer entrepreneurs in the business. For one thing, Lauth took his hydrology seriously. Taking advantage of his proximity to Penn State University, he secured the help of a professor named Richard Parizek. Dr. Parizek was one of the premier ground water hydrologists in the United States, and his program at Penn State was one of the best in the country. Lauth consulted Parizek on which springs to use for his bottled water business and used Parizek's detailed hydrologic and geochemical knowledge to give his product scientific legitimacy.

But Lauth, who had a keen understanding of human nature, knew that effective marketing would require more than scientific legitimacy. It would also need big-time name recognition, and there was no better way to secure this than to sign up celebrity endorsements. During the 1980s, the most revered man in Pennsylvania was Joe Paterno, the legendary head football coach at Penn State. Lauth talked Paterno into being the company spokesman, and AquaPenn was off and running.

But Lauth did one other thing that was even more clever. Taking advantage of Paterno's involvement in AquaPenn, Lauth began hiring ex–Penn State football players to be his marketing representatives. You can imagine how a purchasing agent for a grocery chain in Pennsylvania—who naturally would be a Penn State football fan—would react to a sales pitch from one of Penn State's gridiron heroes. The only questions would be how much shelf space do you want and how soon can you ship? AquaPenn's business took off, first in Pennsylvania of course. But soon, AquaPenn was found in the stores of neighboring states and as far away as Chicago.

It was in this atmosphere of heady success that Ed Lauth and AquaPenn decided to move into Florida and the Southeast. Lauth had heard about a spring that was for sale near Branford, Florida, on the Suwannee River. The main conduit feeding the spring was already tapped by a borehole that, according to the present owner, produced excellent water that was suitable for bottling. Before Lauth would close the deal, however, he sent Bob Hirst, who was AquaPenn's chief technical expert, to check out the spring. Hirst's job was to visit the borehole, gather information about the hydrologic setting, and confirm that the water quality was up to AquaPenn's standards.

On the day that Hirst visited the spring, however, he immediately saw that something was very wrong. It had rained heavily in Florida recently, and the Suwannee River was approaching flood stage. When Hirst was shown the borehole, instead of the clear spring water he expected, the discharging water was the color of tea. Hirst looked at the tea-colored spring water and then looked at the flooding Suwannee River several hundred yards away. He immediately knew what the problem was.

Under normal hydrologic conditions, most rivers in Florida are natural discharge zones for ground water. This is to say that ground water flows from the surrounding higher elevations, where rainfall recharges the underlying aquifer, toward the rivers, where it eventually discharges. But when the water level in a river rises several feet during floods, the direction of water seepage can actually reverse, and river water can move back into the aquifer. That was what was happening here. Suwannee River water containing dark brown dissolved organic matter had been forced into the aquifer by the flood and was now flowing out of the well. Needless to say, this water was wholly unsuitable for bottling, and buying the spring would be a financial disaster for AquaPenn.

Bob Hirst had a problem.

Florida is blessed with a unique confluence of geologic and climatic circumstances that favor the development of springs. These circumstances are not particularly new, having operated over at least the last 80 million years or so. What is now Florida has long been on the trailing edge of North America as the continent has drifted north and west over geologic time. Because of this, tectonic forces have not produced major instances of mountain building near Florida for a long time. So, beginning in Cretaceous time (130–66 million years ago), a large, shallow sea covered all of what is now Florida. Because there were no mountains in the vicinity to provide sand, silt, or clay sediments, the seafloor was covered entirely by the shells of marine creatures. These included corals, microscopic planktonic organisms called foraminifera, clams, and snails, all of which have shells made of calcium carbonate ($CaCO_3$). Gradually, over millions of years, this carbonate shell material accumulated into thick beds of limestone. As this carbonate sediment was deposited, the weight of it depressed the underlying continental crust, forming several basin structures. This, in turn, allowed carbonate material to accumulate to a thickness in excess of ten thousand feet in places.

All this began to change slightly beginning just a few million years ago. Basins that accumulate sediment—such as those underlying Florida—are never simple. Rather, such basins tend to be warped and bent, with some areas subsiding more than others and some areas actually being pushed up. In Florida, there is a geologic structure that has been in place for much of the last 100 million years known as the *Peninsular Arch*, which extends down the center of the Florida Peninsula.[5] Throughout the last 20 million years, the Peninsular Arch has subsided less than the southwest Georgia Embayment to the west, the Southeast Georgia Embayment to the north, and the South Florida Basin to the south. At times, and the present day is one of these times, the Peninsular Arch has actually been pushed up slightly, raising it above sea level. The present configuration of land in Florida owes itself to this slight, and by geological standards it is very slight indeed, upwarping of the crust. This, in turn, has lifted the limestones above sea level, creating the Florida we now see.

Had this newly created limestone terrain been lifted out of the sea and into different climatic circumstances, say like the Arabian Desert, what we know as the Floridan aquifer system would look much different than it does. But much of Florida has a true tropical climate, with an annual rainfall that averages about seventy inches per year. In most parts of the world, this precipitation would collect itself in streams and rivers and run off to the ocean. Not Florida. Because the underlying sands and limestones are so porous and permeable, and because slightly acidic rainfall actively dissolves the limestone, most of the rainwater seeps directly into the ground. Once in the ground, the water is carried off to the ocean beneath the land surface, not over it.

At this point, the Peninsular Arch comes back into play. Some of the highest elevations in Florida occur along the spine of the Peninsular Arch, which stands about a hundred feet above sea level. Rainfall that seeps into the ground at these "high" elevations begins to flow either to the east or to the west beneath land surface. As this water reaches lower elevations near the coasts, it often discharges to springs. Furthermore, because the volume of rain that falls on Florida is so large and because much of this water seeps directly into the ground, the volume of water discharging from the springs can be huge.

The Floridan aquifer system, as the water-bearing limestones underlying Florida are known, consists of numerous geologic formations.[6] There are strict rules governing the naming of geologic formations and hydrologic units in the United States. In general, however, the custom is to name both geologic formations and aquifers (which often include multiple geologic formations) after places. It is forbidden to name rock units or aquifers after people. The naming of most geologic/ hydrologic units is usually a solemn affair, with no room given for frivolity. In the case of the Floridan aquifer, however, a tiny bit of humor managed to find its way into the naming process.

Because much of the water residing in Florida's limestone aquifer was under artesian pressure, the first name given to it was the "principal artesian formations."[7] Later, as the complex nature of the many different geologic formations that made up the aquifer were described in more detail, the term "Floridan aquifer" came into use.[8] Apparently, when George Parker and his colleagues were studying the water resources of the Tampa area, they happened to stay at a particularly impressive hotel called the Floridan Hotel. This hotel, which was built in 1927 and which was then the tallest building in Tampa, was apparently the inspiration for the name Floridan aquifer, Since the hotel was a place, not a person, it was entirely appropriate to use it as a geologic/hydrologic name, and has been used ever since.[9]

The presence of so many spectacular springs in Florida, some of which produce desirable drinking water, provides obvious opportunities for companies in the business of bottling and selling water. Furthermore, because Florida is such a populous state that is hot and humid for much of the year, there is an obvious market for bottled drinking water. The fact that water from the Floridan aquifer has, in some places, undesirable chemical characteristics (it can be hard, highly mineralized, and contain noxious organic carbon and hydrogen sulfide gas) also helps provide demand for low-TDS drinking water. This was the situation in the mid-1990s when Bob Hirst stood near the banks of the flooding Suwannee River and watched tea-colored river water flow out of the "spring" he was investigating for AquaPenn.

Like many CEOs, Ed Lauth was not a particularly patient person. AquaPenn was in a big hurry to locate a water source, build a bottling plant, and get into the market as quickly as possible. Any delay would be bad news, and Ed Lauth did not like bad news. For Bob Hirst to simply fly back to Pennsylvania and tell Lauth the truth—that the spring Lauth was considering was unsuitable—was not the way to make Lauth happy. A better strategy would be to stay in Florida and find a more promising spring source for Lauth consider. Accordingly, Hirst called the office in Pennsylvania, told his secretary that something important had come up, and said not to expect him back for a while.

Then he went to work.

Modern Floridians probably have a better appreciation of ground water, and thus a better understanding of ground-water hydrology, than many other Americans. The reason for this is simple enough. In Florida, almost all the water used for municipal water supply, agriculture, power generation, and mining—which totals about 3.1 billion gallons per day—comes from the Floridan aquifer. Because of its economic importance, the Floridan aquifer is one of the best-characterized, best understood ground-water systems in the world. So, in 1996, when Bob Hirst needed to find a spring source for AquaPenn, there were lots of places he could turn to for information. He visited the U.S. Geological Survey office in Tallahassee, he talked with people from the Suwanee River Water Management District, and he talked with two private consultants. After a week or so of considering and rejecting numerous possibilities, he began to focus on one of Florida's most famous springs, Ginnie Springs, located in Gilchrist County near the Santa Fe River.

People who are familiar with the sport of cave diving, diving into underwater caverns using scuba gear, will immediately recognize the name Ginnie Springs. It was one of the first springs in Florida to develop a diving park and is now one of the best-known diving, swimming, and camping resorts in the United States. People come from all over the world to snorkel in the warm, clear water (the year-round 72°F water appeals to Europeans especially) and to take scuba lessons. For divers who have both the experience and the nerve, there is also the opportunity to explore the underwater caverns that feed Ginnie Springs.

Ginnie Springs is a second-magnitude spring, which is to say that it discharges "only" 51 cubic feet per second, or about 33 million gallons per day. In days past, scuba divers exploring caverns were very much risking their lives, and twenty-seven people are known to have drowned in the cave complex underlying Ginnie Springs. In more recent years, the diving has been made considerably safer by the installation of an iron grate that prevents overadventurous divers from penetrating too deeply into the underwater labyrinth. In fact, Ginnie Springs is now one of the safest diving caves in Florida. But the danger is still there.

One of Ginnie Springs' interesting characteristics, and one that greatly interested Bob Hirst, is the powerful current flowing through the underwater caves. Divers had noticed this long before. But to Bob Hirst, who was interested in locating water suitable for bottling, it suggested something the divers probably never considered. Limestone is relatively soluble in water, which means that groundwater moving though it quickly picks up dissolved solids. However, the rapid rate of water movement through the caverns discharging to Ginnie Springs would tend to limit contact time between the limestone and the water. This, in turn, might mean that the TDS would be low enough to suit the taste of American bottled water consumers. Sure enough, the TDS of Ginnie Springs water turned out to be 160 mg/L, significantly lower than that of much ground water produced from the Floridan aquifer. Hirst decided to take a closer look.

Hirst drove over to Ginnie Springs and asked to see the owner, a man named Mark Wray. Wray was happy to talk, but Bob could tell that he was suspicious about something. Are you working for a foreign company? Wray wanted to know. No, replied Hirst truthfully. What are your brand names? was Wray's next question. Pure American and Great American spring water, Hirst replied, with the emphasis on *American*. Good, said Wray, who was a staunchly patriotic fellow. Let's go to dinner.

That night, Hirst had dinner with Mark Wray, Mark's mother, and Mark's father-in-law and made his pitch. AquaPenn was looking for a source of high-quality drinking water for bottling, he said. At the same time, AquaPenn understood that withdrawing drinking water from the natural outlet of Ginnie Springs was impractical. First of all, people swimming and diving in the spring's basin were a source of fecal bacteria, and no bottled water source can tolerate the possibility of fecal contamination. Second, Ginnie Springs already had a famous and thriving diving, swimming, and camping business. Clearly any new bottling operation could not interfere with the Wrays' ongoing businesses.

Perhaps, Hirst suggested, we could locate one or more of the fractures and caverns feeding the spring on the rise overlooking the river and tap into it with a drilled borehole. Because the volume of water needed for bottling (initially less than 100,000 gallons per day) was trivial compared with the flow in the fractured limestone aquifer (33 million gallons per day), this would not noticeably affect Ginnie Springs itself. Furthermore, because the water would be withdrawn before it got to the spring, the possibility of fecal contamination by swimmers and divers would be eliminated. But there was one considerable uncertainty, Hirst continued. FDA regulations required that calling the bottled product "spring" water meant that any borehole would have to be drilled into the same fractures that actually fed Ginnie Springs. How hard would it be, Hirst wondered, to locate the actual caverns feeding Ginny Spring half a mile away? At this, Mark Wray smiled knowingly. Oh, we'll think of a way, he remarked lightly.

The Wray family and Bob Hirst shook hands on the deal that night.

Where does spring water come from? How deeply does it circulate in the earth? How long does it reside in the earth before it discharges at land surface? People have been asking these questions for thousands of years, mostly without much hope of actually answering them. But because the springs of Florida are so spectacular and because ground water produced from the Floridan aquifer is so economically important, there has been a good deal of effort to answer these questions in Florida. And as it happens, Ginnie Springs is one that has been studied in considerable detail.

In the 1970s, there was a good deal of scientific activity associated with understanding the chemical and geologic processes that control the composition of ground water (chapter 3). There was also a good bit of optimism that these processes could be deduced and cataloged with a good deal of certainty. After all, analytical methods for characterizing ground-water chemistry were getting better and better. As long as we knew accurately what was actually dissolved in water, and as long as we knew the kinds of rocks being dissolved, it would be a simple matter of arithmetic to figure out how much of what rocks and minerals had dissolved.

One of the reasons that question was important was because people were interested in dating ground water. In archaeology, for example, scientists had been using carbon 14 for dating various artifacts, and thus placing them in an accurate chronology, since the 1950s. Why not use carbon-14 to date ground water? After all, carbon dioxide in the atmosphere is a mixture of the isotopes carbon-12 and carbon-13 (both of which are nonradioactive) and carbon-14 (which is radioactive), and the proportions of these isotopes has remained fairly constant over time. Knowing the proportion of carbon-14 in atmospheric carbon dioxide, and knowing the rate that carbon-14 decays (it has a half-life of 5,720 years), it should be possible to estimate the time that has passed between when water seeps into the earth as rainfall to when it discharges from springs or wells.

At first, that was the approach to dating water in the Floridan aquifer.[10] It was recognized right up front, however, that the amount of carbon entering the aquifer via dissolved carbon dioxide in rainwater is "diluted" by carbon dissolved from the carbonate material (limestone) that makes up the Floridan aquifer. Furthermore, because Floridan

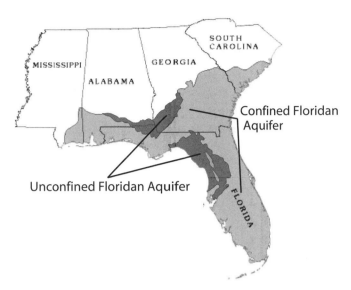

FIGURE 11.1 Confined and unconfined areas of the Floridan aquifer. Source: U.S. Geological Survey.

aquifer limestone is all "dead," which is to say so old that all the carbon-14 has already decayed, there is a huge dilution of the carbon-14 signal associated with recharging ground water. This problem could be handled, however, as long as scientists knew how much limestone or other carbonate materials were dissolving. That turned out to be a difficult thing to figure out. The problem was that limestone ($CaCO_3$) is not the only mineral present in the Floridan aquifer. There is also dolomite ($CaMg(CO_3)_2$), magnesium calcite ($Ca_xMg_{1-x})CO_3$, and gypsum ($CaSO_4$), not to mention particulate organic carbon and a host of trace minerals as well. The upshot was that there are so many different "plausible" sources of carbon dissolving into Floridan aquifer water that figuring out an exact age was simply not possible. It was feasible, however, to estimate a *range* of possible ages.

When rain falls near the Peninsular Arch (near the town of Polk City, for example), a portion of it seeps into the ground and begins a long journey to the coast. This part of the Floridan aquifer is said to be "confined," meaning that the limestone aquifer is overlain by thick and relatively impermeable clay beds (fig. 11.1). Thus, once water enters the Floridan aquifer near the Peninsular Arch, it is effectively trapped and can remain in the ground for thousands of years. This being the case, carbon-14, with its 5,720-year half-life, is ideal for dating the water.

This kind of carbon-14 dating was first applied to Floridan aquifer water beginning in the 1970s. The results suggest, depending on the amounts of various minerals you assume are dissolving so as to "correct" for carbon-14 dilution, that Floridan aquifer water can be many thousands of years old. For example, it takes about 8,000 years for ground water to seep the thirty miles between Polk City and Fort Meade. Similarly it takes about another 4,000 years for it to move from Fort Meade to the town of Wachula. Because of the uncertainties involved, you cannot be exact. But all things considered, it is a fairly good bet that Floridan aquifer water produced in Wachula has been slowly seeping toward the sea for some 10,000 to 15,000 years. This rate of movement, which averages about twenty feet per year, is fairly typical of deep aquifer systems like the Floridan aquifer.[11]

So how about Ginnie Springs? Can the same carbon-14 approach be used to date the spring waters emanating from the many springs thoughout Florida? Unfortunately, the answer is often no. The large springs of Florida most often develop in areas where the Floridan aquifer is "unconfined," meaning the aquifer is not overlain by thick beds of clay characteristic of the Peninsular Arch (fig. 11.1). This, in turn, means that not much time, certainly less than hundred years, passes from when rainwater seeps into the aquifer to when it discharges at the springs. So, if you try to use carbon-14 with its fairly long half-life to date Ginnie Springs water, the answer you get is that the water is younger than about thousand years, which is not particularly satisfying.

There are, however, other methods that can be used to date relatively young ground water. One possibility is the radioactive isotope of hydrogen called tritium (^3H). Tritium is present naturally in the atmosphere but at fairly low levels. In the 1960s, when both the Soviet Union and the United States were regularly blowing up hydrogen bombs in the atmosphere, a huge amount of tritium was released to the atmosphere. Tritium, which has a half-life of 12.4 years, decays much more rapidly than carbon-14. Given the fact that water from Ginnie Springs is relatively young, can tritium be used to date the water?

The answer turns out to be both yes and no. On one hand, ground water that has not been affected by bomb-produced tritium—that is, water that is more than fifty years old—would have tritium concentrations less than 0.2 tritium units (TU). Ginnie Springs water actually has a tritium concentration of about 5 TU.[12] Clearly, then, the water discharging from Ginnie Springs includes water that is less then fifty years old. However, because the amount of tritium in the atmosphere was so variable (it depended on how many bombs were being detonated as rainwater recharged the aquifer), we cannot really get a solid "date" using tritium. But since carbon-14 could tell us only that the water is less than about thousand years old, tritium does narrow it down to being less than fifty years old. Progress has been made.

But tritium is not the only artificial "tracer" that humans have poured into the atmosphere over the last hundred years. One class of chemicals, the chlorofluorocarbons (CFCs), were once widely used as refrigerants for air conditioners and other appliances. Furthermore, because CFCs are so chemically stable, they have tended to accumulate in the atmosphere over time. You may remember that, because CFCs were interfering with the protective ozone layer around the earth, their use was eventually banned by the EPA. But, for the last fifty years or so, rainfall that has been recharging aquifers has contained very small amounts of CFCs. Furthermore, because accurate records of CFC concentrations in the atmosphere are available, it is possible to estimate the age of water based on CFC concentrations. This is exactly what Brian Katz and his colleagues with the U.S. Geological Survey did for Ginnie Springs water and the water of several dozen other springs in Florida, using concentrations of both tritium and CFCs.[13]

Just as is the case with carbon-14, there is uncertainty involved with this method of dating ground water. But when Katz plotted concentrations of tritium versus CFCs, water from Ginnie Springs dated to about twenty years. Similarly, when Katz plotted concentrations of two different CFCs (CFC-11 and CFC-113) against each other, the indicated date was about twenty-five years. Based on this, Katz could reasonably conclude that water discharging from Ginnie Springs is between twenty and twenty-five years old. The same thing turned out to be true for all the springs discharging along the Santa Fe River, all of which indicated ground-water ages of between twenty and twenty-five years.

Thirty years after methods for dating ground water were introduced, it is now apparent that the age of ground water present in the Floridan aquifer varies considerably. In some places, the age of ground water exceeds fifteen thousand years. In others, it is less than twenty years old. All this would be only mildly interesting if it did not immediately explain the observed differences in the chemical quality of Floridan aquifer waters. In places where the ground water is fairly young (Ginnie Springs), the Floridan aquifer produces highly desirable low-TDS drinking water. In other places, where the groundwater is much older

(such as Wachula), Floridan aquifer water is considerably more mineralized and is considered (by some) to be less desirable for drinking.

By the time Hirst returned to Pennsylvania to report to Ed Lauth, he
had all his ducks in a row. He began by showing Lauth a sample of the
tea-colored water he had collected from the borehole near the flooding
Suwannee River. He then showed Lauth a sample of the crystal clear
Ginnie Springs water. Next, he methodically went though the reports
generated over the years by various federal and state agencies as well
as reports written by private consultants. Finally, he left the decision
up to Lauth.

Lauth decided to go with Ginnie Springs.

But there were still several prickly problems that had to be solved.
Chief among these was the necessity of locating the subterranean caverns feeding Ginnie Springs so that a borehole tapping them could be
drilled. Even though the caverns in this system were extremely large
by the standards of most groundwater systems, it would be very tricky
to trace them for half a mile from the springs and intercept them with
a drilled borehole.

There are a variety of geophysical methods that have been developed
over the years for locating underground caves and caverns. Because
limestone is so much denser then water, sound waves projected into the
ground are often "refracted" when they encounter a low-density cave.
By progressively thumping the ground to produce sound waves, and
by moving receivers around to pick up the refracted waves, it is possible to map underground caves. Various other geophysical methods,
including ground-penetrating radar and electrical resistivity methods,
can also be used. But before he went to the expense of deploying such
equipment, and before he hired a driller, Hirst decided to investigate
the existing wells and boreholes on the Wray property.

The results were disappointing. If any of the existing boreholes had
intersected the same caverns and fractures feeding Ginnie Springs,
they should have produced a seemingly unlimited amount of water.
But none did. By now it was clear to Hirst that he would have to find
the caverns on his own and drill a new borehole. It is at this point that
the story takes a bizarre twist. Mark Wray had been watching Hirst's
progress with some interest. And when the existing boreholes failed to
produce the needed quantities of water, he approached Hirst. "When
you come back on your next trip, I'll show you where the caverns are.
Then you can drill a new borehole."

When Hirst returned a couple of weeks later, he found that Mark Wray had drawn a series of parallel lines on the ground using powdered lime, much like the base path lines of a baseball field. "Those are your cavern walls right there," Wray said, pointing matter-of-factly between the lines. "Drill in between them and you'll find the main cavern."

This was too much for Hirst, a practical, no-nonsense rationalist. "How do you know?" he asked.

Wray shrugged and showed Hirst two rods he had brought with him. Each rod was made of clothes-hanger wire, and each was bent at a 90-degree angle. The short part of each rod, the "handle," was about four inches long. The longer part of each rod, the "pointer," was about a foot long. Both wires were shaped like the letter L, in other words, and thus such rods are known as "L-rods." Wray grasped an L-rod in each hand, with the long ends pointing straight ahead of him. As he walked across the first chalk line, the wires he held loosely in his hands twisted and crossed. As he backed up, they straightened again. As he continued walking back and forth between the lines, the wires crossed again and again.

"Those are the cavern walls," Wray repeated.

Hirst's head was spinning. *This is water witching,* he thought to himself. There was absolutely no way he was going to authorize paying a $10,000 mobilization fee to get a drilling rig out to this site and then pay $20 per drilled foot to sink a borehole, based on water witching. Hirst could just imagine what Ed Lauth would say to that.

"I'll tell you what," Wray said, grinning at Hirst's expression. "You get the drilling rig out here, drill the hole, and if it comes up dry, *I'll* pay for it myself. What do you have to lose?"

In the end, the drilling rig was summoned, the borehole drilled, and the caverns found at a depth of about eighty feet. Once the drilling rods were removed, a miniature television camera was lowered into the borehole. The camera showed clearly that the borehole had intersected a cavern a yard or two wide, and the walls of the cavern were at least approximately where Ray had said they would be. The elusive underground caverns had been found.

Hirst pulled Wray aside. "How do those L-rods work?" he asked.

Mark Wray laughed and shrugged. "I have no idea. They just do."

Ginnie Springs is not the largest and certainly not the most well-known spring in Florida. Silver Springs in Marion County, for example, discharges more then 500 million gallons of water per day, a figure that makes it officially the largest spring in the world in terms of average daily flow. Silver Springs is where glass-bottom boats take visitors out to see the cave opening sixty feet below the surface, where they can see thousands of colorful fish swimming to and fro. The waters are so clear that they can also see the bones of ten thousand-year-old animals littering the bottom of the cave at a depth of more than hundred feet. There are also Hornsby Spring, Crystal River Spring, Weeki Wache Spring, Blue Springs (Jackson County), Wacissa Springs, Manatee Springs, and yet another Blue Spring (Volusia County). These are just a few of the more than three hundred recognized springs in Florida.

Florida truly is a land of springs.

It is not surprising, therefore, that AquaPenn was not the only bottled water company investigating the springs of Florida in the mid-1990s. Perrier was actively looking as well. The source Perrier finally settled on was Crystal Springs, near the town of Zephyrhills. Zephyrhills, which styles itself as the "City of Pure Water," fit in well with Perrier's corporate philosophy. Crystal Springs was well known, had a ready-made reputation for pure water, and was located in a rural area (Pasco County) eager to attract business. Today, Zephyrhills spring water is one of the largest-selling bottled waters in the Southeast. In addition, Silver Springs is also used as a source for bottled water sold under a variety of private labels.

Meanwhile, at Ginnie Springs, things were moving rapidly as well. The borehole was completed, underground stainless steel water lines installed to transport the water to the bottling plant, and the plant built. One of the things that had worried Bob Hirst about Florida was the temperature, which hovered in the ninety-degree range for months at a time. When bacteria are warmed, they often take the opportunity to multiply, which could cause problems in the bottling operation. In view of this, Hirst insisted that the water lines at Ginnie Springs be buried fifty inches below land surface (twenty-four inches is standard). This, in turn, would minimize warming as the water flowed to the bottling plant, which would also minimize the growth of microorganisms. In the rough-and-tumble world of bottled water, attention to this sort of detail can make a difference.

The success of AquaPenn in developing the source at Ginnie Springs, and the success of Ed Lauth in building up AquaPenn into an increasingly large and profitable company, soon attracted the attention of another international water company. Groupe Danone, which distributes Evian Spring water, is one of France's oldest and best-known bottled water companies. In the 1990s, Groupe Danone was actively building a presence in the American market, and one way to do that is to acquire established bottled water companies. Accordingly, its representatives approached Lauth about selling AquaPenn. Lauth, the consummate entrepreneur, had to chose between cashing in immediately on the business he had built up over several years or sticking it out for the long term. In the long term, AquaPenn had excellent prospects. But the growth phase was slowing noticeably, and it was growing businesses that really interested Lauth. Finally, after much negotiation, Lauth sold AquaPenn to Groupe Danone. Today, the source at Ginnie Springs—which was so painstakingly located and developed by Bob Hirst—is operated as a joint venture of DS Waters of America and Coca-Cola known as CCDS Waters.

There is a certain romance that surrounds the quest for springs, particularly springs that produce waters with unusual, useful, or even magical properties. That sentiment neatly explains the enduring popularity of stories like Ponce de León and his "search" for the Fountain of Youth. Bob Hirst was certainly not looking for anything magical when he went to Florida to find exceptionally good water, but something that exceptional was not easy to find.

The geologic and hydrologic circumstances that produce spring waters suitable for drinking and bottling are just not very common. In the case of Ginnie Springs, these circumstances involve the recharge of nearly pure rainwater into a highly permeable limestone aquifer and the rapid movement of this water through fractures and conduits. By the time water discharges from Ginnie Springs, twenty years after entering as rainfall, it has been in the subsurface long enough to be cleansed of particulate matter and other contaminants but not long enough to pick up high concentrations of dissolved solids. The result? A pure, relatively low-TDS water that is delightful for drinking.

Many springs in Florida have characteristics similar, but not identical, to those of Ginnie Springs. In many cases, these subtle differences produce spring waters that are not quite as desirable. Sometimes the water has spent longer periods of time in the subsurface and thus has higher concentrations of TDS. Sometimes the water has spent too *little* time in the subsurface and has not been entirely cleansed of particulate organic matter or microorganisms. Sometimes the spring waters discharge in locations that are inaccessible or inconvenient for collecting water. All in all, any one of a hundred different circumstances can prevent a spring from being useful as a source of bottled water.

The story of Bob Hirst and Ginnie Springs is also an example of the kind of scrutiny a potential water source gets before it ever reaches the stage of being bottled. Modern bottling plants cost millions of dollars to build and operate, and it is just good business to look at potential sources very, very carefully before making any investment. In his quest, Hirst relied mainly on the tried-and-true principles of geology, hydrology, geochemistry, and geophysics. But as the incident with Mark Wray and his L-rods shows, water witching can still sneak into the practice of hydrology. Given the enduring association of Florida with the Fountain of Youth, an association that is incurably mystical, perhaps this should not be too surprising after all, even in this day and age of rationality and scientific technology.

Insight can come from anywhere.

12 DESERT CROSSINGS
The Southwest

In later years, Meredith M. Marmaduke would become the governor of Missouri and was considered a man of distinction and standing. On May 24, 1824, however, Marmaduke was just one more young, eager, inexperienced adventurer traveling from Missouri to the fabled city of Santa Fe. Altogether there were "81 persons and 2 servants" in the caravan, along with "2 road waggons, 20 dearborns, 2 carts and one small piece of cannon about 3 lbs." In 1824, the Conestoga wagons that are universally associated with travel across the plains had not yet come into common use in the American West.

The allure of Santa Fe was simple enough. The mines of Mexico produced an abundance of silver, which was then minted into silver "dollars." What the Mexicans lacked, however, was manufactured items such tools, kitchen utensils, and shoes. Enterprising individuals who could deliver these "trade goods" to Santa Fe could exchange them for Mexican silver, which was correspondingly rare in Missouri and the rest of the United States. Two years earlier, a trader named William Becknell had returned to Missouri after one of the first trading expeditions to Santa Fe, leading a witness to record:

> My father saw them unload when they returned, and when their rawhide packages of silver dollars were dumped on the sidewalk one of the men cut the thongs and the money spilled out and clinking on the stone pavement rolled into the gutter. Everyone was excited and the next spring another expedition was sent out.

That sort of thing gets people's attention. Becknell was reputed to have made a profit of fifteen times his initial investment in trade goods, which by any standards is a pretty fair return. All in all, a trader who managed the 1,600-mile round trip from Missouri to Santa Fe could reasonably expect a profit of five to ten times what he was able or willing to invest. That, in turn, guaranteed that young, ambitious adventurers like Meredith Marmaduke would be willing to risk the long and frequently dangerous trek to Santa Fe.

The principal fear of the young men who made up Marmaduke's trading party was the Comanche and Kiowa Indians who lived along the Santa Fe Trail. As the traders were to find, however, their most formidable adversary would be the land itself and the weather that they encountered. The original Santa Fe Trail headed west from Missouri to a trading post named Bent's Fort near present-day Pueblo, Colorado, before turning south. Marmaduke's company, however, had resolved to take a shorter route along what was known as the "Cimarron Cutoff." This route cut diagonally southwest across the plains of southwestern Kansas to the Cimarron River and took about hundred miles off the distance to Santa Fe. While this route was shorter, it also crossed a landscape that was often devoid of water. The term "Cimarron Cutoff" was not the only name for this stretch of the Santa Fe Trail. It was also known as "the dry route." This aptly named part of the trail is what awaited Marmaduke and his similarly inexperienced companions in 1824.

Meredith Marmaduke is remembered in history because he kept one of the first diaries describing travel over the Santa Fe Trail.[1] Like most diarists, he found keeping his journal a monumental chore, and his entries are typically sparse. Most go something like this:

> June 8. Traveled 14 miles, and encamped on one of the branches of the Little Arkansas; killed 3 buffalo and 1 antelope. An alarm was this evening given by our hunters that several hundred Indians were approaching; a party went out to reconnoiter, and found them to be buffalo.

But at the end of June, something happened that caught Marmaduke's attention:

> Tuesday 29th. Travelled about 30 miles, left our encampment at 4 o'Clock A.M. and travelled without making any halt until about 4 o'Clock P.M., without one drop of water for our horses or mules— by which time many of them were nearly exhausted for want of water, heat and fatigue—and many of the men whose water had been drank early in the day, were also very nearly suffocated for want of water—a dog which had travelled with us during our route, fell this day in the Prairie and expired in a few minutes, such was the extreme heat and suffering of the animals—fortunately, for us all at about

4 o'Clock P.M. a small ravine was discovered, and pursued for a few miles, and after digging in the sand in the bottom of it, water was procured in sufficient quantity to satisfy both man & horses but not until after 5 or 6 wells were sunk—and such was the extreme suffering of the animals, that it was with the utmost difficulty that the horses Could be kept out of the holes until buckets could be filled for them— I have never in all my life experienced a time when such general alarm and Consternation pervaded every person on account of the want of water.

In Marmaduke's opinion, finding this muddy water, which could be reached by scraping holes into a dry streambed, was all that saved the lives of the men and animals in the party. But as it happens, this episode has a larger historical significance. It is entirely possible that these five or six hand-dug holes were the first wells dug by Anglo-Americans to tap the great Ogallala aquifer. The Ogallala Formation of Miocene age makes up a good bit of the aquifer, but other geologic formations are also involved, and so the more proper name of this hydrologic unit is the High Plains aquifer.[2] Marmaduke and his thirsty companions seem to have been the first Anglo-American immigrants to encounter the Ogallala aquifer. This discovery would, in time, prove to be far more valuable then all the silver in Mexico.

Marmaduke can certainly be excused for not recognizing the enormous consequences of this discovery. But the Ogallala aquifer, which extends from South Dakota to New Mexico (fig. 12.1), is one of the most important accumulations of fresh water in the United States. Vast stretches of the High Plains of Nebraska, Kansas, Oklahoma, Texas, and New Mexico are, at land surface anyway, entirely devoid of water. But if you happen to probe below land surface, as did the frantic members of Marmaduke's party, you will find a vast sheet of water-saturated sand and gravel that is the Ogallala aquifer.

The Ogallala aquifer had its beginnings in the latest rising of the Rocky Mountains to the west, which began about 17 million years ago. As these mountains were thrust upward they immediately began to erode, sending vast volumes of sediments washing eastward over the plains. These sediments of sand, silt, clay, and gravel were worked and reworked by streams and rivers flowing out of the mountains. For the last 15 million years or so, these repeated washings progressively removed lighter, finer-grained silts and clays, leaving behind the coarse sands and gravels that make the best aquifers. Over time, the sands and

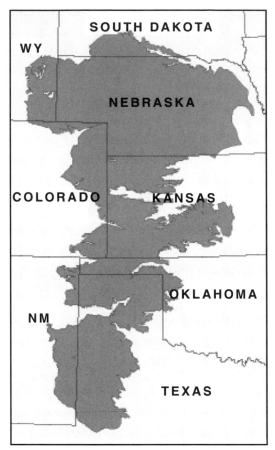

FIGURE 12.1 Extent of the Ogallala aquifer in the United States. Source: U.S. Geological Survey

gravels became saturated with water flowing out of the Rocky Mountains, supplemented by local rainfall as well. This water normally remains hidden below land surface. Its most common manifestation at land surface, however, is as seeps and springs. Much of the Santa Fe Trail in Kansas, Oklahoma, and New Mexico took advantage of springs discharging from the Ogallala aquifer. These springs, having names such as the Lower, Middle, and Upper Springs of the Cimarron River and Cold Spring, were important stopping places along the trail, eagerly anticipated by the thirsty men and animals alike.

The reliance of the Santa Fe traders on ground water seeping from the Ogallala aquifer was natural enough, seeing as it was the only consistent source of water in the area. This reliance on groundwater for sustaining life, however, subtly changed how immigrants to the Southwest thought about water. All the Anglo-American traders who took to the Santa Fe Trail had been raised in the relatively humid climate of the East, and to them seeing water running freely over the land in streams and rivers was as natural as breathing. As they ventured along the Santa Fe Trail, however, they found themselves in a desert where you could walk thirty miles without seeing a single drop of water. The dry riverbeds and washes they passed must have seemed surreal and unnatural to their eyes. Similarly, having to scrape shallow wells in dry streambeds in order to get a drink was a new experience. The Santa Fe traders did not waste time thinking about the strange and exotic ways that water manifested itself along the trail. They scraped their wells, drank the muddy water, watered their horses, and were on their way.

But gradually, over the next hundred years or so, the Anglo-Americans who migrated to the Southwest began to appreciate just how different their water world was from that of the rest of the country. It was not so much that water was *scarce*; rather, it was *invisible*. The surface manifestations of water—rivers, streams, ponds, and lakes—were either absent or much rarer than the settlers were used to. But in the subsurface, which was largely hidden from the eyes of humans, water was actually fairly abundant. The experience of Marmaduke and the Santa Fe traders with the Ogallala aquifer was just one example of this phenomenon. By now, the subsurface nature of the hydrologic cycle in the Southwest has profoundly affected the water consciousness of the people who live there. This, in turn, is of more than just academic interest. It affects the perception and use of drinking water in general and the perceived value of bottled water in particular.

The explanation of the *hydrologic cycle* given in most textbooks goes something like this: Water is evaporated from the oceans by the energy of the sun. This water vapor condenses into clouds, falls as rain or snow onto land, and collects itself into streams and rivers. The water flowing over land surface is universally referred to as *surface water*. A portion of the water falling on the land, however, seeps down below land surface and recharges whatever various geologic formations happen to be there, forming *ground water*. Both surface and ground water are then pulled downhill and downward by the force of gravity, eventually discharging back into the sea (fig. 12.2).

For humans, the part of the hydrologic cycle that is most visible is the rivers and streams flowing over the land surface. Curiously, however,

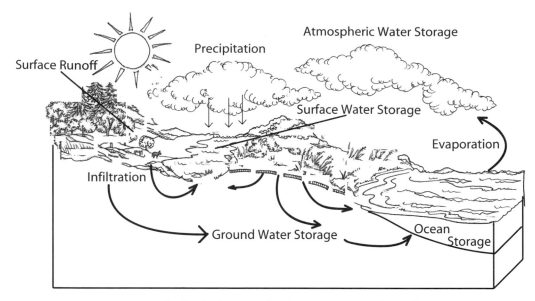

FIGURE 12.2   The hydrologic cycle. Source: U.S. Geological Survey

this highly visible surface water is very much in the minority. If you consider all the fresh water present at any given time in North America, less than 2 or 3% of it resides in rivers or streams. By far the majority of the water is present below land surface, seeping along at a few inches per day in the sediments and rocks that underlie the surface. Because ground water moves so slowly, most of the water discharging back to the ocean (1,300 billion gallons per day, fig. 12.2) is surface water. Thus, while ground water represents a large majority of water *stored* in North America, streams and rivers provide a majority of water *flow*.

In the case of the American Southwest, the surface water component of the hydrologic cycle is highly susceptible to evaporation (fig. 12.2). Whereas annual precipitation in much of the arid Southwest is less then 10 inches per year, the evaporation potential can be as much as 150 inches per year. The net result of this imbalance is that the upper part of the hydrologic cycle—the presence of water flowing in rivers and streams—is cut off for much of the year, effectively removed by evaporation and by seepage into the dry earth. The ground-water component, on the other hand, fed by water seeping into the earth and less affected by evaporation, remains in place. It is, however, largely hidden from human view.

The Ogallala aquifer underlying New Mexico, Texas, Oklahoma, and Kansas is an example of this partially truncated hydrologic cycle. In the higher elevations of New Mexico and Colorado, a fair amount of precipitation falls on a yearly basis, sometimes as much as 30 or 40 inches per year. As this water runs over the landscape, however, it drains into the highly permeable sediments of the Ogallala aquifer, converting from easily observable surface water to hidden ground water. This water continues to seep toward lower elevations, but the surface-water component of the hydrologic cycle is simply missing. Other than the few springs or seeps that pop up when the water table intersects land surface, virtually all the water found in this part of the country occurs below land surface.

The technical problem for the immigrants who moved into Nebraska, Kansas, Oklahoma, and western Texas—an area that was then referred to as the "Great American Desert"—was to somehow access this vast underground reservoir. Most of the early attempts simply mirrored what Marmaduke and his companions did—people simply scraped holes in streambeds and seeps in order to form small basins into which water would collect. But because the Ogallala consists of unconsolidated sands and gravels, and since these are relatively easy to excavate, it was possible to dig shallow wells and line the well walls with laid stone. Such hand-dug wells were not terribly productive, and they were also easily contaminated by human or animal waste, but they worked. Beginning in the 1840s, as American immigrants surged south and west in search of land and gold, hand-dug wells in Kansas became the norm as far as water supply was concerned.

Not all of the hand-dug wells tapping the Ogallala were entirely low-tech affairs. By the 1880s, the era of the oxen-drawn Conestoga wagons was coming to an end, and railroad companies were scrambling to to stake out the most profitable lines. These lines generally followed the old wagon roads, one of which was the Santa Fe Trail. By the 1860s and 1870s, stagecoaches had made their appearance in the Southwest. One of the stage lines in Kansas was owned by a certain Mr. D. R. Green, who established the "Cannon Ball" stagecoach line from Wichita to Dodge City. In addition, Mr. Green's line served points west along the old Santa Fe Trail, one of the stops being in a town that he modestly named Greensburg. By the 1880s, however, it was clear that wagons and stagecoaches were things of the past. The future was going to be in the railroads.

Southwestern Kansas, however, presented some unique challenges for railroads. The general lack of surface water made it difficult to keep the steam locomotives supplied with water. Not a problem, responded the local population of Greensburg; we will dig a well. But not just any well. Because of the need for large volumes of water, the simple small-diameter dug wells used by local farmers were deemed inadequate. Rather, they would dig not just a large well but a very, very large well. This, in turn, would guarantee the kind of water supply needed by railroads.

The "Big Well" of Greensburg, Kansas—reputed to be the largest hand-dug well in the world—was the result. Beginning at land surface with a platform supported by jackscrews, the crews excavated downward into the sands and gravels of the Ogallala aquifer. As the excavation deepened, the jackscrews were lowered and then moved sideways to allow continued excavation. In this way, the platform was gradually lowered into the ground, and the sides of the hole were shorn up with wood planks. Once the water table was encountered, at a depth of about a hundred feet, the sides of the well were cased with laid stone up to land surface. The result was a well 32 feet in diameter, 109 feet deep, and with about 15 feet of water at the bottom. The volume of water stored in a well is given by the equation $V = \pi r^2 d$, where V is the volume of water (cubic feet), r is the well's radius (feet), and d is the depth of water (feet). Given a well radius of 16 feet and a water depth of 15 feet, this translates to 1,222.3 cubic feet, or 9,143 gallons. Nine thousand gallons is a lot of water, and one certainly would expect it to be sufficient to supply steam locomotives with the water they required.

Alas, the Big Well never got to supply the local railroad company—known as the Santa Fe Railroad—with water. A rival company, the Rock Island Railroad, made it to the county line first and won the competition. Accordingly, the railroad line never went through Greensburg. The townspeople were certainly disappointed, but they promptly redirected the Big Well's purpose to becoming their own municipal water supply, which it remained until the 1930s. Historically, however, the Big Well performed—and still performs—the basic function so eagerly pursued by Marmaduke and his well-digging companions in 1824. This was to look below the surface-truncated hydrologic cycle of the Southwest and tap the watery treasure of the Ogallala aquifer. Since the advent of modern drilling technology at the end of the nineteenth century, thousands and thousands of wells have been drilled into the Ogallala aquifer. Today, humans have full access—and in some parts of Texas and Oklahoma perhaps too much access—to the Ogallala. From a historical point of view, however, it is interesting to note that this access began with eighty-three thirsty travelers on the Santa Fe Trail.

When it comes to bottled water, however, the Ogallala aquifer presents certain problems. The problem is not the presence or abundance of springs, which are fairly common throughout the Ogallala's extent. The problem is the chemical quality of the water. Americans generally like drinking water that has fairly low concentrations of total dissolved solids (TDS). Poland Spring water, which since the 1904 World's Exposition in St. Louis has set the standard for American bottled water, has a TDS of about 45 mg/L. In contrast, groundwater produced from the Ogallala aquifer often has a TDS exceeding 200 mg/L, and in parts of Oklahoma and Texas the TDS may be as high as 500 mg/L. Natural spring waters coming from the Ogallala are bottled in some places, but this is rare. Much more commonly, Ogallala waters are chemically treated to lower their TDS and bottled as "drinking waters."

One example of this kind of water is bottled in Clovis, New Mexico, and is aptly named Ogallala Drinking Water. Clovis Bottlers, Inc., which produces Ogallala Drinking Water, uses a fairly standard ten-step process to manufacture its product. The centerpiece of this process is reverse osmosis (RO), which removes dissolved solids from water. Osmosis, you may recall, is the tendency of water molecules to migrate across semipermeable membranes from low-salinity water to higher-salinity water. However, if you artificially pressurize the high-salinity side of the membrane, you can "reverse" this process and make water move to the lower-salinity side. Reverse osmosis is widely used in the bottled water industry to produce low-TDS drinking water from source waters that are not by themselves considered suitable. In the case of many smaller bottlers, however, spring or well waters are used as the source. Clovis Bottlers, for example, uses water from the Ogallala aquifer.

Reverse osmosis, like most water treatment processes, requires multiple steps in order to work properly. The membranes used in the process, for example, are highly sensitive to plugging and must be protected. Clovis bottlers pump water from two Ogallala wells and filter it through a relatively coarse filter (10 microns) to remove large particulate matter that would damage the RO membrane. Second, they use a water softener to replace dissolved iron, manganese, magnesium, and calcium, with sodium. Sodium, as it happens, is easier on the

RO membrane than the other dissolved solids. Next, the sodium-rich water is disinfected by exposure to ultraviolet light (UV) because microorganisms also can clog the membrane. Finally, the water is passed through a fine filter (1 micron) to remove dead microorganisms and any other remaining particulate matter.

Now the water is ready for reverse osmosis, which removes most of the sodium added by the water softener. The water that remains generally has a TDS of less than 10 mg/L and is ready to be stored prior to bottling. The bottling process begins with two more filtering steps, one coarse (10 microns), the other fine (1 micron). Next, the water is disinfected (again) with UV radiation at a wavelength of 254 nanometers. Finally, the water is disinfected (again) with ozone in order to kill bacteria that passed through the filters and survived the UV radiation. It is only now, ten treatment steps later, that the water can be bottled as drinking water.

Clovis Bottlers, Inc., is a typical small operation that serves a distinct niche in the community. Clovis's best customers are the local Native American tribes that allow gambling on their reservations. Clovis produces the drinking water and bottles it with custom labels designed specifically for each casino and/or tribe. This so-called "custom labeling" of both natural and manufactured waters has grown rapidly over the last several years and supports numerous small and medium-size bottled water companies.

The tendency of the hydrologic cycle to be truncated at land surface in the southwestern United States becomes more pronounced as you go west from New Mexico into Arizona, Nevada, Utah, and southern California. Part of this is due to the increasingly dry climate of the area, caused in part by the rain shadow of the Coastal Ranges and the Sierra Nevada in California. But in addition, the distinctive geology of the region plays a role. This part of the country has been extensively faulted over the last 20 million years as the collision between North America and the Pacific Plate has progressed and the Rocky Mountains were thrust upward. In places, blocks of rock have been raised to dizzying heights, causing a series of north-south-trending mountain ranges to develop. In other places, blocks of rock have been dropped lower, creating a series of basins, some of which are today lower then sea level. This "basin and range" geology, when combined with the arid conditions typical of the area, generates hydrologic systems that are confined almost entirely to the subsurface. There are dozens of examples of these truncated hydrologic cycles in the Southwest, created by the distinctive climate and basin-and-range geology. In each case, the local history is inexorably connected with these hydrologic conditions. The city of Phoenix, Arizona, is as good an example of this as any.

The history of Phoenix began long before Columbus made landfall at Española in 1492. As early as A.D. 700, Indians had moved into the Salt River Valley of Arizona and had begun farming the fertile soil they found there. The hydrology of the valley is characterized by water falling as precipitation in the surrounding mountains and collecting into ephemeral streams such as the Salt and the Agua Fria rivers. These rivers, which carry water for only a few weeks of the year, run out onto the valley floor, where the water either evaporates or seeps into the sediments that underlie the valley. These sediments, which are as much as ten thousand feet thick, store vast quantities of groundwater.

The ancestors of the Pueblo Indians who first settled in the valley, however, did not have technology to access this hidden store of water. Instead, they carefully engineered a system of canals to carry the intermittent flow of the Salt River to fields where crops were grown. In years of normal precipitation, this system worked well; they built at least 135 canals that could provide water for the production of crops. However, a devastating drought apparently occurred in the 1400s leading to the abandonment of agriculture. The truncated nature of the hydrologic cycle in the Salt River Valley, where virtually all the available water lies below land surface, was too much for these early Indians. They had to abandon their homes and farms.

The truncated nature of the hydrologic cycle in this part of Arizona also very nearly defeated the first Anglo-American settlers who reached the valley in 1867. Jack Swilling, who had fought for the Confederacy during the Civil War, emulated the earlier Indian practice of diverting water from the Salt River, organizing the Swilling Irrigation Company in 1868. Being a loyal Confederate, Swilling wanted to name the new town Stonewall, after General Thomas "Stonewall" Jackson. Other suggested names for the town included Swilling's Mill, Helling Mill, and Mill City. Finally, a man named Darrell Duppa suggested the name Phoenix, since the new town was springing from the ruins of the former Indian civilization. The new name caught on and was formally recognized in 1868.

With the business of naming the little town settled, it began to grow. The discovery of silver near Tombstone, Arizona, in 1877 led to an influx of miners to the region, who eagerly sought out claims for silver, copper, and gold. Meanwhile, the water resources provided by the Salt River were proving problematic. In wet years, there might be catastrophic floods. In dry years, there was not enough water to go around for growing crops. Building dams on the rivers flowing into the Salt River Valley, which captured and stored water falling in the mountains, helped. What really led to the growth of Phoenix, however, was the discovery of ground water underlying the valley.

With the new drilling technology invented by the fledgling oil industry in the early twentieth century, it suddenly became possible to access the huge reservoir of water that underlay the Salt River Valley. By 1920, these newly drilled wells were producing about 100,000 acre-feet of water per year (an acre-foot is the amount of water needed to flood one acre of land to a depth of one foot and is equal to 325,900 gallons). As agriculture exploded in the valley, especially during the years following World War II, the use of ground water increased to an incredible 2,225,000 acre-feet by 1955. Clearly, tapping the hidden, underground portion of the hydrologic cycle made it possible for Phoenix to grow into the city it is today.

So, with the vast amounts of ground water stored in the desert basins of the Southwest, you might think that they are a natural source for bottled water. To some extent, this is true. People living in the Southwest consume large amounts of bottled water, but most of the natural waters are imported from other regions of the country. What the Southwest does bottle in great quantities is manufactured water. The reasons for this again have to do with the truncated nature of the hydrologic cycle in the basins, human use and reuse of the water that is available, and the resulting effects on ground-water quality.

In a recent study of the water quality of ground water in the Salt River Valley, it was found that the median concentration of total dissolved solids (TDS) was 560 mg/L.[3] That concentration, incidently, exceeds the EPA recommendation of 500 mg/L maximum concentration limit for human drinking water. The lowest TDS concentration measured in the Salt River Valley ground water was 212 mg/L, which is about twice the concentration usually considered suitable for American bottled waters. The maximum measured TDS was an astounding 3,050 mg/L.

The distribution of high-TDS waters was not random but was correlated with recharge to the aquifer that came from irrigation canals and other diversions of surface water. The reason irrigation water has such high TDS concentrations is no particular mystery. In this climate, when water spends any appreciable time at land surface, it begins to evaporate. This, in turn, tends to concentrate whatever dissolved solids are present in the water. Simply by flowing over the land for two or three days before seeping into the earth, the TDS concentration of water may be doubled or tripled. In short, while huge stores of ground water are available in the Salt River Valley and in many other basins in the Southwest, the water quality is not up to the standards most Americans prefer for drinking.

All this illustrates a basic conundrum of the bottled water industry. Americans have particular tastes in drinking water, but much of the water actually available is not up to those standards. The Ogallala aquifer and the basin-and-range aquifers of the Southeast are just the most obvious examples. The fact is, the number of spring and artesian sources that produce water of desirable chemical quality is inherently limited. If bottled water were limited to natural sources, the industry itself would eventually be limited. An obvious alternative is what is practiced by Clovis Bottlers, Inc., which is to use chemical technology to produce a drinking water that mimics the properties of naturally low-TDS spring waters.

This is not a new idea. In the early nineteenth century, when Dr. F. Kreysig and others began applying the new technology of analytical chemistry to spring waters (chapter 3), they were not motivated entirely by intellectual curiosity.[4] Rather, they had the idea that, by knowing what kinds of dissolved solids were present in medicinal spring waters, they could create such waters artificially and sell them. Dr. Kreysig's book is, in many ways, an infomercial for artificially constituted waters concocted by one Dr. Struve of Dresden. Kreysig comments in the preface: "I am bound to bear witness, that Dr. Struve's artificial mineral waters are remedies of the most efficacious kind, and perfect imitations of nature." But, sadly, such artificially constituted mineral waters never really caught on in the nineteenth century. One recurring problem was that the added "minerals" did not dissolve very well, leaving the water appearing cloudy. That, in turn, did not appeal to most water drinkers. The riches that Dr. Kreysig and Dr. Struve doubtlessly hoped for never quite materialized.

By 1994, however, the water market in the world had changed considerably. Bottled water was increasingly popular and profitable. At that time, the bottled water market in America was dominated by low-TDS waters produced predominantly from natural sources. And, as we have seen, these waters are particularly rare in the American Southwest. It was at this point that someone working at Pepsi Cola had an idea similar to the one Dr. Kreysig and Dr. Struve had 170 years earlier. Pepsi's problem, however, was to modify the water by *removing* dissolved solids rather than *adding* them. Accordingly, Pepsi decided to take ordinary tap water from municipal systems, which generally has higher TDS concentrations than many bottled-water drinkers like, and strip out the dissolved solids using reverse osmosis technology. That, in turn, would produce a low-TDS drinking water similar to such waters as Poland Spring. The technology Pepsi used was not new either, being essentially the same as that used by tiny Clovis Bottlers, Inc. Then the water could be packaged in attractive bottles with blue labels—carefully mimicking those used by natural spring waters—and sold through Pepsi's formidable marketing network. Like any new product, the question came up as to where to do the market testing.

The answer was the Southwest.

Pepsi's introduction of Aquafina—as it named its manufactured water product—in 1994 jolted the bottled water industry. Pepsi already had a massive distribution network, and since distribution is the most important part of selling single-serving PET-bottled water, Pepsi was perfectly placed to get into the business. The fact that it also had access to beverage-manufacturing and bottling technology helped as well. But perhaps most important of all, Pepsi had a long tradition of using clever—some would say ruthless—marketing strategies. Aquafina ads poked fun at the elitest image of Evian, Aquafina sponsored the NCAA basketball tournament, Aquafina contributed to the United States' World Cups teams. The idea was to identify Aquafina with a healthy and very American lifestyle. Pepsi also structured its contracts with convenience store owners so that Aquafina was the only bottled water that could be sold out of Pepsi's coolers.

All this worked spectacularly well. By the year 2000, Aquafina had become the number four producer of bottled water in America, with a 7.8% market share.[5] By 2003, Aquafina was the best-selling bottled water in America, with 11.3% market share.[6] In essence, Pepsi Cola had realized Dr. Kreysig's dream, conceived in the 1820s, of manufacturing drinking water and making a lot of money doing it.

But while naturally occurring low-TDS spring waters are rare in the Southwest, they are not absent entirely. Furthermore, they often occur in unusual and unexpected places. Consider, for example, Death Valley, California.

The hydrologic story of Death Valley, at least for Anglo-American immigrants, can be traced to 1849, when gold was discovered in California. The road west to California began in Missouri and actually shared parts of the old Santa Fe Trail before heading northwest. In the fall of 1849, about hundred wagonloads of immigrants struggled into Salt Lake City intent on reaching California. The problem was, it was too late in the year to make it through the Donner Pass. The Donner party had become stranded at the pass just a few years earlier (1846), and the memory of that disaster was still fresh in people's minds. These forty-niners would have to wait for spring to continue their journey.

This put the little town of Salt Lake City in a bind. The year's agricultural surplus was sufficient to feed the townspeople and their livestock for the winter, but they had not counted on four hundred additional mouths to feed. The Mormon fathers of the town were as compassionate as anyone to the stranded immigrants, but they could see that having them stay for the winter might lead to disaster. Fortunately, there was an experienced guide in Salt Lake by the name of Jefferson Hunt who had twice traveled over the "Old Spanish Road" leading to California and the little town of Los Angeles. The city founders convinced Hunt to guide the immigrants south. This would relieve pressure on the fragile economy of Salt Lake City, and it would save time for the travelers, who were desperate to reach the goldfields of California. So, in November of 1849, about hundred wagons and four hundred people left Provo, Utah, heading for Los Angeles.

Because of his long experience, Jefferson Hunt knew better than to try to hurry. The deserts ahead would not provide much feed for the oxen, and it was far better to take a leisurely pace rather than exhaust the animals at the beginning of the trek. But the gold seekers did not want to wait. They wanted to get to California fast. Rather then going south, they wanted to go west. So-called cutoff trails, much like the Cimarron Cutoff of the Santa Fe Trail, were always the subject of speculation among immigrants. And, as it happened, the wagon train was overtaken by a mule pack train headed due west for the goldfields whose owners intended to go through the "Walker Pass" of the Sierra Nevada. That was enough for the impatient immigrants. About fifty wagons forsook Captain Hunt and followed the mule train west, directly into Death Valley.[7]

Contrary to what you might think, water is actually fairly abundant in Death Valley, as it often is in basin-and-range terrains. The basin that is Death Valley collects rainfall and snowmelt in the surrounding mountains over an area of about 8,700 square miles of California and Nevada. Even though rainfall averages only four or five inches per year, if you take that much water over an area 8,700 square miles, it adds up to a lot. Probably less then 5% of this water recharges the underlying geologic units and begins to move toward the floor of the valley, but even that is a lot of water. As this water seeps downward, it intersects the various faults that formed the valley in the first place, rising to the surface as springs. The most spectacular example of this is found at the foot of the Funeral Range, where springs provide large quantities of warm but drinkable water. All in all, the impatient immigrants who wandered into Death Valley in 1849 actually could count on finding isolated springs in most parts of the valley.

But the presence of springs did not mean that their water supply problems were solved. The immigrants quickly learned that the mule trail they had counted on could not accommodate their Conestoga wagons. Furthermore, many of the springs they found were merely seeps that produced only dribbles of water. This, in turn, meant that it was impossible for all of the fifty or so wagons to stay together in one group. The spotty availability of water, and the equally spotty availability of grass for the oxen, meant that the wagons had to separate in order to survive. And separate they did, with various groups heading in different directions, each of which adopted different survival techniques.

Not all these survival techniques proved to be effective. One group of eleven young, unmarried men abandoned their wagons and resolved to hike through Walker Pass unencumbered by anything other than what they could carry. That proved to be a mistake. Although there was water to be had from various springs along the way, the springs were too far apart. A man on foot could not carry enough water to stay hydrated and healthy in this desert environment. In the end, nine of the eleven men died on the journey. You might think that such young, healthy, strong men would be the most likely to survive the rigors of Death Valley. Their choice of a water-carrying strategy, however—hand-carried bottles and canteens—doomed them. In the 1860s, miners in the Argus Range west of Death Valley reported finding the skeletons of the men who had made up the "lost patrol," huddled in a circle apparently trying to shelter from the wind.[8] How the two survivors escaped is still a matter shrouded in mystery. In later years, neither of the two men could bear to speak about their ordeal.

The immigrants who held on to their wagons fared better then the "lost patrol." One important reason for this was that their wagons carried water barrels, and this carefully stored water could sustain the travelers as they trudged between the isolated springs in the valley. There were several different groups of wagons. One group from Kansas was known as the "Jayhawkers," another was the "Georgians," and another group is generally referred to as the "family wagons."[9] One family of this group, the Wade family, deserves particular mention. Of all the immigrants, the Wades learned to manage the water supply problem most efficiently and effectively.

Several things about the Wades were unusual. For one thing, they were not American but English. And although their four children had been born in America, the Wades all thought of themselves as being English. They certainly had the quiet, bulldog determination of the breed. For another thing, Mr. and Mrs. Wade did not particularly care to socialize with the other immigrants. As the trek through Death Valley progressed, the Wades, their four children, and the two teamsters they employed became more and more self-sufficient. When the rest of the family wagons finally ground to a halt, thwarted by the towering heights of the Slate Range, the Wades continued plodding to the south. Two intrepid scouts, Lewis Manly and John Rogers, went ahead of the marooned family wagons promising to return with help, which they eventually did against overwhelming odds. The Wades, however, considered Manly and Rogers's chance of success to be too small and preferred to rely on their own system of travel.

The system that the Wades developed as conditions worsened consisted of stopping at whatever water hole or spring could be found and sending out scouts to find the next water hole. Only after a new source had been located, and the information communicated back by means of signal fires, did the Wades fill their water kegs and plod on to the next water hole.[10] In this way, the Wades made their way southward, eventually crossing the Old Spanish Road, which was now well marked by the passage of Jefferson Hunt's wagons a few weeks earlier. Of the fifty or so wagons that entered Death Valley in 1849, the Wade wagon was the only one that made it to Los Angeles intact. All the other survivors had to walk out. This was partly because of the Wades' dogged, determined approach to travel. But it also reflected their solution to the water supply problem. Their success, which contrasts markedly with the failure of the "lost patrol," involved many different factors. One factor was the Wades' approach to finding and—just as important, storing—supplies of water.

Much of the spring water encountered by the Death Valley immigrants in 1849 had water quality problems similar to those found in the Salt River Valley of Arizona and indeed most of the Basin-and-Range Province of the Southwest. However, some of the spring waters emanating from the high altitudes on the flanks of the basins are relatively unmineralized and produce delightful drinking water. In Death Valley, for example, springs producing low-TDS water are found on the flanks of the Panamint Mountains. The remoteness of these locations, however, precludes bottling this water. In other parts of southern California, however, the interaction of mountains with the local climate produces similar good-quality waters that are used for bottling. The fact that these waters are rarer than bottling-quality waters in other parts of the country actually increases the value of the sources that can be used. Take, for example, Mount Palomar in southern California.

The name Palomar refers to the flocks of band-tailed pigeons that live on the mountain of the same name; it seems to mean something close to "pigeon house" in the language of the local Native Americans. Mount Palomar itself is an isolated mountain that rises to an elevation of 6,126 feet above sea level. The elevation difference between the mountain and the surrounding deserts produces an almost magical transformation in climate. As you climb Mount Palomar on California S7, the landscape begins as a sagebrush desert, transforming first to grassland and then to pine forests as you go higher. Finally, as you get to the crest of the mountain, the forest turns into a lush canopy dominated by oak trees. For many hundreds of years before the Spanish padres and Anglo-Americans arrived in the vicinity, these oak trees produced acorns, a staple food for the local Pauma, Yipeche, La Joya, Potrero, Rincon, Pala, Pechanga, Aguanga, Puerta La Cruz, and Puerta Nofia Indians. The sheer number of Indian tribes that lived nearby is ample testament to just how productive these oak forests were. The Indians gathered the acorns during the fall, ground them into flour using mortars and pestles, and carried the flour down to the valley below for their winter food supply.[11]

The oak forest that covers Mount Palomar reflects the basin-and-range hydrology of the area. During El Niño years, when moisture is abundant, it is not unusual for Mount Palomar to receive fifty or sixty inches of precipitation. Even in non-El Niño years Mount Palomar will get thirty inches of precipitation. This abundant water, in turn, allows the growth of the water-loving oak trees. Mount Palomar is underlain mostly by granites that, near land surface anyway, tend to be highly fractured. These fractures collect the melting snowpack in the spring, diverting meltwater from the surface and pulling it downhill. As these fractures intersect land surface on the flanks of the mountain; the water feeds dozens of springs. This water, which probably has a residence time in the granite aquifer of less then a few years, is largely unmineralized and is perfect for the low-TDS taste of American bottled water consumers.

But while this water is perfect for bottling, getting it to market is a major challenge. For one thing, most of Mount Palomar is either national forest property or Indian reservations. There is literally nowhere to locate a private bottling plant. Springs, and boreholes tapping into the granite fractures feeding the springs, however, do not take up much room. Over the years, one bottling method that has been developed involves filling specially designed tankers with water and transporting the water to bottling plants in more convenient locations. Mt. Palomar water, for example, is pumped from wells on the mountain, transported thirty-five miles to the town of Escondido, on the desert floor, by specially designed tanker trucks and bottled there. This, in turn, is the most common practice for bottling water in much of the Southwest. Locating bottling plants on the ranges where precipitation falls and where spring waters of sufficient quality exist is often not economically practical. Collecting spring waters in the mountains and transporting them to bottling plants, as is done by Mt. Palomar and by Arrowhead as well, is a more common practice. Although the geology and hydrology of the western and southwestern United States limits the availability of high-quality spring waters suitable for bottling, they are there.

And their scarcity makes them all the more desirable.

13 SILVER CLOUDS BELOW
California and the Pacific Northwest

By nature and necessity, Jean de La Pérouse was a cautious man. In this year of 1786 his two tall ships were marvels of modern technology, but they still moved at the whim of wind and tide. Furthermore, La Pérouse was in unknown waters, sailing south along the coast of Oregon and northern California. The unknown was something he and his crew were used to by now, having explored and mapped in the Pacific Ocean for the last few years. The experience of being utterly alone on a vast and sometimes hostile ocean had taught La Pérouse that it was not wise to take chances. Nevertheless, there before him was the unexplored coast of California, and he very much wanted to see it. As it happened, his wish would be fulfilled.

On September 6, La Pérouse wrote in his ship's log:

> At two o'clock we were about a league distant from Cape Blanco [a league is about 3 miles], which bore north-east by east. I continued to run along the land, standing to the south-south-east. At the distance of three or four leagues, we perceived only the summits of the mountains above the clouds. . . . Uncertain of the direction of the coast, which had never been explored, I kept under an easy sail to the south-south-west.

In other words, although La Pérouse wanted to look at the land, he was not going to risk his ships to do it. Furthermore, the clouds and mists that regularly blanket the coast of northern California were rolling in, making it dangerous to approach the coast.

The next day, however, clearing weather and curiosity led Pérouse to try again. This time, he was rewarded by a strange and awe inspiring sight. His ship's log reads:

> I continued to steer so as to get nearer the land, from which I was only four leagues distant at the approach of night. We then perceived

a volcano on the summit of the mountain which bore east from us. The flame was very vivid; but a thick fog soon concealed it from our sight. Deeming it prudent again to increase our distance from the land, as I was apprehensive, that, by following a course parallel to the coast, I might fall in with some rock. . . .

La Pérouse and his men, entirely by chance, were the first Europeans to observe an erupting volcano in the Cascade Range.[1] It is not clear which mountain was erupting at the time, but it probably was Mount Shasta. Given his recorded position near Eureka, California, and standing a few miles out to sea, he would have been able to see a major eruption at either Mount Shasta or Mount Lassen. But, alas, the fogs rolled in again and the cautious La Pérouse continued south, making landfall at Monterey on September 15. Fortunately, following this particular voyage, La Pérouse sent his logs and charts to Paris for eventual publication. If he had not this glimpse of the active volcanoes that characterize the American Northwest would have been lost forever. Two years later, La Pérouse sailed off into the South Pacific to continue his explorations and was never seen again.

The unknown can be dangerous, even when you are careful.

The volcanoes that form the Cascade Mountains of the American Northwest are notable for their frequent eruptions, the violence of those eruptions, and their sheer physical beauty. There are few sights more awe-inspiring then seeing Mount Hood or Mount Rainer from the air, where their peaks often stand well above the clouds. In the 1960s, this sentiment was captured by the poet John Denver when he sang about climbing the Cascade Mountains and seeing the silver clouds below.

The clouds are an important a part of the story. When moisture-laden air sweeping off the Pacific Ocean encounters the Cascades, it is pushed upward thousands of feet. As the air rises and cools, clouds form, and the resulting precipitation blankets the landscape with rain and snow. This rainfall and snowmelt collects into streams and rivers, giving the Pacific Northwest one of the most reliable and abundant sources of water in the world.

It is fitting, therefore, that the name "Cascades" given to the mountain range refers directly to water. When Lewis and Clark reached the Northwest in 1804, they were carried down the Columbia River on the last leg of their journey to the Pacific Ocean. This wild ride, which for the next thirty years was the only known route to the Pacific from the

Missouri Territories, began to be referred to as "the cascade." It was just one more step to call the surrounding mountains, and particularly the volcanic peaks, the Cascade Mountains. They have been called that ever since.

We have already seen how springs have a powerful affect on the human imagination. Mountains, with their lonely isolation and dangerous beauty, have a remarkably similar affect. Whether it was Moses on Mount Sinai, Satan tempting Jesus on a mountaintop, the Hindus venerating Kailas, or the Japanese revering Mount Fuji, mountains have always been associated with the divine in human imagination. It is not too surprising, therefore, that the snow-covered beauty of the Cascades should inspire these feelings as well. But when you factor in the fiery power, the awe-inspiring terror, and the sheer magnificence of volcanic eruptions, the impact on the human psyche can be profound.

Consider, for example, Mount Shasta.

There are numerous springs on the flanks of Mount Shasta and the surrounding peaks, (as on all the volcanoes that make up the Cascade Range). These mountains, and the springs they produce, were important to the numerous tribes of Native Americans who lived in the vicinity of Mount Shasta. As such, it was natural that these people required an explanation as to their origin. One traditional Native American story, which speaks to these origins, goes something like this:

Long ago, when the Great Spirit lived in the heavens, he decided to create the world. To do so, he used a sharp stone as an auger and bored a hole in the sky. He then poured snow and ice through the hole until he had created a great mountain—Mount Shasta—that reached nearly to heaven. With the mountain built, the Great Spirit then stepped down upon the newly made earth and proceeded to create life. He pressed his fingers into the ground here and there causing the first trees to appear. He then made the sun shine in order to melt the snow and ice so the water could nourish the trees. He then gathered some of the leaves of the trees and breathed on them, making the first birds. The Great Spirt also gathered sticks fallen from the trees and broke them into pieces. The small pieces became small animals such as mice and rabbits. The medium pieces became larger animals like deer and elk. But the largest pieces of all became the largest of all animals: the grizzly bear. The grizzly was such a magnificent creature that the Great Spirit gave it dominion over all the other plants and animals that had been created. With his creation complete, the Great Spirit hollowed out Mount

Shasta and made it his wigwam. Bringing his family down from heaven to live there, he started a fire to keep them warm. The smoke from the Great Spirit's fire could be seen coming out of the top of Mount Shasta for miles around.

One winter, when it was especially cold and windy, a great storm blew off the ocean and began to rage around Mount Shasta. During the storm, the fire hole in his wigwam's roof became blocked, and the Great Spirit sent his daughter up to clear it so the smoke from their fire could escape. Before she went, he sternly warned his daughter not to look out, lest the North Wind should seize her. The little girl did as she was told, but as she reached the summit, her curiosity got the best of her and she eased her head out to look at the world. When she did, the North Wind grabbed hold of her hair, dragged her out of the mountain, and sent her tumbling down the side in the ice and snow. The little girl lost consciousness as she fell, finally coming to rest at the base of the mountain.

As it happened, an old grizzly bear was hunting near the base of the mountain and came across the unconscious girl. Being a kind bear, the grizzly gently picked her up and carried her home in his arms. In those days, grizzly bears walked upright on their hind legs, used their paws like hands, and spoke to each other. The grizzly's wife soon grew to love the little girl, nursed her at her own breast, and raised her like her own cubs. After many years, the little girl grew into a radiant young maiden, the grizzlies' oldest son fell in love with her, and the couple were married. Their children, the offspring of the Great Spirit and the grizzly bear, became the first people. This family lived happily for many years at the base of Mount Shasta.

But as the years went on, the mother grizzly, who had raised the Great Spirit's daughter to womanhood, grew old and was coming to the end of her life. Before she died, the mother grizzly knew she should tell the Great Spirit that his daughter was alive and well. Accordingly, she sent a grandson up above the clouds to tell the Great Spirit. When the Great Spirit learned that his beloved daughter was alive, he was wild with joy and rushed down the mountain to find her. So great was his speed as he ran down the mountain that he melted snow and ice in his path and caused springs to issue forth from the ground.[2]

That was the origin of Mount Shasta's springs.

This story is properly classified as a myth. A myth is a traditional story whose purpose is to explain otherwise inexplicable natural phenomena. This particular myth addresses the origin of Mount Shasta, its springs, and the origin of humanity as well, putting each of these phenomena in a context that Native American people could understand. Furthermore, the myth allays fear. In this day and age of scientific sophistication, it is hard to imagine just how terrifying an active volcano must have been to prehistoric people. Fear is an uncomfortable emotion, and it is not one that humans like to live with. One solution to this problem would be to simply move away from the volcanoes, and doubtless some Native Americans did just that. However, that would also mean doing without the abundant water, fertile land, and game-filled forests that surrounded the mountain. Another solution would be to learn to live with the fear. And the best way to live with fear is to understand its source. Having traditional stories that explain puzzling and dangerous natural phenomena, thereby assuaging the fear they engender, is a basic human coping mechanism that is practiced in every culture of the world.

If you think about it like that, the story of the Great Spirit and Mount Shasta explains a lot. For example, it explains why the mountain was made in the first place (so the Great Spirit could step down from heaven), it explains why the mountain was observed to smoke (it was the fire of the Great Spirit's wigwam), and it explains the presence of the ever-important springs (a remnant of the Great Spirit's charge down the mountain to find his long-lost daughter). Finally, as is common in myths, it suggests the comforting notion that people are descended from the Great Spirit himself. By tying all this together in an understandable, comforting framework, it helped ease the anxiety about living near a volcano. Moreover, it is a cracking good story, one that a skillful storyteller could use to mesmerize the village children and their parents as well. But more than anything, this story gave comfort to people living in a mysterious, dangerous, and confusing world. As such, this myth was a lot more than an amusing story. It was an important part of the Native Americans' survival strategy.

Another explanation as to the origin of Mount Shasta and its springs has to do with the semisolid, relatively thin (that is, a few kilometers thick), and ever moving plates of rock that cover the surface of the earth.[3] The interior of the earth—which includes the upper and lower mantle, and the inner and outer core—contains significant amounts of radioactive elements. As these elements decay over time they produce heat. This heat, in turn, is dissipated by driving convection cells (circulating currents of hot fluid) in the mantle. These convection cells, in turn, slowly move the plates that make up the earth's crust, and these plates move in various directions relative to each other. A few hundred miles off the coast of Washington and Oregon, for example, these forces are pushing the Juan de Fuca Plate toward the North America Plate. Because the rocks making up the floor of the Pacific are denser than the rocks making up North America, the seafloor is being *subducted*, or pushed underneath, North America. As these rocks are subducted, they partially melt beneath North America, producing water-laden magma (molten rock). This newly created magma then rises toward land surface, where it occasionally erupts as volcanoes. Farther south, off of the coast of California, the smaller Gorda Plate is also being pushed under North America. Material derived from the Gorda Plate has partially melted at depth, pushed to land surface, and created volcanic mountains at Mono Lake, Mount Lassen, and Mount Shasta.

As you might expect, the production and eruption of molten rock varies over time. Because of this, Mount Shasta is not one volcano but several.[4] The oldest volcanic rocks in the area are dated to about 500,000 years ago, and different cones have been forming in slightly different places ever since. Over time, these cones have been variously eroded and modified by subsequent volcanic eruptions. The oldest cone, called the Sargent's Ridge Cone, has been subjected to several periods of glaciation and erosion and is barely visible. More recent eruptions have produced separate cones called Cinder Cone, Black Butte, and, most spectacularly, Shastina. The present summit of Mount Shasta, called the Holcum Cone, began forming only about 8,000 years ago. Since then, it has erupted about ten times. The most recent eruption, in the late eighteenth century, was probably the one witnessed by La Pérouse in 1786.

This long and complex geologic history affects the hydrology of the region as well. Snow falling on Mount Shasta supports the presence of five small glaciers. The snow and ice, however, periodically melts, often resulting in catastrophic landslides. Shasta Valley, for example, is underlain by the remnants of several of these landslides.[5] Less catastrophically, snow melting in the highlands seeps into the underlying volcanic rocks and flows downward beneath land surface. The rocks that form from the thick and viscous lavas that erupt from the Cascades volcanoes tend to be highly fractured and porous. Sometimes, the surface of a lava flow solidifies first, forming a hard crust under which molten lava continues to flow. This, in turn, forms "lava tubes" that, once the lava cools and becomes solid rock, are natural conduits for flowing water. Where these conduits intersect land surface, springs develop. Because the water issuing from these springs is fairly young—after all, it is largely melted snow—it has not dissolved very much of the surrounding volcanic rock. This combination of circumstances produces cool, crisp water that contains little in the way of dissolved solids or microorganisms. The town of Dunsmuir, nestled on the western flank of Mount Shasta, gets its water supply from the lava tube–fed Mossbrae Springs, advertising it as "the best water in the world." Not surprisingly, this water has been bottled and sold over the years as well, most recently under the name Vasa Natural Spring Water.

That was the origin of Mount Shasta's springs.

This story, which explains the creation of both Mount Shasta and the surrounding springs, is the result of scientific rationality, and most modern Americans would not consider it a myth at all. Interestingly, however, this story has several features characteristic of myths. It certainly explains the presence of Mount Shasta and its springs, putting them in a context that people can understand. It also is entertaining. The idea of plates colliding, the seafloor diving underneath North America, the production of molten lava, and the eruptions of fiery, destructive volcanoes has all the drama of any myth. The story is also comforting. The knowledge that the source of the volcano's destructive power is a predictable natural phenomenon, unrelated to the arbitrary anger of malevolent spirits, has removed a good bit of fear people otherwise would feel.

Just like the Native Americans before them, people living in the Pacific Northwest have to deal with the certain knowledge that Cascades volcanoes erupt regularly, that they sometimes explode, and that these explosions can kill people. The eruption of Mount St. Helens in 1980 was just the most recent example of this. Living with this ever present danger is bearable, however, if the cause is understood. Most people who live near Cascades volcanoes are aware of the potential danger, but they have a good bit of *faith* that scientists will give them ample warning of any impending eruptions. The people living near Mount St. Helens, for example, had weeks of warning before the final explosion, and most of them wisely left in time.

The operative word here is faith. It is entirely true that the geologic history of Mount Shasta has been painstakingly assembled over the years by geologists employing rigorously rational methods. But rationality, for all its usefulness, never eliminates uncertainty. The warnings about the imminent eruption on Mount St. Helens were indeed accurate, but only to a point. Everybody expected and assumed that the volcano would erupt *upward*, where the cone vent was. None of the volcanologists monitoring the mountain, for all their technical skill, could have predicted that the mountain would explode *sideways* in the direction that it did. When the mountain did explode, the sideways blast caught an unfortunate number of people by surprise, and this contributed significantly to the death toll of fifty-seven.

But while the rational, geologic "story" of Mount St. Helens does not explain everything, it does explain a lot. It explains why the Northwest has so many explosive volcanoes and why other parts of the country do not. It explains how these volcanoes are related to the plate movements that cause earthquakes along the west coast. It explains why there is not just a single cone at each mountain but many smaller cones as well. Most important, it provides a framework within which future eruptions can be predicted. Numerous seismometers constantly monitor earth movements in the Cascades that could spell new eruptions, and it is highly unlikely that one will take us by surprise. Finally, this story has the more modest benefit that it explains the excellent drinking waters produced by the springs on the flanks of Cascades volcanoes.

This spring water affects the ebb and flow of the bottled water industry in many ways, but one of the more interesting has to do with the perennial competition between Pepsi and Coke. In chapter 12 we saw how Pepsi stole a march on its rival to grab a profitable foothold in the business of PET-bottled drinking water beginning in 1994. Coca-Cola, long used to being number one in the U.S. beverage industry, was not amused and immediately began plotting ways to compete with Pepsi. Pepsi's Aquafina, by virtue of its earlier entrance into the market, held a significant sales lead (7.8% market share) over Coca-Cola's Dasani drinking water (3.7% market share) in 2000.[6] Clearly, Coca-Cola faced a formidable uphill battle to catch up if it simply tried to imitate Pepsi's product.

One obvious approach was for Coca-Cola to create a drinking water product that was different from, and hopefully better than, Aquafina. Coca-Cola decided that, in addition to using reverse osmosis to lower TDS concentrations, it would add a "proprietary" formulation of minerals that would make the water taste better. The result was Dasani, which was introduced in 1999. But Coca-Cola did not stop there. In 2003, it made a strategic alliance with DS Waters of North America, which was named CCDS. With this alliance in hand, Coca-Cola began selling DS bottled spring waters (which includes Ginnie Springs of Florida) along with Dasani in the thousands of coolers it owned across the country. This enabled Coca-Cola to compete directly with Pepsi in the manufactured drinking water business (Dasani versus Aquafina), but it also brought spring water into the picture. Doubtlessly, Coca-Cola had marketing research indicating that some percentage of the market had a preference for natural spring waters. Adding DS's spring waters to Coca-Cola's formidable marketing network was one very good way to capture market share from Pepsi. Furthermore, this would help DS Waters compete with its rival Nestlé. All in all, it was a very clever marketing ploy.

And as it happened, one of the first spring waters to show up in Coca-Cola's coolers was Crystal Geyser, once an independent bottler now in the fold of DS Waters. One of the sources of Crystal Geyser spring water is in the little town of Mount Shasta, nestled high on the western flank of the volcano.

Unlike Jean de La Pérouse, Sam Brannan was not a cautious man. He had been born in 1819, the son of a respectable Irish farmer who had settled in Maine. Farming, however, was too tame for young Sam, who early on decided to take up the printer's trade. At the age of twenty-three, Sam moved to New York, where he became the publisher of a Mormon newspaper. Not one to quibble about theology, Sam adopted the Mormon faith in order to secure the publisher's position.[7]

The 1840s were not a happy time for the Church of Latter-Day Saints. Moving from place to place, the Mormons were systematically persecuted everywhere they tried to settle. When their prophet Joseph Smith was murdered by a mob, it became clear that the Mormons needed to find a more congenial place to live. Brannan, along with Brigham Young, were named to lead expeditions westward. Brigham Young chose to go overland toward Utah. Brannan, on the other hand, opted to charter a ship to go to California. In 1846, Brannan and 236 men, women, and children embarked from New York on the steamship *Brooklyn* headed around South America to Yerba Buena, a tiny hamlet that would later take the name of San Francisco.

Once in California, Brannan's band went right to work building a new life for themselves, their families, and their church. For his part, Brannan went into the newspaper business, founding the *California Star* in 1849. This was a fortunate turn of events because it was just in time to report the discovery of gold. In fact, several of Brannan's Mormons were working at John Sutter's mill when the discovery was made. Brannan had no interest in digging gold, but he was perfectly placed to tell the world about it in his newspaper. Furthermore, he had the foresight to buy up many shovels, pans, clothing, and other items the miners would need. It was a classic. Brannan's newspaper stories enticed a flood of fortune seekers to California's new goldfields. Once they arrived, Brannan sold the newcomers the supplies and equipment they would need to go dig it up. Soon, Brannan had four stores, cornering a good deal of the retail market in San Francisco. Between the newspaper, the stores, and other erudite real estate investments, Brannan rapidly acquired wealth. By 1850, he had become one of California's first millionaires, a distinction of wealth that was far rarer in the nineteenth century than it is now.

Like many of the newly rich of the California Gold Rush, Brannan found it something of a challenge figuring out what to do with his sudden wealth. Never one to sit still, he took his wife, Ann Eliza, and their four children to Europe. As was the custom in those days, Brannan's family spend a good bit of time at various spas and baths. Brannan apparently enjoyed the easy splendor and sophistication of these "watering places." On his way back home, he also happened to visit Saratoga Springs, New York, then the finest and most exclusive spa in the United States. All this made an enormous impression on him. And, as it happened, it set the stage for the next great quest of his life.

Upon returning to California in 1851, Brannan became interested in some hot springs that had been discovered in the northern Napa Valley at the foot of Mount St. Helena. These hot springs had been a favorite of the local Native Americans, who valued them for their medicinal properties, calling them names such as "Tu-la-ha-lu-si" (the beautiful land) or "Coo-lay-no-maock" (the oven place). With hot springs and spas being so fashionable in Europe and in the eastern United States, Brannan was quick to see the potential for building a resort near the burgeoning new city of San Francisco. His grand vision was to build a "Saratoga of the Pacific" that would be the equal of any spa in Europe or America.[8]

In 1859, Brannan acquired two thousand acres of land surrounding the springs and went to work. By the time the spa opened in 1862, he had built a hotel and twenty-five cottages. All this was done on a magnificent scale suitable to the taste of wealthy San Franciscans, who then eagerly embraced the European concept of "taking the waters." The story of how the spa got its name may not be entirely true, but it is too good not to repeat. One day, Brannan, who by now was no longer a Mormon (he seems not to have paid his tithes), was drinking whiskey with some of his friends, telling them about his grandiose plans. The hot-spring resort he was building, he said, would be superior even to New York's

Saratoga. Deep in his cups, he raised his arms and declared, "I will make it the Calistoga of Sarafornia." Blinking, he considered the spoonerism he had just uttered. "Calistoga, Calistoga!" he cried. "That's it."

It has been Calistoga ever since.

The same geologic processes of subduction and partial rock melting that formed the Cascades and the Coastal Ranges of California, Oregon, and Washington also created hundreds of hot springs in the Pacific Northwest. The Napa Valley of California is a structural trough, underlain by fractured rocks that make a conduit for bringing deep, hot waters to land surface at a variety of places including Calistoga. There is a description of these springs written by the author and poet Robert Louis Stevenson in 1880. Stevenson suffered from tuberculosis and had come to California for his health. While visiting the upper Napa Valley, he and his wife spent some time at the site of the abandoned Silverado Mine near Calistoga. He later wrote about his impressions of the area in a little book titled *Silverado Squatters*. In this book, Stevenson describes the hot springs as follows:

> The whole neighbourhood of Mount Saint Helena is full of sulphur and of boiling springs. The Geysers are famous; they were the great health resorts of the Indians before the coming of the whites. Lake County is dotted with spas; Hot Springs and White Sulphur Springs are the names of two stations on the Napa Valley railroad; and Calistoga itself seems to repose on a mere film above a boiling, subterranean lake.[9]

In the past, these thermal waters had seeped through the underlying sediments to form pools of mud and hot water. Native Americans greatly valued these hot mud baths for their medicinal benefits. Beginning with Bannan's spa, however, the waters were collected first by conduits and later by drilled boreholes to more efficiently control the hot waters. Also, Brannan managed to build a railroad from San Francisco to Calistoga at considerable public expense. With the railroad came thousands of visitors. Against all odds, Calistoga had succeeded.

But Brannan's lack of caution finally cost him. He had a tendency to drink too much whiskey, and a tendency to dally with women other than his patient but proud wife. In 1870, Ann Eliza's patience ran out. She divorced him and received half of his estate in settlement. That, in turn, forced Brannan to sell his holdings in Calistoga at a considerable loss. Brannan latter declared that Calistoga "was the greatest business mistake which eventually contributed to my financial downfall."

When Brannan died in 1889, it was said that he was "penniless but owed no man."

The unknown can be dangerous, especially when you're not careful.

Like much of what goes on in California, the history of bottling the mineral waters of Calistoga differs considerably from that of the eastern United States. After the introduction of chlorination in eastern cities beginning in 1913, the use and popularity of bottled water declined precipitously. In California, however, the mineral waters from the springs of the upper Napa Valley were still held in high esteem. Furthermore, the many visitors to the springs often came away with a taste for mineral waters. The fact that they were widely considered to be good for the health was also a factor. So, beginning in 1919, a woman by the name of Maude Luella Akerman and some of her friends started the Calistoga Bottling Works and began supplying San Francisco with Calistoga water. This may have been the first woman-owned water-bottling company ever to go into the business in the United States, which is an interesting testament to changing social mores in the early twentieth century. The fact that this was done by independent-minded Californians, who often seem to be on the cusp of social change, is no particular surprise.

Over the next several years, many of the various health spas in the Napa Valley started similar operations. There was Vichy Springs (Napa County), Samuel Soda Bottling Works (St. Helena), C. Somps Mineral Water (Napa County), Aetna Mineral Water, Priest's Natural Soda, and Tolenas Soda Water, to name a few. These days, the principal remains of these now defunct bottling operations are the distinctive glass bottles they produced, which are highly prized by bottled collectors. One such mineral-water entrepreneur, named Giuseppe Musante, started the Calistoga Mineral Water Company in 1920 and began delivering his water to the state fair in Sacramento in a ramshackle old truck. His hard work and perseverance were soon rewarded. Giuseppe's water won two gold medals for "Purity and Excellence" in 1924 and 1925 at the state fair.

It is safe to say that the market for mineral water—defined as having a total dissolved solids content of greater than 250 mg/L—is not very large in the United States these days. Since 1995, sales of "sparkling water," or naturally carbonated waters such as Saratoga Springs and Calistoga, have decreased precipitously. The reason, of course, is the continued American taste for low-TDS drinking waters. In the year 2000, "sparkling waters" accounted for less than 3% of the volume of domestic bottled waters.[10] This decline has put significant pressure on all bottlers of mineral waters, including America's oldest bottled water, Saratoga Springs. But here again, California has run against the national trend. There is a small but devoted following of Calistoga Sparkling Mineral Water in the Pacific Northwest. As is the case in much of Europe, this mineral water is prized for its unique taste, and, with a twist of lime, it is often used as a substitute for alcoholic drinks at fashionable cocktail parties.

Consistent with its corporate strategy to acquire springs with a long and interesting history, Nestlé now owns Calistoga Sparkling Mineral Water. Nestlé, in turn, has built a high-volume state-of-the-art bottling plant to carry on the tradition of bottling Calistoga mineral waters. Significantly, however, most of the water volume bottled at this plant is low-TDS spring water collected in the mountains surrounding the Napa Valley, transported to the plant in water trucks, and bottled under labels that include Calistoga Mountain Spring Water and Arrowhead Mountain Spring Water. It is difficult to say what the ultimate fate of sparkling mineral water will be in the United States. But as long as a few sources like Calistoga and Saratoga Springs manage to hang on by their fingernails, there is hope that mineral waters in America may survive the shifting sands of taste and fashion.

More bottled water is consumed in California than in any other state of the Union. In the year 2000, Californians consumed approximately 1.2 billion gallons of bottled water, just about double the amount consumed by Texans, who are number two. A good bit of this is explained by the fact that California has the largest population of the fifty states. In terms of per capita consumption, California was actually number two, at 36.1 gallons per person in the year 2000, slightly behind Arizona at 39.6 gallons per person.[11] Nevertheless, it is clear that Californians are particularly fond of bottled water, and it is worth delving into just why this is so.

Part of the reason certainly has to do with climate. Much of California is hot and very dry for most of the year. In this sort of climate, staying properly hydrated is a necessity of life, and the people have adjusted accordingly. Drinking bottled water is just one way, and a particularly convenient way, to stay hydrated. Another reason has to do with fashion. As we have seen previously, the fashionability of drinking water has come and gone several times over the last four-hundred years. Furthermore, keeping up with the latest trends—indeed, setting those trends—is very much a part of California culture. As bottled water was being reinstated as fashionable in the late 1970s, it was entirely natural that California would play a large part in the new trend.

But there are several other reasons why bottled water is so popular in California relative to other parts of the country. One has to do with hydrology. In the basin-and-range geology of southern California, the Coastal Ranges that line the Pacific, the Sierra Nevada of eastern California, and the Cascade Range in northern California all trap moisture coming off the Pacific Ocean. Furthermore, because this water falls at such high altitudes, and because of the steepness of the mountains, it tends to run off fairly quickly. This minimizes contact time with the underlying rocks and soils, producing the low-TDS waters that Americans tend to like. It is just an accident of nature that the most populous state happens to have a hot, dry climate and happens to have an unusually productive source of desirable drinking water. But people cannot be expected to climb mountains every time they want a drink of water. Consequently, the custom of collecting these waters and transporting them to cities for sale became customary in California very early on. The modern fashionability of bottled water that developed in the East during the 1980s simply reinforced a long-standing practice in California.

Another reason has to do with geology. For the last hundred million years or so, the west coast of North America has ground over the top of the Pacific Basin. This series of collisions and subductions has contributed to raising the Rocky Mountains, generated hundreds of basins and ranges, and formed the Coastal and Cascade mountain ranges. In addition, these processes have also contributed to piling up the remnants of volcanic islands, oceanic sediments, and oceanic crust onto the coast of California. These so-called "exotic terrains" baffled geologists for the better part of a hundred years before the new concept of plate tectonics began to make sense of them.[12] This geologic diversity, and the consequent diversity of rock types found in California, produces a wide variety in the chemical composition of spring waters. Thus, the granites of the Sierra Nevada produce low-TDS calcium bicarbonate waters, the hot springs of the Napa Valley produce high-TDS sodium chloride waters, and springs on the flanks of the Cascades volcanoes produce waters that are intermediate between these two extremes.

One example of how this geologic diversity affects the chemical composition of spring waters is Adobe Springs, located in a remote, mountainous area west of Modesto, California. The source of the water is the surrounding mountains, which trap moisture. But because these mountains are made of rocks that once lay on the floor of the Pacific Ocean, only to be "scraped" off onto California's coast, they bear the chemical signature of that history. When seawater circulates through rocks and sediments on a tectonically active seafloor, the magnesium present in seawater tends to be stripped out and accumulates in the rocks. Such magnesium-rich rocks and sediments were deposited on California's coast and later raised into mountains. As rainfall interacts with these rocks, their abundant magnesium is dissolved, producing distinctive magnesium-rich water that forms springs. Adobe Springs taps this water, which can contain up to 110 mg/L of magnesium. (In contrast, most bottled waters have magnesium concentrations of just 1 or 2 mg/L.) This high concentration of magnesium, which purportedly has a variety of health benefits, is the basis for marketing Adobe Springs bottled water in California. The real story is that, by virtue of its geologic history, there is a greater variety of spring water composition in California than in any other region of the United States.

Another reason Californians are so fond of bottled water has to do with California's history and culture. Ever since the days of the forty-niners, Californians have done things in their own unique way, for their own unique reasons. We saw how Calistoga mineral waters were first bottled in 1919, just when bottled water was largely going out of use on the east coast. Calistoga is not the only example of how Californians ducked the trend of decreasing bottled water use in the early and mid-1900s. Even during the 1950s and 1960s, several bottled water companies—notably Sparklett's and Arrowhead—were tooling along in fine fashion, oblivious to what was going on in the rest of the country. This water was bottled almost entirely in bulk for home or business delivery, and in California's hot, dry climate was a popular source of drinking water. So, when the bottled water fashion of the late 1970s began in New York, it did not seem strange at all to Californians. In fact, there were probably many who viewed this renewed fashion as the rest of the country following California's lead—which Californians see as the natural order of things.

Finally, there is environmental awareness to consider. It is largely forgotten these days, but California suffered very early on the ravages of water pollution. In the late 1800s, gold was extracted from sediments at the foot of the Sierra Nevada and other mountain ranges using a technique known as "hydraulic mining." In its crudest form, hydraulic mining consisted of trapping water from a stream, pressurizing it, and using hoses to blast sediments into gold-gathering sluices. This was a very cheap and efficient way of separating gold dust from the surrounding sediments. It also created an incredible mess. It destroyed whole portions of the landscape, it dumped huge volumes of sediment into rivers, and it created a water pollution problem of epic proportions.

Californians were all for mining gold and getting rich, but it was impossible to ignore the environmental damage the hydraulic mining was causing. The loads of sediment that were filling riverbeds raised water levels in the rivers, and this inevitably led to several catastrophic floods. After a particularly bad flood in 1875, the towns of Marysville and Yuba on the Bear River were heavily damaged. This led the local farming community to file suit in Yuba City to stop the hydraulic mining.[13] In 1879, the judge in the case ruled in favor of the farmers, saying the miners had "not acquired any right to use the bed of Bear River nor the beds of its tributaries as a place of deposit of their mining tailings." So, long before the term "environmental movement" was even coined, Californians were engaged in technical, legal, and social efforts to protect the quality of their waterways and the water they contained.

This was partly why the water delivery businesses continued to operate in California in the early twentieth century. Very simply, there was a demand for clean water that was prompted at least in part by California's water pollution problems. But even more, this history helps explain why Californians have been, and remain, so environmentally conscious. This consciousness is firmly rooted in California's history and is one factor in the present popularity of bottled water.

The natural history of springs and spring waters is a small part of the human experience. In California, for example, the discovery of gold and the subsequent Great Migration largely defines the region's past. This precipitated the war with Mexico, generated decades of legal wrangling over land ownership, and produced a population determined to do things its own way. But many of these characteristics — some would say peculiarities — of California life and politics are reflected in the people's collective water consciousness. From the mystical origins of springs, to the early regulation of mine-tailing disposal, to a preference for spring waters collected in the mountains and trucked to the cities, many of California's customs — customs that are reflected throughout the Pacific

Northwest—make perfect historical sense. In this way, California is no different from any other part of the country. It is just a simple fact that attitudes, beliefs, and customs surrounding water reflect a region's history. It's like an old man remembering how, as a little boy, he had once peered into a pond to glimpse his reflection.

It shows us who we are, and what we have been.

14 ZEN AND THE ART OF WATER QUALITY
What Makes "Good" Water Good?

Since it was founded in 1678, Charleston, South Carolina, has had problems with its drinking water. When English settlers first reached what was to become Charleston Harbor in 1668, they initially picked a spot on the west side of the Ashley River for settlement. That proved to be bad judgment. The site was low, poorly drained, and much of the available water was brackish and of poor quality. Partly because of the poor water supply, the settlers suffered dreadfully from a variety of miasmal diseases. But even worse, the site was hard to defend from the local Native American population, who were not particularly happy about having new and uninvited neighbors.

So, in 1678, the colony moved across the Ashley River to a peninsula that offered higher ground and much better protection against the frequent raids of the Native Americans. Even better, the peninsula turned out to be underlain by a bed of clean quartz sand about twenty feet thick. This sand, in turn, was underlain by a bed of black clay. Rain falling on the peninsula seeped into the sandy sediments and was trapped by the underlying clay. The settlers soon found that they could easily dig wells ten or fifteen feet into the sand, line the sides with stone, and procure an abundant supply of excellent drinking water. Their new security, combined with a reliable source of clean water, was the best of all possible worlds, and the little town began to thrive.

All was well until about 1750, when an unexpected calamity arose. In the words of a Charleston municipal report:

> But as habitations were gradually built up and the population increased, it was noticed that the water in the wells, especially in the more populous portions, was rapidly losing its pristine purity, and was becoming hard, impotable, and injurious to health. The evil went on increasing and spreading with the growth of the City. . . . The wealthier citizens began to gather the rain-water that fell on

their roofs into water-tight cisterns, mostly underground, in order to preserve it for domestic purposes. As the evil continued to increase in the wells, such cisterns came gradually into general use among the middle classes, and finally even among the poorest, until a cistern for rain-water became a necessary adjunct to a dwelling of any kind in Charleston.[1]

This "evil" was the result of hundreds of unlined privies used to dispose human and animal sewage. In effect, the Charlestonians were using their sandy aquifer both as a source of drinking water *and* as a sewage disposal system. These clearly incompatible uses lasted for only a few years, and, by 1800, rain-fed cisterns were the main source of drinking water in the city.

Nevertheless, Charleston continued to thrive, and by the early nineteenth century South Carolina had become the wealthiest state in the Union. This was due mostly to agriculture, which produced an abundance of cash crops including rice, indigo, tobacco, and cotton. To make matters even better, gold was discovered in the Carolina Piedmont in 1827. This precipitated a fevered gold rush, and between 1829 and 1858 South Carolina produced more than seventy thousand troy ounces of gold.[2] With all this wealth pouring through the port of Charleston, the city now had the means to procure a better source of water than rain-fed cisterns. London, England, had recently managed to drill a 400-foot well that produced an abundant supply of water. Paris, France, had drilled wells in excess of 1,800 feet deep and found excellent water supplies. So, went the thinking, if London and Paris could drill deep wells for water supply, so could Charleston.

Beginning in 1823, numerous attempts were made to drill deep wells in Charleston, most of which ended in failure. The problem was that Charleston is underlain by sediments of the Atlantic Coastal Plain, some of which were so tightly cemented by calcite that they were very difficult to drill through. Furthermore, most of the sediments underlying the city were impermeable clays that did not yield water. This meant it was necessary to drill through the clays and hope to find some deeper sands that would produce water. In 1849 and again in 1856, drillers managed to complete two small-bore wells in some thin sands found at depths of 1,260 and 1,230 feet respectively. However, these wells produced only a few gallons of water per minute, hardly the volumes needed to supply Charleston with water.

It was not until 1878 that a well driller named Fleming Spangler finally succeeded, drilling a deep well located in Marion Square in Charleston. Spangler's well was 1,970 feet deep, having managed to reach a thick layer of sand that yielded an abundant supply of water. Furthermore, this water flowed naturally from the well under artesian pressure. The initial flow rate was officially measured to be 250 gallons per minute. Fifty-five years after the great well-drilling endeavor was undertaken, Charleston had finally succeeded in locating a reliable source of water.[3]

The availability of clean, fresh water in the middle of Charleston was a new thing in 1878, and the good citizens were thrilled. The well water was quickly pronounced to be healthy in all regards, much more so than rainwater stored for days or weeks in moldy cisterns. Water flowing from the well was piped to a small fountain at Cannon Park on Calhoun Street, and soon people were lining up to fill containers for home use as drinking water. In time, collecting water at the "Calhoun Street Fountain" became a Charleston tradition. In addition to providing a source of water, it was a convenient place to meet with friends and acquaintances and chat about the events of the day. Soon, longtime residents of the city acquired a taste for the fountain's water, preferring its flavor to that of all other water.

The water itself was being produced out of a geologic horizon that would later be named the Middendorf aquifer. The sands of the Middendorf were laid down about 70 million years ago during Upper Cretaceous time. The mountains to the west were undergoing one of their periodic bursts of uplift, and the sediments that poured out from the highlands accumulated on a series of deltas reaching out into the Atlantic Ocean. The Middendorf aquifer represents a period of sedimentation when particularly course-grained sands were being deposited. After the end of the Cretaceous (65 million years ago), sea level rose again, resulting in the deposition of about 1,500 feet of clayey material in the vicinity of Charleston.[4] These thick clays contributed to the difficulty of reaching the water-bearing sands, and this is one reason it took so long to drill the Marion Square well.

While 250 gallons per minute was a lot of water, it was not enough to supply everybody in Charleston. More wells were needed, and new ones were drilled into the water-bearing Middendorf sands in Martin Park (completed in 1885), at Nassau Street (1887), at George Street (1907), and at Charlotte Street (1911). Unfortunately, the city engineers soon learned a basic lesson of well hydraulics. As more wells were put into production, the artesian pressure diminished accordingly. Each successive well yielded less and less water. The city tried a variety of other water sources, including building a dam on Goose Creek north of Charleston, which went into service in 1904. However, a storm destroyed the dam in 1916, and Charleston's hunt for water continued. The problem was not finally resolved until 1938, when a twenty-mile-long tunnel was built to the nearby Edisto River. This tunnel carries water underneath the Ashley River to Charleston, where it is treated and distributed. The Edisto River Tunnel, which is an engineering marvel, is what finally solved Charleston's water supply problem.

But by now many of Charleston's residents had become accustomed to collecting water from the Calhoun Street Fountain. In addition, long-time Charlestonians considered it to be tastier and healthier than Edisto River water. In this regard, however, Charleston's taste in water quality was out of step with the rest of the country. By 1920, the American preference for drinking water with low concentrations of total dissolved solids (TDS) was firmly established, particularly in the Northeast. Water produced from the Marion Square Well, on the other hand, had a TDS of 1,100 mg/L, easily qualifying it as a mineral water. Having drunk the water now for two generations, however, the Charlestonians would not be swayed. Their well water, they were sure, was the best in the world. It was what they had grown up with, they were used to it, and they just liked it.

None of this would have mattered if Charleston had not experienced a development boom beginning in the 1960s. The invention of air conditioning, the soft sea breezes, and the beautiful low-country charm began to draw more and more people to the Charleston area. The Isle of Palms and Mount Pleasant, located across the Cooper River north of Charleston, grew particularly rapidly. Since the Edisto Tunnel did not extend under the Cooper River in those days, engineers again began drilling wells into the deep Middendorf aquifer to provide water for these new communities. This water had the same chemical composition as water from the Marion Square well, the water that native Charlestonians loved so well. There was just one small problem. When people moving into Mount Pleasant—folks who were largely from the Northeast—first tasted the water, their reaction was always the same.

They hated it.

From the point of view of someone moving from New York City, there was a lot to hate. New York City municipal water, largely drawn from reservoirs in the Catskill Mountains, is the kind of low-TDS, moderately soft drinking water that most Americans prefer. When people from the Northeast first tried Mount Pleasant's high-TDS and extremely soft water—it contained as much as 450 mg/L of sodium—they could not help but wrinkle their noses in distaste. Not only did it taste funny (it's too "soapy," they complained), but it was so soft that it actually made bathing difficult. Even after you thought you had rinsed off all the soap, a vigorous rub could bring back a lather. "It makes you feel too slippery" was a common complaint.

All this fuss greatly amused the Charlestonians, who, just like the Native Americans two centuries earlier, were not sure they liked the influx of more people into their part of the world. "If you don't like the water, go back home" was a common sentiment. Throughout the 1970s and into the 1980s, Mount Pleasant's water woes, or at least its *perceived* water woes, continued. Today, thanks to reverse osmosis treatment and water imported from Charleston, Mount Pleasant's municipal water quality is more in line with that of the rest of the country, and complaints have eased. But for a long time, the dichotomy between the people who loved Middendorf aquifer water (native Charlestonians) and those that hated it (transplanted northerners) was striking. Even if you overlooked the obvious regional prejudices, it was still a fact that everybody was talking about the very same water.

How can *the same water* taste good to some people and bad to others?

The "taste" and odor of water is something that has been the subject of close study by engineers over the last fifty years or so. Municipal water-treatment facilities try hard to produce a product that people like, and the operators of these facilities are very sensitive to complaints. Nobody likes to have their customers unhappy, and when it comes to water, the quickest way to make customers unhappy is to produce water that tastes or smells "bad." But to address complaints about water taste, it is first necessary to describe what water tastes like in terms more illuminating then "good" or "bad." Engineers are nothing if not systematic, and so over the years they have doggedly worked toward ways to describe the taste of water.

One method, used by the American Water Works Association (AWWA), literally revolves around commonly held perceptions of taste (sweet, sour, salty, bitter), odor (earthy, musty, chlorine, septic, etc.), as well as the way water "feels" in the mouth (tingling, drying, metallic, etc.). The theory is that people's *perception* of these properties is

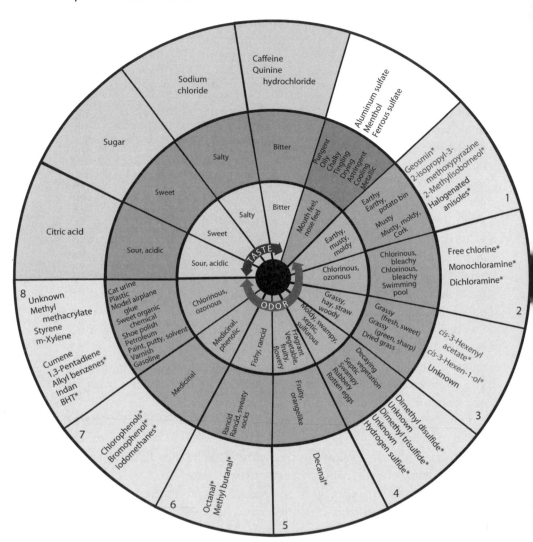

FIGURE 14.1 The taste and odor of water. The inner wheel indicates categories, the middle wheel indicates descriptors, and the outer wheel indicates reference standards. Source: The American Water Works Association

relatively consistent, and thus can be used to describe different waters in a systematic way. The "wheel" used to describe the taste and odor of water is shown in figure 14.1. In the middle of the wheel are various perceptions of taste, odor, and feel. On the outside of the wheel are the various potential causes of those perceptions. One of the things this diagram shows is just how many different perceptions of taste and odor there really are. But even more, it shows how many possible causes of these perceptions there are as well. Considering that most people think that water should not have any taste or odor to begin with, you can begin to appreciate just how problematic all this is for engineers operating water-treatment plants.

But there is a real difference between *describing* how waters tastes or smells and explaining *why* some people like some properties and dislike others. The story of Charleston and Mount Pleasant illustrates the basic conundrum. By all accounts, the water produced by the Marion Square well has a slightly "salty" taste, which is entirely consistent with the high TDS of the water and the relatively high concentrations of sodium and chloride (fig. 14.1). All this is well and good. But it does not explain why the native Charlestonians "like" that salty taste and why transplanted northerners "dislike" the very same taste. If preferences in the taste of water were determined entirely by water chemistry (high TDS, low TDS, etc.), then everybody's preference would be fairly similar. Clearly that is not the case.

The answer has to lie deeper.

The question as to what makes one thing good and another thing bad is a very old one. It particularly intrigued philosophers in ancient Greece, and some very smart people including Aristotle, Socrates, and Plato weighed in on it. Over the centuries, all this led to a branch of philosophy called *aesthetics*, or the study of what makes some things good and other things not good. Philosophy does not get a lot of attention from most Americans these days, which is actually too bad. All of mathematics and much of scientific rationalism are based on principles worked out over the centuries by diligent philosophers. Luminaries like Immanuel Kant (Cartesian coordinates) and Isaac Newton (calculus) considered themselves primarily to be philosophers, and they thought of their scientific inquiries as being secondary to philosophy. But no matter. All it takes is one boring, incoherent philosophy class in high school or college to drive most people away from this ancient and honorable discipline for a lifetime.

One person who was not driven away from philosophy was Robert M. Pirsig, who in the early 1970s wrote a book titled *Zen and the Art of Motorcycle Maintenance*.[5] Against all odds, and against the better judgment of the many publishers who rejected it for publication, the book became a best seller and one of the defining "cult" books of the 1970s. The reason for its cult status was that the main character, who calls himself Phaedrus (from one of Plato's dialogues), starts thinking about the problem of what makes some things good and other things bad. He thinks about the problem so deeply and so obsessively that he eventually drives himself insane, landing in a mental hospital where he is subjected to electrical shock therapy. The therapy produces a more docile individual who, rather than continuing Phaedrus' fevered quest for truth, simply gives up. This newly made person gets out of the hospital, gets a job, gets married, and tries mightily to remain "normal" for the rest of his life. That pursuit of normalcy, as you might expect, eventually puts him at odds with his eleven-year old son. But, while making a cross-country motorcycle trip with his son, the older, "Phaedrus" personality begins to reawaken, inexorably pushing its way to the surface. In the end, Phaedrus defeats the made-up personality that society created for him and resumes his quest for understanding. That victory, in turn, earns Phaedrus the respect of his troubled son, allowing them to reconnect.

On this journey, Phaedrus manages to work out a philosophical framework for describing what he calls Quality, or that elusive essence that separates what is good from what is not good. That framework, in turn, goes a long way toward explaining why water produced from the Middendorf aquifer can be "good" to the Charlestonians and "bad" to the Mount Pleasanters at the very same time.

Phaedrus began his musings by wondering whether Quality exists in objects (like water) or whether it is entirely subjective, existing only in minds of people (their "taste" in water). At first glance, the idea that Quality depends on the chemical properties of water seems obvious. For most Americans, high-quality water must have relatively low concentrations of TDS. If you consider the Charleston conundrum, however, the problem with this thinking becomes obvious. What do you do with people like the Charlestonians who actually *like* high-TDS water? And it is not just the Charlestonians who fit into this category. European consumers are particularly fond of high-TDS mineral waters and cannot fathom why Americans like such bland, flavorless, low-TDS waters. Clearly, this elusive Quality cannot reside entirely in the chemical composition of the water itself. There has to be something else going on.

On the other hand, you might think that Quality is entirely subjective, residing exclusively in the minds of individual consumers. Superficially, that is the easiest way to explain why Charlestonians, Mount Pleasanters, and Europeans can love or hate the very same water. But again, that does not quite stand up. For one thing, there are clear chemical differences between various waters that are easily measured. Furthermore, some properties of water—especially the presence or absence of dangerous fecal bacteria—are entirely invisible and can be determined only by laboratory analysis. So while water preferences certainly exist in the minds of consumers, there are very real chemical and biological properties involved with what is good. Clearly, water Quality cannot depend entirely on the mind of the consumer alone.

As Phaedrus pondered these lines of inquiry, he began to wonder whether Quality could be defined at all. If Quality did not depend entirely on the properties of the object itself (the water) or on the predilections of the observer (the drinker), perhaps it was something that simply could not be defined. That would put Quality in the category of *infinity*, which mathematicians can show is undefined. But as he pondered these lines of inquiry, he had a sudden burst of insight. Quality, Phaedrus realized, depends on an *interaction* between an object and an observer. Quality is not a *thing*, Phaedrus thought; it's an *event*. Quality is what happens when someone with a particular need (a more or less thirsty person) comes into contact with an object that can relieve that need (a glass of water). Furthermore, since the need of the observer and the properties of the water can vary enormously, the resulting Quality Event also varies enormously. For someone having a fashionable dinner party, rusty tap water that smells of chlorine would have very low Quality. That very same water, however, would be a blessing for someone dying of thirst in a desert. The definition of Water Quality, therefore, is constantly shifting and changing. At any particular time, Quality depends on the water *and* on the drinker *and* on the circumstances surrounding the interaction.

All this goes a long way toward explaining why the Charlestonians had such a different perception of Middendorf Aquifer water than the transplanted northerners. When the Marion Square well was completed in 1878, the only other sources of drinking water in Charleston were rain-fed cisterns. Water stored in cisterns often acquires a musty taste, and it frequently contains unpleasant microorganisms, including potentially dangerous fecal bacteria. The water flowing out of the Marion Square well, since it came from a very ancient, very deep artesian aquifer, was entirely free of fecal bacteria. By definition, therefore, the Quality of Marion Square well water was immediately higher than the quality of cistern-stored rainwater. In time, the distinctive taste of this high-TDS water became associated with Quality in the minds of

Charlestonians, which entirely explains their enduring fondness for the water.

People raised in the Northeast, however, had very nearly the opposite experience. Because of the bedrock geology of New England and because of its humid climate, the water people were used to drinking had low concentrations of TDS. Only water that had been heavily contaminated by various human activities had a high TDS. For these folks, therefore, the distinctive taste of high-TDS water produced by Mount Pleasant's wells could mean only one thing. It was bad.

So the great Charleston–Mount Pleasant water quality conundrum is not a conundrum at all. Not only does it make perfect sense, but it illustrates a broader truth concerning drinking water. On one level, chemical properties (high or low TDS) and biological properties (the presence or absence of fecal microorganisms) are certainly part of the picture. But every single person in the world is carrying around a different set of experiences and expectations regarding those properties. In effect, everybody has their own "filter" through which every drink of water passes, and every single person will render a different Quality assessment accordingly.

It is just as well—and certainly no accident—that humans have developed such a flexible way of judging water quality. The reason is that water can contain so many different kinds of dissolved solids and suspended matter that the possible variations and permutations are infinite. As rainfall condenses out of clouds, all potential drinking water starts with a fairly uniform, fairly dilute, composition. There are variations in the chemistry of precipitation, of course, but they are not usually substantial. In violent storms at sea, sea spray can be carried up to the clouds, and the resulting precipitation has a slightly higher TDS than clouds formed over land masses. But in general, precipitation that falls on the earth is pretty close to pure distilled water, generally having a TDS under 15 mg/L.

It is when newly fallen precipitation begins interacting with the earth that the real changes in water chemistry begin. In some places, precipitation falls on relatively insoluble crystalline rocks, and the water that runs off into streams and rivers remains fairly low in TDS. New England is a good example of this. In other places, Florida is a good example, water falls onto soluble limestones that are quickly dissolved. But while ground water percolating through the Floridan aquifer may pick up higher concentrations of dissolved solids, it is also cleansed of dissolved organic matter. Florida is covered by decomposing organic matter, and surface waters are often colored by dissolved and particulate organic matter. Ground waters, such as those discharging from Silver Springs and Ginnie Springs, have been thoroughly filtered and are crystal clear. The chemical composition of drinking water—an important component of its Quality—depends partly on such earth-water interactions.

Then there is the issue of water that seeps into the extreme depths of the earth. Most of the water falling on land surface discharges into adjacent streams and rivers within a few days or weeks. The small percentage of water that seeps deeply into the earth, however, has an added opportunity to pick up dissolved solids. In the end, there is a virtually endless variety of water chemistries available for human consumption. As we have seen, deciding which among these is "good" to drink depends on what that composition happens to be *and* on the specific needs of the people doing the drinking.

But in many respects, this apparent variety is misleading. While it might be true that the chemical and biological characteristics of drinking water vary enormously across the country, how much does this variability mean to the individual consumer? After all, if you live in Florida, you are going to be limited to the ground or surface water that has interacted with the underlying limestone of the Floridan aquifer and with the overlying mantle of tropical vegetation. If you live on the High Plains, you very likely will be limited to water from the Ogallala Aquifer with its often high concentrations of TDS. If you live in southern California you are limited to municipal water that has probably been imported from northern California. In other words, much of the variety available in drinking water around the country is inherently limited by water distribution systems. Furthermore, if the available water does not meet your personal definition of Quality—which is what happened to the people moving from the Northeast to Mount Pleasant—then you're just out of luck.

That is where bottled water enters the picture. From the very beginning of the American bottled water industry in the 1820s, when teamsters would drive wagons into the Pennsylvania countryside, fill their barrels with spring water, and deliver it to paying customers in Philadelphia, the real product that was being sold was choice. Municipal drinking water available in cities prior to the days of modern water treatment was always chancy. Having the option of having reliably clean drinking water delivered to your house, where it generally appeared on the table at suppertime, was part necessity and part luxury.

But the real reason people were willing to buy it was that it gave them a choice.

Although the bottled water industry, the bottling methods and materials, and the products available have changed enormously over the years, the basic dynamic of offering choice in drinking water remains intact. Nowadays, thanks to the dramatic improvements in municipal water treatment, the choice is no longer between safe and dangerous. Rather, if people have a predilection for water from the French Alps, they can have Evian bottled water virtually anywhere in America. If they fancy low-TDS water from Poland Spring, they can have that too. If they happen to like mineral waters, they can have those produced from Saratoga Springs or Calistoga.

All of which explains a lot about the present popularity of bottled water. On average, the typical American consumed 22.6 gallons of bottled water in 2003, making it the number two nonalcoholic beverage (behind carbonated soft drinks) in the United States. In the year 2000, 94.4% of this bottled water was low-TDS drinking water, 2.9% was domestically produced sparkling mineral water, and 2.7% was imported sparkling mineral water. Of the low-TDS drinking water, fully one-third (33.5%) was sold in handheld PET bottles. However, almost one-third (29.5%) of bottled water was delivered in bulk, usually in five-gallon bottles, to individual homes or businesses.[6] If you lay the potential variety of available bottled waters on top of the variety of available well waters, municipal waters, and home treatment and filtration systems, Americans have more choice in their drinking water now than any other people at any time in history. Furthermore, given that Quality is inseparable from individual tastes and predilections, it follows that the quality of drinking water in America is at an all-time high.

But variety in drinking water is under assault, from a variety of circumstances. Take, for example, the entry of Coca-Cola and Pepsi into the industry. Prior to 1994, neither company was even in the bottled water business. By 2003, Aquafina (11.3% market share) and Dasani (10.0% market share) were the number-one-selling and number-two-selling bottled waters in America. And they are not done yet. The goal of both Pepsi and Coca-Cola—which is entirely understandable—is to try to capture as much of the water market as possible.

This has greatly changed the dynamics of the bottled water industry in America. Thirty years ago, the industry consisted of hundreds of small independent bottling companies selling bulk water in coolers.

Now, most bottled water is sold in handheld PET bottles, a business dominated by a few large companies. By the year 2000, the more traditional players in the bottled water market, the Perrier Group (29.4% market share), Danone Waters (15.0% market share), and Suntory Water Group (9.0% market share) were scrambling to keep up with Coca-Cola and Pepsi. Since 2000, Groupe Danone and Suntory have merged and have made a strategic alliance with Coca-Cola along the way. Similarly, the Perrier Group, now in the fold of the Nestlé Corporation, has come to its own arrangements with Coca-Cola as well. All this has led to less diversity in the variety of available bottled waters and a consequent loss of choice on the part of consumers.

Is the time coming when our only choices for water will be between two tap waters, Aquafina and Dasani?

The answer is probably no, and the reason has to do with water quality. If people living on opposite sides of a river in Mount Pleasant and Charleston cannot agree on what is or is not "good" water, what are the chances that people from the Northeast will agree with people from the Southeast? What are the chances that the tastes of midwesterners will coincide with those of people living in the Pacific Northwest? What are the chances that Californians will ever agree with anybody? In short, it is not going to happen. As long as individual and regional tastes differ, and as long as people have a fondness for the history and tradition of local spring sources, there will be a market for variety. That variety, in turn, will continue to be supplied by numerous small water bottlers serving "niche" markets. There is a natural human fondness for variety, and at some point that dynamic is likely to limit consolidation of the drinking water industry.

Drinking water in the United States, and not just bottled water, is riding a wave of popularity that seems perfectly natural to most modern Americans. But as we have seen, the popularity of drinking water has risen and fallen numerous times over just the last few hundred years alone. It is inevitable that, at some point, bottled water use will peak and then decline. Who knows whether that will happen in the near or far future? But it certainly will happen. The last time this happened (1913), it was largely due to the chlorination revolution in municipal waters. It is entirely possible that new technological developments, such as designer home treatment systems, will emerge and overwhelm the bottled water industry. If and when that happens, bottled water will once again fade into the shadows of history. It is entirely possible that, fifty years from now, the colorful PET bottles so ubiquitous today will be collector's items, monuments to an old-fashioned and obsolete industry.

We began this natural history by wondering just why Americans, who have access to limitless volumes of healthy and virtually free municipal water, would ever spend money for bottled water. The answer is that bottled water companies—along with municipal water suppliers, home-based water treatment systems, water stores, and privately owned wells to name a few—are not just selling water. They're selling variety. They're selling choice. They're selling Quality.

And there will always be a market for that.

NOTES

1. WATER FROM THE HEART

1. M. N. Baker, *The Quest for Pure Water*, volume 1, second edition, *The History of Water Purification from the Earliest Records to the Twentieth Century* (Denver: The American Water Works Association, 1972), p. 342.

2. Mark Shippen, "Reflections from the Depths of a Water Jar, *Ceramics Monthly*, April 2000, pp. 40–43.

3. Ibid.

4. Ibid.

5. Baker, *Quest for Pure Water*.

6. Ibid., p. 13.

7. M. Green and T. Green, *The Good Water Guide* (London: Rosendale Press, 1985), p. 26.

8. F. Kreysig, *A Treatise on the use of natural and factitious waters of Carlsbad, EMS, Marienba, &c. &c.*, translated from German by W. F. Bekenn (London: S. Highley, Publisher, 1824).

9. Green and Green, *Good Water Guide*, p. 26.

10. Baker, *Quest for Pure Water*, p. 342.

11. Green and Green, *Good Water Guide*, p. 26.

2. MYTHS AND MYSTERIES

1. Cecil Munsey, *The Illustrated Guide to Collecting Bottles* (New York: Hawthorn Books, 1970).

2. J. Bord and C. Bord, *Sacred Waters: Holy Wells and Water Lore in Britain and Ireland* (London: Granada Publishing, 1985).

3. Ibid., p. 4.

4. R. Lanciani, *Ancient Rome in the Light of Recent Discoveries* (Boston and New York: Houghton, Mifflin and Company, 1898).

5. J. M. Mackinlay, *Folklore of Scottish Lochs and Springs* (Glasgow: William Hodge & Co., 1893), p. 25.

6. Ibid., p. 131.

7. Bord and Bord, *Sacred Waters*.

8. F. D. Adams, *The Birth and Development of the Geological Sciences* (New York: Dover Publications, 1938), p. 427.

9. Ibid.

10. Ibid., p. 429.

11. Ibid., p. 431.

12. Ibid.

13. Ibid., p. 447.

14. Ibid.

15. Ibid., p. 451.

16. D. B. Stevens and M. D. Ankeny, "A Missing Link in the Historical Development of Hydrogeology," *Ground Water* 42 (2004): 302–309.

17. J. Johnstone, *An Account of the Most Approved Mode of Draining Land; According to the System Practised by Mr. Joseph Elkington, Late of Prinethorp, in the County of Warwick* (Edinburgh, Scotland: Mundell and Son, 1797).

18. S. Winchester, *The Map That Changed the World* (New York: HarperCollins Publishers, 2001).

19. O. E. Meinzer, *The Occurrence of Ground Water in the United States, with a Discussion of Principles*, U.S. Geological Survey Water Supply Paper 489 (Washington, D.C.: U.S. Government Printing Office, 1923).

20. S. N. Davis and R.J.M. DeWiest, *Hydrogeology* (New York: John Wiley & Sons, 1966).

21. P. E. LaMoreaux and J. T. Tanner (eds.), *Springs and Bottled Waters of the World* (Berlin: Springer-Verlag, 2001).

22. D. C. Prowell, *Preliminary Geologic Map of the Barnwell 30' × 60' Quadrangle, South Carolina and Georgia*, U.S. Geological Survey Open-File Report 94-673, Atlanta, Ga., 1994.

23. Ibid.

24. Winchester, *Map*; Prowell, *Preliminary Geologic Map*.

25. The chemistry of the Healing Springs has been investigated by Peter Stone of the South Carolina Department of Health and Environmental Control. Stone's initial hypothesis was that Healing Springs water was entirely shallow recharge moving through the Upland and Tobacco Road Sand units. However, analysis of the water revealed a higher alkalinity and an older carbon-14 age date than Stone expected. David Prowell, who has mapped this area for the U.S. Geological Survey, had previously noted the presence of carbonate material in the Dry Branch Formation, and suggested that dissolution of these limestones could form conduits that connected

deeper, older ground water with the Healing Springs. The tentative consensus of Stone, Prowell, and other geologists is that the Healing Springs discharge waters are a mixture of young, shallow sources and older, deeper sources. As of this writing, that is the best explanation for the origin of the Healing Springs that science can give.

3. MEDICINES AND MIRACLES

1. F. Kreysig, *A Treatise on the use of natural and factitious waters of Carlsbad, EMS, Marienba, &c. &c.,* translated from German by W. F. Bekenn (London: S. Highley, Publisher, 1824).

2. Ibid., p. 72

3. Ibid., p. 118.

4. Ibid., p. 120.

5. Ibid., p. 7.

6. W. Back, E. R. Landa, and L. Meeks, "Bottled Water, Spas, and Early Years of Water Chemistry," *Ground Water* 33 (1995: 605–614).

7. Ibid.

8. Ibid.

9. S. N. Davis and A. G. Davis, "Saratoga Springs and Early Hydrogeochemistry in the United States," *Ground Water* 35 (1997): 347–356.

10. Back, Landa, and Meeks, "Bottled Water."

11. Davis and Davis, "Saratoga Springs."

12. S. R. Stoddard, *Saratoga Springs, Its Mineral Waters* (Glens Falls, N.Y.: Published by the author, 1806).

13. J. H. Steel, *An Analysis of the Mineral Waters of Saratoga and Ballston with Practical Remarks on their Use in Various Diseases, Containing Observations on the Geology and Mineralogy of the Surrounding Country, with a Geologic Map,* second edition (Albany, N.Y.: Packard & Van Benthuysen, 1819).

14. Ibid.

15. B. C. Renick, *Base Exchange in Ground Water by Silicates as Illustrated in Montana,* U.S. Geological Survey Water-Supply Paper 520 (Washington, D.C.: Government Printing Office, 1925), pp. 53–72.

16. Ibid.

17. V. Seaman, *A Dissertation on the Mineral Waters of Saratoga including an Account of the Waters of Ballston,* second edition (Printed and sold by Collins and Perkins, No. 189 Pearl Street [Albany?], 1809).

18. W. Back, "Hydrochemical Facies and Ground-Water Flow Patterns in Northern Part of Atlantic Coastal Plain," U.S. Geological Survey Professional Paper 498-A, 1966.

19. I. I. Chebotarev, "Metamorphism of Natural Waters in the Crust of Weathering," *Geochimica et Cosmochimica Acta* 8 (1955): pt. 1, pp. 22–48; pt. 2, pp. 137–170; pt. 3, pp. 198–212.

20. Back, "Hydrochemical Facies."

21. J. H. Feth, C. E. Robertson, and W. L. Polzer, "Sources of Mineral Constituents in Water from Granitic Rocks in Sierra Nevada, California and Nevada," U.S. Geological Survey Water-Supply Paper 1535-I, 1964.

22. R. M. Garrels and F. T. Mackenzie, "Origin of the Chemical Compositions of Some Springs and Lakes," in *Equilibrium Concepts in Natural Water Chemistry*, Advances in Chemistry Series 67 (Washington, D.C.: American Chemical Society, 1967), pp. 222–242.

23. G. W. Putman and J. R. Young, "The Bubbles Revisited: The Geology and Geochemistry of 'Saratoga' Mineral Waters," *Northeastern Geology* 7, no. 2 (1985): 53–77.

24. Ibid. Concentrations of carbon dioxide (CO_2) in water are often reported as "partial pressures," or pCO_2, and given in units of atmospheres. Water in equilibrium with atmospheric carbon dioxide has a pCO_2 of 0.0033 atm, which is much lower than the concentrations in many Saratoga Springs waters. The high pCO_2 of Saratoga Springs waters is why they effervesce.

25. D. C. Siegel, K. A. Lesniak, M. Stute, and S. Frape, "Isotope Geochemistry of the Saratoga Springs: Implications for the Origin of Solutes and Source of Carbon Dioxide," *Geology* 32 (2004): 257–260.

26. Ibid.

27. Steel, *Analysis*.

28. Davis and Davis, "Saratoga Springs."

29. D. C. Siegel, "Personal Reflections on Saratoga Springs, New York: Hydrogeological and Horse Racing 'Hot Spot' of the East," *Ground Water* 42 (2003): 141–143.

30. J. R. Smith, *Springs and Wells in Greek and Roman Literature: Their Legends and Locations* (New York and London: G. P. Putnam's Sons, The Knickerbocker Press, 1922).

4. THE URNS OF CANA

1. *What Life Was Like on the Banks of the Nile, Egypt (3050–30 BC)* (Alexandria, Va.: Time Life Books, 1997).

2. G. C. Nelson, *Ceramics: A Potter's Handbook* (New York: Holt, Rinehart and Winston, 1971).

3. Alfred Mallwitz, "Cult and Competition Locations at Olympia," in W. J. Raschke (ed.), *The Archaeology of the Olympics* (Madison: University of Wisconsin Press, 1988).

4. Nelson, *Ceramics.*

5. Mallwitz, "Cult and Competition Locations."

6. Cecil Munsey, *The Illustrated Guide to Collecting Bottles* (New York: Hawthorn Books, 1970).

7. Hugh Tait, *Glass: 5,000 Years* (New York: Harry N. Abrams, 1991).

8. Ibid.

9. Munsey, *Illustrated Guide.*

10. Ibid.

11. Ibid.

12. Ibid.

13. Ibid.

14. Larry Freeman, *Grand Old American Bottles* (Watkins Glen, N.Y.: Century House, 1964).

15. Munsey, *Illustrated Guide.*

16. Freeman, *Grand Old American Bottles.*

17. Michael Polak, *Antique Trader Bottles Identification and Price Guide*, fourth edition (Iola, Wis.: KP Krause Publications, 2002).

18. Munsey, *Illustrated Guide.*

19. Jim Dorsch, "Route Choices," *Bottled Water Reporter*, June/July 2000, pp. 17–22.

20. "It's Only Water, Right?" *Consumer Reports* 65, no. 8 (August 2000): 17–22.

21. S. C. Nagel, F. S. vom Saal, K. A. Thayer, M. G. Dhar, M. Dechler, and W. V. Welshons, "Relative Binding Affinity–Serum Modified Access (RBA-SMA) Assay Predicts the Relative *in Vivo* Bioactivity of the Xenoestrogens Bisphenol A and Octylphenol," *Environmental Health Perspectives* 105 (1997): 70–76.

22. J. Ashby, H. Tinwell, and J. Haseman, "Lack of Effects for Low Dose Levels of Bisphenol A and Diethylstillbestrol on the Prostate Gland of CF1 Mice Exposed *in Utero*," *Regulatory Toxicology and Pharmacology* 30 (1999): 156–166; S. Z. Cagen, J. M. Waechter, Jr., S. S. Dimond, W. J. Breslin, J. H. Butala, F. W. Jekat, R. L. Joiner, R. N. Shiotsuka, G. E. Veenstra, and L. R. Harris, "Normal Reproductive Organ Development in CF-1 Mice Following Prenatal Exposure to Bisphenol A," *Toxicological Sciences* 50 (1999): 36–44.

23. Ray Rowlands, "Going Global," *Bottled Water Reporter*, June/July 2002, pp. 15–19.

5. HIDDEN LIFE, HIDDEN DEATH

1. John Snow, *On the Mode of Communication of Cholera* (London: John Churchill, Publisher, 1855).

2. N. Howard-Jones, "Robert Koch and the Cholera Vibrio: A Centenary," *British Medical Journal* 288 (1964): 379–381.

3. M. Bentivoglio, "Filippo Pachina: A Determined Observer," *Grain Research Bulletin* 38, no. 2 (1995): 161–165.

4. R. R. Colwell, "Global Climate and Infectious Disease: The Cholera Paradigm." *Science* 274 (1996): 2025–2031.

5. A. Huq and R. R. Colwell, "Vibrios in the Marine and Estuarine Environment: Tracking *Vibrio cholerae*," *Ecosystem Health* 2 (1996): 198–214.

6. S. M. Faruque, Asadulghani, A. R. Alim, M. J. Albert, K. M. Islam, and J. J. Mekalanos, "Induction of the Lysogenic Phage Encoding Cholera Toxin in Naturally Occurring Strains of Toxigenic *Vibrio cholerae* 01 and 0139," *Infection and Immunity* 66 (1998): 3752–3757.

7. K. O. Stetter, "Hyperthermophiles in the History of Life," in G. R. Bock and J. A. Goode (eds.), *Evolution of Hydrothermal Ecosystems on Earth (and Mars?)* (West Sussex, England: John Wiley & Sons, 1996).

8. S. G. Wadhwa, G. H. Khaled, and S. C. Edberg, "Comparative Microbial Character of Consumed Food and Drinking Water," *Critical Reviews in Microbiology* 28 (2002): 249–279.

9. S. C. Edberg and M. J. Allen, "Virulence and Risk from Drinking Water of Heterotrophic Plate Count Bacteria in Human Population Groups," *International Journal of Food Microbiology* 92 (2004): 255–263.

10. Ibid.

11. J. T. Lisle and J. B. Rose, "*Cryptosporidium:* Contamination of Water in the USA and UK: A Minireview," *Journal of Water Supply and Research Technology Aqua* 44 (1995): 103.

12. H. Leclerc and M. S. Da Costa, "The Microbiology of Natural Mineral Water," in D.A.G. Senior and P. R. Ashurst (eds.), *The Technology of Bottled Water* (Boca Raton, Fla.: CRC Press, 1998).

6. THE WINDS OF FASHION

1. T. J. Stiles, *The Colonizers, in Their Own Words* (New York: The Berkley Publishing Group, 1998).

2. Gregg Smith, *Beer in America: The Early Years, 1587–1840* (Boulder, Colo.: Brewers Publications, 1998).

3. C. A. Wilson, *Food and Drink in Britain, from the Stone Age to the 19th Century* (London: Constable and Company, 1973).

4. Ibid.

5. Dale Taylor, *The Writer's Guide to Everyday Life in Colonial America* (Cincinnati: Writer's Digest Books, 1997).

6. Smith, *Beer in America.*

7. W. Back, E. R. Landa, and L. Meeks, "Bottled Water, Spas, and Early Years of Water Chemistry, *Ground Water* 33 (1995): 605–614.

8. Carl Bridenbaugh, *Early Americans* (Oxford: Oxford University Press, 1981).

9. Ibid.

10. Ibid.

11. Ibid.

12. Back, Landa, and Meeks, "Bottled Water"; S. N. Davis and A. G. Davis, "Saratoga Springs and Early Hydrogeochemistry in the United States," *Ground Water* 35 (1997): 347–356.

13. Davis and Davis, "Saratoga Springs."

14. John Glenn and N. Taylor, *John Glenn: A Memoir* (New York: Bantam Books, 1982), p. 225.

8. THE BATTLE OF ICE MOUNTAIN

1. D. H. Getches, *Water Law in a Nutshell* (St. Paul, Minn.: West Publishing Co., 1997).

2. Ibid.

3. Ibid.

4. A. W. Creech and R. D. Dowdy, Jr., "Camp Holly Springs, Henrico County, Virginia, USA: A Case Study in 'Springhead' Protection," in P. E. LaMoreaux and J. T. Tanner (eds.), *Springs and Bottled Waters of the World* (Berlin: Springer-Verlag, 2001).

5. W. M. Alley, T. E. Reilly, and O. L. Franke, "Sustainability of Ground-Water Resources," U.S. Geological Survey Circular 1186, Denver, Colo., 1999.

6. Ibid.

7. Robert Glennon, *Water Follies: Groundwater Pumping and the Fate of America's Fresh Waters* (Washington, D.C.: Island Press, 2002).

8. S. S. Hutson, N. L. Barber, J. F. Kenny, K. S. Linsey, D. S. Lumin, and M. A. Maupin, "Estimated Use of Water in the United States in 2000," U.S. Geological Survey Circular 1268, 2004.

9. K. N. Eshleman, *Bottled Water Production in the United States: How Much Groundwater Is Actually Being Used?* (Alexandria, Va.: Drinking Water Research Foundation, 2004).

9. AN ENDLESS SEA

1. V. L. McGuire and J. B. Sharpe. "Water-Level Changes in the High Plains Aquifer—Predevelopment to 1995," U.S. Geological Survey Water-Resources Investigations Report 97-4081, 1997.

2. R. H. Dott, Jr., and R. L. Batten, *Evolution of the Earth*, fourth edition (New York: McGraw-Hill, 1988).

3. O. E. Meinzer, "The Occurrence of Ground Water in the United States, with a Discussion of Principles," U.S. Geological Survey Water-Supply Paper 489, 1923.

4. O. E. Meinzer, "Large Springs in the United States," U.S. Geological Survey Water-Supply Paper 557, 1927.

5. H. Ries and T. L. Watson, *Engineering Geology* (New York: John Wiley & Sons, 1913).

6. H. E. Thomas, *Ground-Water Regions of the United States — Their Storage Facilities*, volume 3 of *The Physical and Economic Foundations of Natural Resources*, U.S. 83rd Congress, House Committee on Interior and Insular Affairs, 1952, pp. 3–78; R. C. Heath, "Ground-Water Regions of the United States," U.S. Geological Survey Water-Supply Paper 2242, 1984; W. Back, J. S. Rosenshein, and P. R. Seaber (eds.), *The Geology of North America*, volume O-2, *Hydrogeology* (Boulder, Colo.: The Geological Society of America, 1988); J. A. Miller (ed.), *Ground Water Atlas of the United States* (Reston, Va.: U.S. Geological Survey, 2000).

7. Heath, "Ground-Water Regions."

10. GRANITES AND GLACIERS

1. H. A. Poole and G. W. Poole, *History of Poland* (Mechanic Falls, Maine: Poole Brothers Publishers, 1890; reproduced by Poland Spring Water Company, Poland Spring, Maine); M. Robbins and C. Robbins, *Poland Spring: Walk Hand in Hand with History from the 1790s to Today* (Poland Spring, Maine: Poland Spring Inns, n.d.).

2. Poole and Poole, *History of Poland*.

3. R. H. Dott, Jr., and R. L. Batten, *Evolution of the Earth*, fourth edition (New York: McGraw-Hill, 1988).

4. Ibid.

11. THE LAND OF SPRINGS

1. R. H. Fuson, *Juan Ponce de León and the Spanish Discovery of Puerto Rico and Florida* (Blacksburg, Va.: The McDonald & Woodward Publishing Company, 2000).

2. T. M. Scott, G. H. Means, R. C. Means, and R. P. Meegan. "First Magnitude Springs of Florida," Florida Geologial Survey Open-File Report No. 85, 2002.

3. Ibid.; J. C. Rosenau, G. L. Faulkner, C. W. Hendry, and R. W. Hull, *Springs of Florida*, Florida Geological Survey Bulletin No. 31, revised

(Tallahassee, Fla.: State of Florida Department of Natural Resources, 1977).

4. Fuson, *Ponce de León*.

5. J. A. Miller, *Hydrogeologic Framework of the Floridan Aquifer System in Florida and Parts of Georgia, Alabama, and South Carolina*, U.S. Geological Survey Professional Paper 1403-B (Washington, D.C.: U.S. Government Printing Office, 1986).

6. Ibid.

7. V. T. Stringfield, "Artesian Water in the Floridan Peninsula," U.S. Geological Survey Water-Supply Paper 773-C, 1936, pp. C115–C195.

8. G. G. Parker, G. E. Ferguson, S. K. Love, and others, "Water Resources of Southeastern Florida," U.S. Geological Survey Water-Supply Paper 1255, 1955.

9. Miller, *Hydrogeologic Framework*.

10. L. N. Plummer, "Defining Reactions and Mass Transfer in Part of the Floridan Aquifer," *Water Resources Research* 13 (1977): 801–812.

11. L. N. Plummer, D. L. Parkhurst, and D. C. Thorstenson, "Development of Reaction Models for Ground-Water Systems," *Geochimica et Cosmochimica Acta* 47 (1983): 665–686.

12. B. G. Katz, H. D. Hornsby, J. K. Bohlke, and M. F. Mokray, "Sources and Chronology of Nitrate Contamination in Spring Waters, Suwannee River Basin, Florida," U.S. Geological Survey Water-Resources Investigations Report 99-4252, 1999.

13. Ibid.; B. G. Katz, J. K. Bohlke, and H. D. Hornsby, "Timescales for Nitration Contaminations of Spring Waters, Northern Florida," *Chemical Geology* 179 (2001): 167–186.

12. DESERT CROSSINGS

1. S. G. Hyslop, *Bound for Santa Fe: The Road to New Mexico and the American Conquest, 1806–1848* (Norman: University of Oklahoma Press, 2002).

2. J. A. Miller (ed.), *Ground Water Atlas of the United States* (Reston, Va.: U.S. Geological Survey, 2000).

3. R. J. Edmonds and D. J. Gellenbeck, "Ground-Water Quality in the West Salt River Valley, Arizona, 1996–98—Relations to Hydrogeology, Water Use, and Land Use," U.S. Geological Survey Water-Resources Investigations Report 01-4126, 2001.

4. F. Kreysig, *A Treatise on the use of natural and factitious waters of Carlsbad, EMS, Marienba, &c. &c.*, translated from German by W. F. Bekenn (London: S. Highley, Publisher, 1824).

5. Beverage Marketing Corporation, *Bottled Water in the U.S., 2001 Edition* (New York, 2001).

6. Beverage Marketing Corporation, *Bottled Water in the U.S., 2004 Edition* (New York, 2004).

7. John Southworth, *Death Valley in 1849: The Luck of the Gold Rush Emigrants* (Bishop, Calif.: Chalfant Press, 1978).

8. Ibid.

9. Ibid.

10. Ibid.

11. B. Litchfield (ed.), *Palomar Mountain Views* (Palomar Mountain Volunteer Fire Department, 1982).

13. SILVER CLOUDS BELOW

1. Michael Zanger, *Mt. Shasta: History, Legend & Lore* (Berkeley, Calif.: Celestial Arts Publishing, 1992).

2. Ibid.

3. S. L. Harris, *Fire Mountains of the West: The Cascade and Mono Lake Volcanoes* (Missoula, Mont.: Mountain Press Publishing Company, 1988).

4. R. L. Christiansen and C. D. Miller, "Volcanic Evolution of Mt. Shasta, California," *Abstracts with Programs*, Geological Society of America, Cordilleran Section Meetings, vol. 8, no. 3 (1976): 360–361.

5. D. R. Crandell, C. D. Miller, H. X. Glicken, R. L. Christiansen, and C. G. Newhall, "Catastrophic Debris Avalanche from Ancestral Mount Shasta Volcano, California," *Geology* 12 (1984): 143–146.

6. Beverage Marketing Corporation, *Bottled Water in the U.S., 2001 Edition* (New York, 2001).

7. Kay Archuleta, *Early Calistoga: the Brannan Saga* (Calistoga, Calif.: Illuminations Press, 1991).

8. Ibid.

9. R. L. Stevenson, *Silverado Squatters* (1880; reprinted for the Silverado Museum, St. Helena, Calif., 1974).

10. Beverage Marketing Corporation, *Bottled Water 2001*.

11. Ibid.

12. J. A. McPhee, *Assembling California* (New York: Farrar, Straus and Giroux, 1993).

13. J. S. Holliday, *Rush for Riches: Gold Fever and the Making of California* (Berkeley, Calif.: Copublished by the Oakland Museum of California and the University of California Press, 1999).

14. ZEN AND THE ART OF WATER QUALITY

1. P. N. Lynch, C. V. Shepard, and J.F.M. Geddings, *Artesian Wells, 1823–1879*, Municipal Report of the City of Charleston, S.C., 1881.

2. C. H. Murphy, *Carolina Rocks* (Orangeburg, S.C.: Sandlapper Publishing Co., 1995).

3. Lynch, Shepard, and Geddings, *Artesian Wells*.

4. G. S. Gohn, "Studies Related to the Charleston, South Carolina, Earthquake of 1886," U.S. Geological Survey Professional Paper 1313, Reston, Va., 1983.

5. R. M. Pirsig, *Zen and the Art of Motorcycle Maintenance* (New York: Bantam Books, 1974).

6. Beverage Marketing Corporation, *Bottled Water in the U.S., 2001 Edition* (New York, 2001).

INDEX

ABOUT THE AUTHOR

Francis H. Chapelle has been a research hydrologist for the U.S. Geological Survey since 1979. He received B.A. (music) and B.S. (geology) degrees from the University of Maryland, and M.S. and Ph.D. degrees (geochemistry) from the George Washington University. His research interests center on how microbial processes affect the chemical quality of ground water in both contaminated and pristine environments. He has authored more than 120 scientific papers and a textbook (*Ground Water Microbiology and Geochemistry*, John Wiley & Sons, 2000) on these subjects. In addition, he has written a book for the general reader, *The Hidden Sea* (National Ground Water Association, 2000), describing the history of various mystic and rational approaches to understanding ground-water systems, and how the idiosyncrasy of aquifers often complicates efforts to assess and clean up environmental contamination.